A HISTORY OF TRUST IN ANCIENT GREECE

A History of Trust in Ancient Greece

STEVEN JOHNSTONE

The University of Chicago Press   CHICAGO AND LONDON

STEVEN JOHNSTONE is associate professor in the Department of
History at the University of Arizona. He is the author of *Disputes and
Democracy: The Consequences of Litigation in Ancient Athens*.

The University of Chicago Press, Chicago 60637
The University of Chicago Press, Ltd., London
© 2011 by The University of Chicago
All rights reserved. Published 2011.
Printed in the United States of America

20 19 18 17 16 15 14 13 12 11   1 2 3 4 5

ISBN-13: 978-0-226-40509-4 (cloth)
ISBN-10: 0-226-40509-5 (cloth)

Library of Congress Cataloging-in-Publication Data

Johnstone, Steven, 1959–
A history of trust in ancient Greece / Steven Johnstone.
p. cm.
Includes bibliographical references and index.
ISBN-13: 978-0-226-40509-4 (cloth : alk. paper)
ISBN-10: 0-226-40509-5 (cloth : alk. paper) 1. Trust—Greece—History.
2. Trust—Economic aspects—Greece. 3. Trust—Political aspects—
Greece. 4. Democracy—Greece. 5. Greece—Civilization—To
146 B.C. 6. Greece—Economic conditions—To 146 B.C. I. Title.
DF231.2.J64 2011
938—dc22
2011007969

♾ This paper meets the requirements of ANSI/NISO z39.48-1992
(Permanence of Paper).

Adam, *you*!

CONTENTS

PREFACE

Henry Adams remarks:

> A parent gives life, but as parent, gives no more. A murderer takes life,
> but his deed stops there. A teacher affects eternity; he can never tell
> where his influence stops. A teacher is expected to teach truth, and may
> perhaps flatter himself that he does so, if he stops with the alphabet or
> the multiplication table, as a mother teaches truth by making her child
> eat with a spoon; but morals are quite another truth and philosophy is
> more complex still. A teacher . . . makes of his scholars either priests or
> atheists, plutocrats or socialists, judges or anarchists, almost in spite of
> himself. In essence incoherent and immoral, history had either to be
> taught as such—or falsified.[1]

This relationship between teacher and student may have existed in
Adams's time, but it is much too intimate and unpredictable to be tol-
erated in our own. The state demands docile workers, students long for
well-paying jobs, and teachers balk at accepting the troubling influence
that comes with relinquishing control. No one wants a teacher who creates both tyrants and philosophers, equally useless.

The same objections do not apply to an author. The change from
teacher to author, from students to readers, restores the erratic and profound possibilities of the relationship. If an author disavows the disciplin-
ing of his readers, if he refuses to impose the etiquette of coherent history
and emancipates his readers to forge their own truth, if he imagines that
his book, instead of remaking readers in his own image, might free them
even to confound him, he recognizes that the readers' freedom and even
transformation comes not from the author's imposing it but through their
struggling themselves to make meaning out of history. An author's work
provides only the materials or possibility of transformation; your mode
of reading—of historical realism, of contemporary relevance, of theo-

retical reflection, of literary enterprise, of scholarly debate, of pleasure, of irony—directs the outcome.

The following pages, then, are written for those readers who do not demand tidy instruction but crave the materials of meaning, who treat a book less as a power than as a provocation, and who do not care to be imprisoned by the limits of the author's imagination—or are willing, for the time, to think like this.

ACKNOWLEDGMENTS

Ten years is a long time for a war, for a homecoming, for a book. For me the last decade has been much more a marvelous journey than a struggle, mostly because of the hospitality I've received along the way.

What most writers crave is time. Four organizations offered generous fellowships that allowed me harbor to research and to write this book: the Center for Hellenic Studies, the Institute for Research in the Humanities at the University of Wisconsin (Madison), and the John Simon Guggenheim Memorial Foundation; in each case, the College of Social and Behavioral Sciences at the University of Arizona supplemented the fellowship. I am deeply grateful to these organizations.

In a time when libraries face large budget cuts, I think it's important to acknowledge that research like this would not be possible without robust research libraries and helpful staffs. I would like to thank the libraries and librarians at the Center for Hellenic Studies, Georgetown University, the University of Wisconsin, Columbia University, and especially the University of Arizona (whose librarian on one occasion even allowed me to exceed the limit of 250 books checked out at one time).

Several people have actively worked to support this project, and I would like to thank Josh Ober, Ian Morris, Michael Gagarin, Leslie Kurke, Matthew Christ, Sarah Deutsch, Chris van den Berg, and the anonymous readers for the press. While in residence at the Center for Hellenic Studies and at the Institute for Research in the Humanities I enjoyed and benefited from my colleagues, particularly Sandy Blakely and Andy Merrills. I have been privileged to speak to and receive comments from audiences at the University of Notre Dame, Columbia University, Wellesley College, Victoria College (University of Toronto), and the University of Arizona, and I thank those who invited me.

I thank my colleagues in the Department of History at the University of Arizona who, just as I was beginning to contemplate this journey, inexplicably rescued me from the Sea of Adjuncts, then gave me tenure, and put up with me both leaving and staying around. Thousands of conversations with my colleagues, and with my students too, have sustained me intellectually over the last decade and have no doubt influenced this book in subtle and unacknowledged ways.

I am grateful for the care shown for this book by the people at the University of Chicago Press, particularly Susan Bielstein, Margaret Mahan, and Carol Saller.

Finally, this book is much more of a collaboration than the single author's name would indicate. While having coffee and reading the newspapers at our oak kitchen table in the morning, or over dinner out on the patio on a warm Tucson evening (listening to the train whistles and the silence), or while walking—randomly exploring D.C. or Madison, or going from home to campus—or (too often, I know) when I'd barge into your office and interrupt your work because I had an idea I had to urgently talk about, Adam you've been my best audience, best editor, best critic, and best friend. It's true! You've read all of this many times, and I can't even absolve you from the remaining errors (as one politely should) because I can't separate you from any of it. You understood this project better than anyone, sometimes even better than I do, and the initial inscription is not just a dedication but also an acknowledgement that I wrote this with and to the smartest and most generous person I know.

CHAPTER I

Introduction

Greeks thought a lot about the heap (σωρός, *soros*). Some ancient philosophers used the heap to critique the arbitrariness of boundaries and definitions. They offered this paradox:[1] Any heap (of, say, grain) has a specific (if actually uncounted) number of kernels, so you can take away a kernel and it will still be a heap. But then take away another, and another, and so on. You reach the point where either a single kernel makes up the heap (absurd!) or you have to define the number of kernels that constitutes a heap, an arbitrary and indefensible boundary. (Why would one hundred grains of wheat be a heap, but not ninety-nine?) The heap, an essentially unbounded object, counterpoises what is limited. For Greeks, measure (*metron*) relied on an exact boundary to create fullness, a filling to the brim.[2] Although full measures could be counted as units, measure itself was not quantitative; it was qualitative, the quality of completeness. The contrast between the unbounded and the limited drives the mythic showdown between two prophets, Calchas and Mopsos, recounted in a preserved fragment of a sixth-century poem ascribed to Hesiod.[3] Calchas defies Mopsos with an enigma: "Amazement seizes my soul at how many figs this wild figtree has, tiny though it is. Can you say the number?" Mopsos responds by first seeming to concede the contest—"The number is infinite"[4]—then veers from counting figs to measuring them—"but the measure is a medimnos. And just one fig is left over which you could not add to it." Mopsos here revolutionizes the problem of naming the number: admitting that the number of figs is incalculable, he nevertheless introduces the medimnos, a standard measure of volume. Calchas's challenge requires a number, but Mopsos does not return the number of figs—as, for example, the Delphic oracle claimed to know the number of grains of sand[5]—but the number of measures, "1 medimnos + 1 fig." Because "the number of measure seemed to them to be true," Calchas, overthrown by his own dare, dies. The boundedness of the measure makes possible the enumeration of the uncountable by shifting the unit from the fig to the medimnos. The medimnos was a measure that had an exact limit—you could not add even one more fig—but to a heap you could pour on any number of grains without altering, violating, or destroying its nature. A measure defined a precise fullness, but a heap—unmeasured, uncounted, unlimited—represented abundance.[6]

This book is a heap.

Both economics and politics flourished in ancient Greece because of novel systems of impersonal trust. If personal trust refers to confidence vested in an individual because of particular familiarity, impersonal trust denotes the ways that abstract systems allow people to routinely interact, even with strangers, *as if* they trusted one another. Ancient Greece saw the proliferation of such abstract systems—money, standardized measurement, law, rhetoric, and so forth—which profoundly affected people's lives from the most public settings to the most intimate. Understanding these systems as sets of practices—what people did as opposed to their psychological dispositions—this study analyzes how they functioned and their effects.

Although sociologists often take the prevalence of impersonal networks as a mark of modernity,[7] ancient Greeks routinely interacted in ways mediated by complex, abstract systems. Theirs was not—or not essentially—a "face-to-face" society but a society constructed of a range of relationships, from the intimate to the objective. Nevertheless, these abstract systems operated and were limited in historically specific ways. Money, for example, did not exert a universally depersonalizing effect, nor did the fact that Greeks had standard measures imply that they used them in the same ways we do. Indeed, abstract systems acted sometimes to depersonalize relationships, but sometimes to *repersonalize* them, that is, to allow novel personal investments and trust that would not have been possible otherwise. In many cases, then, you should not understand personal trust as an original condition supplanted by the operations of abstract systems (as a lost state of nature), but rather as an effect of such systems.

The heapiness of this book derives in part from the ways I have treated theory. I have used theoretical and comparative insights to inspire questions and hypotheses with respect to the evidence from ancient Greece in an attempt to generate novel and productive lines of inquiry. I have relied on these theoretical insights not as frameworks on which to stick evidence, but as scaffolding to be removed as the evidence accumulates. (I'm not denying that the initial theoretical positions have informed the answers, but these initial positions themselves are not my fundamental objects of inquiry.) This book, then, does not attempt to articulate a totalizing model either of trust or of Greek society. Nor to test a contemporary theory or model against the ancient evidence. Nor to apply a theory to the ancient evidence (as sometimes happens "to fill gaps"). Nor to use ancient evidence to illustrate a universally true theory. I do think, however, that using theory to generate questions can open up new vistas on the past as well as link sometimes separate fields.

In this book I rely on a particular analytical vocabulary to frame my questions, especially three terms: trust, systems, and practice.

Trust. While I treat personal relationships of trust, I focus more intently on trust lodged in impersonal systems that allowed people, strangers even, to interact *as if* they trusted each other. I have borrowed this distinction between personal and impersonal trust from sociologists writing about the modern world, especially Niklas Luhmann and Anthony Giddens.[8] For these writers, impersonal or generalized trust—trust reposed in abstract systems like money or law—renders marginal or even irrelevant usual notions of personal trust: indeed, you drive without worrying about whether you can trust the people speeding almost directly at you; you hand large amounts of your money over to complete strangers (tellers) in a bank without a moment of doubt; you go into buildings designed and put up by people you know nothing about; you interact confidently all the time with strangers in the world. Those who repeatedly fail to do this (who will not drive or fly, who will not use credit cards or banks or even currency itself, who will not rely on the police or the government in any way), those who will not act within systems are generally treated not as distrustful but as insane. For social theorists like Luhmann and Giddens, the prevalence of impersonal trust uniquely marks the everyday activities of modernity. Without disputing the special nature of the modern world (as a historian, I approach all worlds as distinctive), that is, without simply assuming that the Greeks were like us, retrojecting our world back onto theirs, I'm asking: How did systems of impersonal trust, such as they were, work in classical Greece? Although this book concentrates on the history of these systems, it also considers personal relationships of trust. Even in the modern world, the suffusion of systems has not rendered personal trust obsolete. Giddens acknowledges the complex relations between personal and impersonal trust: he argues that personal trust undergirds the ability to trust systems, that systems often depend on "gatekeepers," individuals with whom you may develop a personal relationship (e.g., your doctor), and that systems may allow the cultivation of novel, even radical forms of personal trust. And this raises a second question: What were the relations between abstract systems and personal trust in classical Greece?

When I began this project, I was enticed by the work of scholars of the contemporary world who link personal trust nurtured in the institutions of civil society to the success of democratic politics. Robert Putnam, for example, argues that robust relationships of personal trust, nurtured in the voluntary associations of civil society (churches, clubs, etc.), are necessary to allow citizens in modern democracies to trust and engage with each other.[9] Relationships in civil society create "social capital," a generalized attitude of trusting, which gets transferred to and used in democratic political settings. For Putnam, our age has seen a decline in personal relationships (hence his concern about those who go "bowling alone"), causing a weakening of democratic engagement.

At first glance, such a model would seem relevant for ancient Greece. Aristotle, after all, imagined the relationships among citizens of the polis as a *koinonia*, a community based on affection or shared regard (*philia*). This emphasis on personal relationships accounts for his famous claim that the ideal polis would not be too large: citizens need personal knowledge of each other's character.[10] Following in this tradition, several historians of ancient Athens have located the sources of democratic political power in civil society, seeing the roots of political cooperation in the personal bonds cultivated in other groups and institutions.[11]

Yet as I worked on the history of trust, the limitations of this model became apparent. For the modern period, certainly, many scholars have not been convinced that a robust civil society promotes a democratic political order. Some have pointed out that the theory does not explain the causal mechanism; indeed, it often relies on "social capital," a metaphor, to insinuate a moneylike fungibility.[12] Others have noted that empirical research rarely bears out the theory.[13] For my purposes, moreover, the theory seems to generate few compelling questions, perhaps in part because it already presumes an answer (that civil society determines political engagement). But it is also the case—and this would be an empirical conclusion from the second half of this book—that the successful functioning of the political system should and can be explained in the first instance by the composition of that system itself. Greek citizens ran their cities successfully not because they were especially disposed to personally trust one another but because the political system—the protocols of working on boards, the legal mechanisms of political accountability, and, most of all, rhetoric—allowed them to act as if they did.

A history of trust is also a history of distrust. You can treat these as opposites, or as functional equivalents. Both, after all, arise from personal familiarity and provide resources for making decisions and taking actions.[14] My point here isn't exactly taxonomical; rather, it's that distrust is not always and necessarily dysfunctional, and that there are contingent, unpredictable, and historically specific relationships between trust and distrust.

Systems. I'm not committed to any particular systems dogma (e.g., functionalism), but I find the idea of systems analytically prolific because it raises profound questions about how to understand the past. I would note in particular three topics broached by systems analysis: complex relationships, expertise, and emergence.

The analysis of systems prompts you to think about relationships, not (or not just) entities. Aristotle's analysis of the oikos, the household, in book 1 of his *Politics*, does this. He cleverly decomposes the oikos into three parts, which consist not of people but of relationships: master-slave, husband-wife, father-children.[15] But his account of these relationships could be more complex in two ways. First, he treats them as exclusively hierarchical (they are forms of ruling),[16] but thinking in terms of systems allows for more complex configurations. In reality, there were reciprocal elements to each relationship.[17] Second, an analysis of systems points to the interconnections among relationships. Aristotle describes the differences between the three he considers, but does not consider how one might affect another. Thinking of them as a system encourages understanding relationships as dynamic rather than static.

Systems have complex relations to expertise. On the one hand, systems often concentrate expertise in a few authorities, allowing most people to interact in routine ways. Consider here the Greeks' economic system, in which a limited number of experts—people who knew how to mine, smelt, mint, and verify silver coins—enabled others to use these coins without having to consider their intrinsic value on each occasion. On the other hand, for a system to work, people need general competence in the relevant skills, though this is usually a less burdensome requirement than the dispersed expertise needed in the absence of a system. (Think of the difference between knowing how to use coins and knowing how to make them.) The combination of concentrated expertise and general competence allows the majority of people to act in routine ways that limit the need for both dispersed expertise and personal trust.

The emergent effects of systems offer a fecund analytic for understanding trust because of its potential to illuminate the complex relations between trust and abstract systems. Emergence describes ways in which the whole exceeds the sum of its parts. Thus, for example, the dynamics of climate cannot be reduced to (though they depend upon) the interactions of molecules. Emergence has both an epistemological aspect (the behavior of the system cannot be predicted from the behaviors of the parts) and an ontological one (the interactions of the parts cause outcomes that the serial addition of the parts could not). Recognizing that systems may create effects unlike any of their components or inputs raises the possibility that people's trust in abstract systems is an emergent property of those systems, not a precondition of them. If emergence points to the ways in which systems create (rather than require) impersonal trust, it also suggests that complex impersonal systems can transform the conditions and configurations of personal trust as well. The work of Giddens shows that the abstract systems of modernity have altered and intensified the most intimate relations. One thing to look out for, then, is how abstract systems in ancient Greece may have impelled a *repersonalization* of social relationships.

Practice. In analyzing these systems, I have found particularly helpful Pierre Bourdieu's elaboration of the idea of practice.[18] Bourdieu articulated the notion of practice out of dissatisfaction with structuralist accounts of society, which tend to be static, monolithic, and mechanistic. Practice, in contrast, which names an ordinary person's unselfconscious ability to do what he or she does, attempts to allow for the uncertainty, contingency, and trickiness of ordinary life. It attempts to restore agency to people by shifting from a notion of rules that govern action to an idea of strategies that people can take up at times and in ways of their own devising. This focus on practice attempts to account for both structure (there are only so many practices, each with its own logic) and individual agency.

Focusing on various practices entails three consequences. First, I'm offering not a story of agents (a traditional narrative history) but an analysis of the conditions that made agency possible. Second, practices often involve people using things, whether physical things like coins, standardized measuring vessels, writing instruments, or shipping containers, or intellectual things like money values, or rhetorical language. These things, however, are not themselves determinative but take on importance depending on how they're used. Third, I'm fundamentally interested in how people relate to each other through what they do. I treat practices as essentially social.

The heaviness of the book also derives from the ways I have treated evidence. Because I use the idea of trust analytically less as a rigid criterion, pruning away everything unrelated, than as a fecund problematics, the idea of trust generates myriad questions to pose to ancient evidence. This has had the dual effect of offering new insights into some texts that may have become threadbare from familiarity, and also of encouraging the search for new evidence. At times the absence of limits in this inquiry has awed me a little—what text, however obscure, long, or seemingly irrelevant could I safely fail to ransack? Following the sources has also meant that my analyses of them have attempted to present them in their full and sometimes confounding complexity, even when this goes beyond the question of trust. One friend who read this manuscript remarked, "You historians are in love with evidence!" It's true, and if I've lingered over their description, I hope you'll share some of my bedazzlement.

This study concentrates on the Greeks of the classical and early Hellenistic periods, roughly the fifth and fourth centuries BCE.[19] Its chronological scope was determined by the disposition of available evidence. Before about the mid-fifth century, Greeks did not put up many stone inscriptions or write much prose. Consequently, my history of trust describes how these systems operated in the classical period, not how they developed earlier on. The amount and quality of evidence available from the classical period allows for a fineness of analysis that is mostly impossible for earlier centuries. Sacrificing detail and a degree of probability, you could profitably trace the origins of these systems back into the archaic period. That would result in a different book.

On the later end, Alexander's conquest of the Greeks and of most of the eastern Mediterranean in the late fourth century, the advent of the Hellenistic period, marks the end of this study, in part because the availability of evidence changes (inscriptions remain abundant, but some prose sources, such as legal speeches, become scarce), and in part because the large Hellenistic monarchies that ruled Greeks changed the political and social conditions of life. In the classical period, most Greeks lived in relatively small, autonomous political units, cities usually, but sometimes federations of towns or regional states. Politics, economics, religion, and other activities were dispersed, and the scale of their organization was small. Hellenistic kingdoms did not put an end to local activities—indeed, they relied on and promoted the business of cities—but they did introduce organizations of a scale unknown to Greeks of the classical period. So continuities existed alongside radical innovations. When I have included evidence from the Hellenistic period, I have attempted to account for both the similarities and the differences.

I have not relied on (though I have occasionally cited) sources later than the Hellenistic period, unless they are clearly quoting an earlier author. The problem with these late sources (including Plutarch, Diodorus, or Pollux, all a few hundred years later, to the *Suda*, more than a millennium after the fact) is not so much that they're inaccurate but that it's often impossible to assess their accuracy. Using evidence conservatively, I have not relied on restored portions of fragmentary inscriptions, where the restoration of the lost part carries a substantial amount or a critical part of the meaning. Again, the problem with these restorations is that the probability of their being right cannot be gauged. In some instances, despite the urge to know, it's better to remain agnostic.

The availability of evidence has also guided the geographic emphases of this book. Athens stands out because of a number of related factors: the exceptional size of the city (at least a quarter of a million people in the whole of Attica, the area around Athens), its unusual wealth (not just from tribute paid by other Greeks in the fifth century, but from its rich silver mines, and the situation of its port, Piraeus, as an important entrepôt), its military power, its unparalleled erection of inscriptions, its attraction as a cultural center, and the canonization of the city and its writers by later Greeks and Romans. In what follows I treat Athens as neither consistently unique nor always representative, but as sometimes one, sometimes the other, often in between.

As the heap contrasts with the measure, so this book stands in relation to a traditional monograph, which aims at a totalizing completeness. The latter achieves its perfection by defining a precise boundary, then including everything within and excluding everything outside this perimeter. Compassing such a threshold is both powerful and artificial—powerful because it allows a synoptic view of a complex phenomenon, but artificial because it invariably lops off meaningful relationships which exceed the threshold. Indeed, the attempt at completeness can end up defeating itself; whatever is excluded can call into question the adequacy of the definitions that make fullness possible.

In analyzing trust and systems, the chapters of this book move generally from economic practices to political ones.

In chapter 2 you start in the center of the city, in the agora, the marketplace. The ways that Greeks of the classical period used minted coins, a specific material form taken by the abstract system of money, profoundly shaped personal relationships in the agora, not only differentiating sellers from buyers but also conferring on sellers a particular advantage: more secure knowledge about the value of what they would receive in any transaction. Sellers sought to exploit, and buyers to neutralize, this information advantage in the conventional forms of negotiating a deal. The generalized trust in money here created a specific form of personal distrust—buyers distrusted sellers—which the practice of haggling encoded. Thus, many Greek marketplace regulations, usually understood as attempts to control prices, seem equally aimed at overcoming or at least compensating for the asymmetric positions of sellers and buyers and at restraining or eliminating haggling, which is the practical manifestation of this asymmetry.

Archaeologists have uncovered and extensively documented the measures and weights used by Greek cities, and they have elaborated the particular standards of each city, but no one has really asked how or how often Greeks actually used standardized measures, the subject of chapter 3. Evidence for the extensive trade in grain suggests that on the wholesale level, expert traders did not use standard measures, indeed did not measure at all, but instead used their expertise to gauge amounts by the size and number of shipping containers (in this case, bags). While inscriptions show that city officials often measured grain with standard measures, they also show that this was a slow, expensive process, required of public officials because of the rigorous mechanisms of accountability imposed on them. Laws that enforced the use of standard measures in the agora (but nowhere else) attempted to mitigate the asymmetry of the relationship between buyer and seller.

You get to peep inside the oikos in chapter 4. Little evidence suggests that Greek households, most of which depended significantly on farming for their livelihood, relied on abstract systems to organize their economic activities. Insofar as the widespread use of standard measures and accounting has often been compelled by the state, the typical structure of Greek taxation (and also of rent collection) functioned successfully without imposing either. In keeping track of stuff, households relied not on written accounts and standardized measures but on containers and an art of allocating that accommodated supply, time, need, and pleasure. A flexible system, containerization allowed the household head either to extend trust to the members of the oikos or, if he distrusted them, to manage supplies himself.

Chapter 5 hustles you back to the agora, returning to the practices of assigning money values, this time in political contexts. In contrast to haggling, an interpersonal method of valuing, cities usually trusted individuals to unilaterally value their own goods, whether for taxes denominated in money values (e.g., import duties) or for distinguishing citizens by wealth. Greeks used money values both to commensurate (as in haggling or collecting taxes) and to create thresholds of incomparability (as between different classes of citizens). The history of schemes of classifying citizens at Athens shows an evolution from citizens as valuing subjects to citizens as valued objects, whereas an inscription from the North African city of Cyrene shows in detail how the latter worked in practice.

With chapter 6, the book completes the shift from the economic to the political, now examining the protocols that allowed citizens to act in groups. In Athens and elsewhere, government officials typically served not individually but on boards, often with strangers and only for a year. Scholars have slighted the activities of these boards, probably because at Athens at least the Assembly and the courts seem to have held more power. Yet these offices had real responsibilities, including (perhaps most significantly) the board of ten generals. In the absence of preexisting personal relationships of trust, the rituals and protocols associated with working in small groups allowed board members to powerfully act together by creating both equality and the opportunities for leadership. Boards decided not so much by majority rule as by consensus building, a process revealed in Xenophon's extensive account of the deliberations of the leaders of the Ten Thousand.

Just as groups acted together, so they could be held liable together, as will be seen in chapter 7. In general, Greeks remained flexible on whether people in groups should be liable individually or collectively, but the latter option often prevailed. Analyses of several Athenian trials, including the condemnation of the generals after the battle of Arginusai, shows how this system responded to the problem of each member denying responsibility for the group's action, as well as the challenge of gathering sufficient information to distribute liability proportionally. The threat of holding all members equally liable demanded that each member scrutinize and trust the others, and it seems to have promoted solidarity and consensus. Collective liability can be understood as part of the democratizing tendency to give equal shares, a practice Xenophon critiqued not so much as unfair as unproductive.

Having considered the linguistic codes that allowed people to interact in the agora and on boards, you end in chapter 8 in the courts and the Assembly, witnessing the most powerful ancient system of language, rhetoric. Instead of taking up the perspective just of the speaker and treating rhetoric as a powerful instrument of persuasion, I emphasize the activity of the audience as well, suggesting that rhetoric was a linguistic system that allowed very large groups to decide things by transforming and simplifying them. While speakers insisted on their own trustworthiness, they affirmed it through rhetoric; so a generalized trust in the system preceded and established trust in specific speakers. Rhetoric constituted relationships among citizens—not just between a speaker and a listener, but among the members of the judging audience—that were abstract, impersonal, and powerful.

Heraclitus: "The fairest order in the world is a heap of random sweepings."[20]

CHAPTER 2

Haggling

Haggling transformed the fundamental structural asymmetry created by coinage, the difference between sellers and buyers, into a distinct cultural practice of conflict. Although money constituted an abstract system that depended on a generalized trust, money did not simply (or mainly) depersonalize the relationship between buyer and seller; rather, by encoding these structurally differentiated positions as conventional interpersonal conflict, it repersonalized the relationship through buyers' distrust of sellers.

Coinage differentiated roles in economic exchanges. On the most basic level it defined buyers and sellers: buyers gave coins for stuff, sellers gave stuff for coins. More than this, however, coinage endowed these buyers and sellers with different amounts of information about the transaction. Economists often note that coinage lowers transaction costs relative to bartering, especially information costs. In bartering, because both parties know more about their own goods than about the other's, each faces significant information costs; that is, it requires expertise, investigation, and testing, to evaluate what you are getting from the other party in the exchange. This need for reciprocal investigation plays out in a scene of Euripides' *Cyclops*: When Odysseus arrives on the Cyclops' island, he begins to negotiate with Silenus for food. He asks for bread, but Silenus replies they only have animal products: meat, cheese, and milk. Odysseus demands: "Show them. Light suits merchandise."[1] Silenus asks how much he'll pay; Odysseus says he has no money (gold), but he barters with wine, praising its source (the son of Dionysus) and its quantity. Then he offers a sample taste to Silenus, who replies: "That's fair. A taste calls forth a sale."[2] Both parties test the other's goods.

Compare this to money sales: Here buyers (those giving coins) face the same information costs as in barter, but sellers do not, because they can trust the value of coins. (By the fourth century, the Athenian polis provided a coin tester, probably in the agora, to check any suspected coins.)[3] Thus, although coinage may have lowered transaction costs, as economists claim, it did so differentially, creating significant information asymmetries between buyers and sellers.[4] The buyer's lack of information about the quality of the goods underpins much of the concern about the agora and what went on there.[5] The problem of information and value (*axia*) is at the heart of the Platonic dialogue *Hipparchus*.[6] The young man conversing with Socrates indignantly complains that "lovers of gain" profit from things they know are worthless[7]—apparently at the expense of those who do not have this knowledge. This asymmetric structure of information created by coinage lies behind the persistent distrust of sellers and the identification of people with the buyer.[8]

This fundamental structural asymmetry was enacted as conflict through haggling. It is important to recognize the dynamics of this translation. Haggling was a coherent and independent cultural practice, such that it cannot be simply reduced to the underlying differentials, neither one-to-one nor wholly. Indeed, buyer and seller engaged in a practice that had many elements with no obvious functional relation to the parties' underlying structural positions. Thus, although the structural differentiation of buyers and sellers concerned their access to information, hagglers often did things that were not about finding or concealing knowledge—for example, they engaged in repartee.

Haggling should be studied, then, both as an economic activity and as a cultural practice. Many traditions of economic analysis have slighted haggling, often, as Vivienne Brown has shown, because analysts have assumed that abstract forces (supply and demand, competition, etc.) determined the real price and haggling either merely revealed it or deceitfully perverted it.[9] But there are signs that this idealist position is giving way. (The position is idealist because what's ontologically primary is something abstract, like supply and demand, and not particular people doing or thinking particular things.) Certainly there has been a tradition in anthropology of closely analyzing the actual forms of marketplace transactions.[10] Even within the discipline of economics itself the impulse of what's called New Institutional Economics—recognizing that no market is perfect and paying attention to the specific configuration of transaction costs in each case[11]—allows for a more careful analysis of haggling. While I hope this chapter contributes to what may be called the history of pricing,[12] my intention is not to reduce haggling to pricing. For my project, what people said and did is as important as the price they agreed on.

Haggling highlights the complex relations between trust in abstract systems (in this case, money) and trust in persons. It's often said that money depersonalizes, but money did not (or not especially) depersonalize the relation between buyers and sellers in Greece. Indeed, while coinage depended on a generalized trust to operate (the belief that others would continue to accept coins at a relatively steady value), it also had complex, uneven, and surprising effects: coinage created information asymmetries, which intensified personal relationships by exacerbating buyers' distrust of sellers. The system of trust in money repersonalized market relationships by creating new pools of distrust.

In this chapter I describe the scene of haggling, the agora, paying particular attention to the relative unimportance of status—to the ways, that is, that people in the market were defined primarily as buyers or sellers. I then examine the lack of information faced by buyers about the goods they sought , a problem which suffuses stories about sophists' fees. Next, I turn to the cultural form into which this conflict was translated, namely haggling, probing the comic representations of haggling in an attempt to analyze its procedures and protocols and the ways it encoded conflict. Finally, turning to political economy, I consider the ways in which cities attempted to control or moderate this conflict, which they did at times by trying to balance out the information asymmetry (probably not very successfully) and more often with schemes to dampen or even eliminate haggling itself.

Before heading out to the agora, however, it's worth considering how the process of shopping in the contemporary world differs from the Greek. Because in almost all contexts today sellers post prices (and this is true even when negotiations are common, as with houses or cars), your initial move as a shopper is a solitary calculation: considering the price. The present ubiquity of posted prices dates back only a century or two. Fixed prices were an effect of the standardization of goods due to industrial production, the increasing size of retail establishments, and the reluctance of owners to delegate the task of bargaining to employees, especially to the young women who staffed nineteenth-century department stores. Although (as economists note) such fixed prices impose a cost on sellers,[13] they allow the indefinite expansion of the retail enterprise by solving the problem of trust inherent in delegation. Nowadays, in small stores or those dedicated to "service," buyers may interact with a seller (or a seller's representative), but this interaction is rarely a negotiation of price. Instead of negotiating with a seller over price, buyers today navigate between different sellers of the same or similar goods looking for the best price, an *extensive* as opposed to an *intensive* process. This contrasts with contemporary bazaars in other cultures, where anthropologists' descriptions suggest that intensive negotiations with a single seller are more common.

Buyers and Sellers in the Agora

The activities of buying and selling not only organized the agora but also defined the people there. While other activities—especially religious and governmental—occurred in the agora and left their imprint, the economic ones were essential.[14] Economic activities did not just happen; rather, they imparted both a spatial and a social organization. Other statuses mattered—gender, citizenship, freedom—but they mattered in the context of the two fundamental roles of the agora, buyers and sellers.

The agora constituted a spatial organization of exchange.[15] Although *ergasteria* (workshops where things were both made and sold) could be located elsewhere, they tended to cluster around the agora as they did, for example, in Olynthus.[16] Ancient sources speak as if the Athenian agora was also highly organized internally,[17] with different wares sold in separate quarters, though modern scholars doubt it was quite as tidy as that.[18] Indeed, while some retail establishments were fixed (*ergasteria* in houses or permanent buildings, for example), others could move: some vendors sold from booths (*skenai*), carts (*hamaxai*), or trays (*teliai*).[19] Merchants who appeared at temporary venues, like the festival at Eleusis, must have been using such portable equipment.[20] Finally, merchants and craftsmen might sometimes travel to find customers,[21] even making house calls (though the evidence suggests this was usually done at the invitation of the household head).[22]

Most Greek households depended on exchanges in the market. However seriously Greeks took the ideology of household *autarkeia*, self-sufficiency, only the richest or the very poorest could have approached this condition. Most people, even most farmers, relied on others to produce at least some of what they used or ate: fish, pottery, charcoal and firewood, metal tools, meat, salt, and even grain.[23] The author of one treatise on household management specifically referred to the system of selling off produce and buying what you need later, thus obviating the need for a storehouse, a system he characterized as "Attic."[24] Indeed, the agora, especially at Athens, seemed to provide a fantastic abundance of goods. Xenophon asked: "Those who want to buy or sell without delay, where could they succeed better than at Athens?"[25] While modern scholars have inventoried the goods and service available for sale,[26] ancient writers made a minor literary genre of such catalogues: of kinds of sellers,[27] of products from various cities,[28] of produce available out of season,[29] of food for sale in times of peace.[30] In Aristophanes' *Acharnians*, as Compton-Engle has argued, the agora fulfills the dream of food automatically presenting itself to be eaten.[31]

People of all sorts—male and female, slave and free, foreign and local—

jostled promiscuously in the agora,[32] and all of these might act as sellers or buyers. We know quite a bit about the status of sellers, who were not all free men. Aristophanes' plays show free women selling bread, other food items, and flax cloth.[33] Athenian laws, legal speeches, and inscriptions demonstrate their presence as well.[34] Women tended to concentrate on selling products that corresponded to their activities in the oikos,[35] but also those that required little capital investment in either equipment or stock.[36] We know, too, that non-Athenian men and slaves sold things.[37] While many sellers made the things they sold, some merchants' sole labor was to sell the products of others. Indeed, Plato treats middlemen, people who buy from farmers and craftsmen and sell to everyone, as the normal kind of vendor (*kapelos*).[38] Proprietors of *pantopolia*, a kind of general store known for its variety of goods (everything from hoplite armor to ocher),[39] probably made few, if any, of their goods.

If you needed skill or capital to be a seller, almost anyone, you might suppose, could be a buyer—it didn't matter who you were if you had money. Not only free men went shopping, but slaves of both sexes, often alone at the behest (and with the money) of their owners.[40] But the meager evidence that free women went shopping (in Athens at least) has led one historian to suspect that shopping "was not the routine task of Athenian housewives."[41] The obvious sources fail to offer much: Aristophanes never constructs a scene in which women shop, though he refers to them having small amounts of money and buying little treats.[42] Xenophon's schematic account of the household puts the wife in charge of expenditures,[43] but it also sticks her firmly indoors; when his character Ischomachus thinks he needs something, he sends the slave shopping.[44] And Theophrastus implies that husbands often bought things when he represents a pestering wife asking: "What have you brought me from the marketplace?"[45] Other comedies provide glimpses, and there's Aristotle's famous remark that in democracies it's impossible to prevent the wives of poor men from leaving the house.[46] The challenges of the evidence about whether free women went shopping (and similar questions, as, for example, whether women went to the theater)[47] derive, I suspect, not from the absence of women but from (what I would call) a regime of invisibility, which reflects less what women did or didn't do than how men perceived and described the world. Some historians have argued that Athenian ideologies of the seclusion of free women and, indeed, of the inviolability of the oikos do not for the most part accurately represent reality.[48] I would add that the omissions in our sources are themselves significant phenomena.[49]

Thus in a broad sense, economic activities imparted a promiscuous social organization to the agora, especially in contrast to formal institutions of government, which excluded women, slaves, and noncitizens.[50] Such statuses mattered, of course, insofar as they affected a person's control of money; so female entrepreneurs tended to cluster in trades that required the least capital investment. But the primary organizing social relationship of the agora was none of these statuses; rather, it was the dynamics of the interactions between buyers and sellers, especially the practice of haggling.

Buyers' Ignorance

In meeting sellers, buyers faced a confounding problem: they might not fully understand the nature of the seller's goods until after the transaction, when they could possess, inspect, and use them. Xenophon's treatise *On Horsemanship*, a how-to manual for horse owners, illustrates this problem in detail: Almost one fifth of it consists of advice about examining horses for "someone who intends not to be cheated in buying a horse."[51] Buyers often experienced this asymmetry of information as a problem of trust, linking doubt about the goods to suspicion of the seller. To analyze the dynamics of this relationship between buyers and sellers, I examine the stories told about sophists charging their pupils fees.[52] Professional educators, the sophists appeared during the second half of the fifth century and offered to teach many skills: rhetoric, military tactics, even virtue itself. Although these goods were more intangible than most, they presented similar problems to buyers.

From the perspective of the buyer (and the discourse assumes the perspective of the buyer) the fundamental problem was knowing the quality of the commodity, in this case the sophist's instruction. Plato develops this at length in a scene in his *Protagoras*: Hippocrates, son of Apollodoros, awakes Socrates before dawn, agog to be introduced to the great Protagoras pronto. Attempting to dampen the young man's zeal, Socrates asks if he would so readily entrust his body to another before examining everything, taking counsel with his friends and relations for many days.[53] Socrates then initiates such an examination: "Doesn't the sophist happen to be a kind of wholesaler or retailer of wares from which the soul is nourished?"[54] Socrates analogizes instruction of the soul with nourishment of the body: Vendors of food ignorantly praise everything they sell, and unless you happen to be a doctor or trainer you don't know whether it's good or bad.[55] As Socrates analyzes it, the problem for buyers is knowledge of the goods:

> When you buy food or drink from a merchant or peddler, it's possible to take it away in containers other than your body. Before you take it

into your body by eating or drinking, if you store it at home, you can
deliberate, consulting with an expert about what ought to be eaten and
drunk, and what not, and how much and when.[56]

Moreover, insofar as some sophists claimed to teach virtue, there was a
neat conundrum about their pay (*misthos*) and the quality of their goods:
if a student tried to weasel out of the fee and the sophist sought to compel payment, it was apparent that the sophists hadn't really taught virtue
at all, and hence didn't deserve the fee.[57]

This problem contains two analytically distinct, but practically wed,
phenomena: the difficulty buyers have in assessing the quality of goods
before purchase, and the challenge of trusting the seller. It's possible to
imagine a solution to the dilemma by treating it not as a problem of trust
(of the seller) but of information (about the commodity). Xenophon takes
such an approach in recommending a strategy for forestalling disputes
over the value of training:

> As he sends out his slave [to learn] a skill, so he ought to send out [his
> horse] only after he's written down what it will need to know when it's
> returned. For these notes will remind the horse trainer of what it's nec-
> essary to take care of if he hopes to get his *misthos*.[58]

The written memo attempts to give the buyer of services some assur-
ance about their nature. This solution emphasizes information in establishing a contractually equal relationship between buyer and seller. The
buyer trusts the written contract as much as he does the other party (and
the seller does, too, since he apparently collects his pay at the end of the
training).

Absent such a written guarantee, buyers focused their doubts on the
personal trustworthiness of the seller. For the sophist to ask for payment
before the training implied that he did not trust his pupil. Isocrates denounced such behavior:

> The most ridiculous thing is that [sophists] don't trust the people from
> whom they receive [their pay], the ones to whom they are about to hand
> over the discipline of justice. They put their students' money in escrow
> with people they have never taught; while they're planning prudently
> for their own security, they're doing the opposite of what they profess.
> It's allowable for those who educate in other subjects to be overly ex-
> acting on points of disagreement, since nothing prevents those who are
> skilled in other matters from being dishonest concerning the contract.
> But isn't it absurd when those who inculcate virtue and moderation
> don't trust those whom they teach most of all?[59]

The practice Isocrates describes—the pupil pays before the training, but the fee is held in escrow until it's complete—would seem designed to mitigate the problem of trust entailed in the timing of the payment. Nevertheless, although Isocrates represents the issue as the sophist's failure to trust, things look different from the point of view of the students, who are the buyers: even with the fee in escrow, they are required to trust the seller, the sophist, whose refusal to extend trust counts against their good faith.

Protagoras is reported to have relied on a different practice: he reposed his trust entirely in the student. Aristotle asks:

> Who assesses the value, the one who gives away or the taker? For the giver would seem to entrust it to the other. They say that Protagoras did just this: whenever he taught anything, he ordered the student to value the worth of what he thought he had learned, and give him that much. But in such circumstances, some people prefer the idea of "*misthos*" for a man."[60]

Aristotle here delineates two practices of valuing in exchanges. In the latter, which he calls *misthos*, quoting a corresponding proverb,[61] the parties agree to the price before the exchange, and the seller of services does not need to trust the buyer.[62] The Protagorean solution, however, takes the teaching of virtue seriously by shifting the risk to the sophist, who now trusts his students (and, by implication, his own educating) completely. This procedure entails several changes. First, the price is determined after the pupil has received his instruction, so that he has full knowledge. Second, the price is named by the buyer, not by the seller, an alteration not quite as drastic as it first appears. When the seller named the price, the buyer still assented. But this points to the most fundamental change in the Protagorean practice: the buyer names the price *unilaterally*. The method of commensurating the labor and the fee is radically subjective and represents in action Protagoras's most famous saying, "Man is the measure of all things."[63] In the Protagorean scheme, the value of the knowledge or labor is whatever the buyer says it is.[64]

These stories reveal that buyers approached exchanges feeling disadvantaged by their relative ignorance of what was being sold. The nature of a sophist's teaching may be more uncertain than the nature of, say, wheat, but (as I argue in chapter 3) in ancient Greece no goods adhered to quality standards, so that they were all (to some degree) dubious. The asymmetry of knowledge was, in many situations, a problem of personal trust (or distrust). Xenophon offers a solution, the written guarantee, which does not depend on personal trust, but there's no evidence that his recommendation was normally followed. More commonly, uncertainty about the goods prompted a distrust of the seller. The Isocratic practice attempted to allay distrust by having a third party hold the fee; the Protagorean attempted to overcome both ignorance and distrust.

An Ethnography of Haggling

Most of the evidence I use below for understanding the practice of haggling comes from Greek and especially Athenian comic writings. But you might ask: Can you take scenes from comedy as reliable depictions of real life? Might not the literary genre—and not some correspondence to the actual world—explain the ways that characters talk? You certainly need to attend to the generic features of comedy, yet one of these was the superimposition of one recognized discourse on another or its transposition to an alien context. The incongruity was funny. Thus, the comic effect depended the audience detecting the characteristics of haggling. Comedy did not invent but drew on, stylized, and heightened the verbal cleverness of haggling. This approach aligns with the attempts of other Greek historians to use the evidence of comedy to say something about society.[65]

Many Greeks considered the agora a place for cheating: "People go to the agora and . . . practice deception in selling and buying. The person who has deceived the most, he's the one who's admired."[66] But while the general claim might apply to both shoppers and merchants, specific complaints applied exclusively to the latter. It was alleged that sellers sometimes resorted to downright crookedness, that they bamboozled buyers by switching between different currencies during the negotiations over price,[67] that they showed you the good stuff but then switched it and gave you the bad,[68] that they misrepresented or watered down the product,[69] that they used short measures.[70]

The primary problematics of shopping in ancient Greece, however, concerned the necessary but dubious negotiations between buyer and seller, as shown by an analysis of tactics available to each party. There seem to have been few if any posted prices in Athens. For sellers, the methods of advertising were limited. While they would display their goods (sometimes, it was suspected, with the best ones up front),[71] the best way to attract attention was to shout. Thus, hawkers' shouting filled the central city: "Buy charcoal!" or vinegar or oil.[72] Such spiels could indicate the quality of the goods as well: a fish seller might ballyhoo his anchovies as sweeter than honey. (This observation sets up Antiphanes' joke that the dealers in honey might as well shout that their product was as rotten as anchovies.)[73] Some sellers swore an oath to the quality of their goods, the most disreputable tactic of all, according to Plato.[74] While sellers attempted to attract customers, buyers initiated the negotiations—and did so by first asking the price.[75]

To the potential buyer's initial inquiry, merchants could respond in a number of ways. As you can see in the collection of complaints about fish sellers at the beginning of Athenaeus, book 6, some merchants responded nonverbally. These comic caricatures reveal that the sellers' bearing constituted one of their tactics. Sellers might feign deafness,[76] stay seated,[77] hang their heads down (in guilt, Amphis says, over their murderous ways),[78] raise their eyebrows and lower their eyes,[79] or frown.[80] Negotiations in the market, then, were not merely verbal but also incarnated, enacted through bodies. If fish sellers were said to be Gorgons who turned customers to stone because they charged so much,[81] the smiling glance of an eel itself could make a buyer pay almost any price.[82]

Sellers responded verbally, too, of course. For a merchant to refuse to name a price, asking customers instead how much they'd pay, was considered pigheaded or grouchy (αὐθάδης).[83] Whether they adopted a brusque or jovial manner,[84] once sellers had named a price they fiercely resisted the demand to lower it.[85] An anecdote from Aristotle's *Constitution of the Naxians* shows merchants responding to counteroffers by threatening to end the negotiations altogether.[86] This story highlights an important point about haggling: the refusal to negotiate could itself be a tactic within negotiations. It also shows that the language of bargaining could include stock phrases common among many merchants, as Aristotle reports: "Whenever [people on Naxos] ... would make a low offer on something being sold, it was the custom of the sellers to say that they would prefer to give [the fish] to Telestagoras [a local grandee] than to sell it at that price."[87] In the game of bargaining in the agora, however ritualized, success depended on mastery of the conventions, especially the patter.

Buyers and sellers negotiated, then, not (or not only) by exchanging numbers, which converged on the final price, but by using gestures and language, both cunning and conventional, to cap and forestall each other. Buyers less experienced in the conventions of haggling might feel disadvantaged. Ostensibly for such people, Lynkeos, the brother of the ruler of Samos and a student of the philosopher Theophrastus, wrote a *Treatise on Shopping*, dedicated to a friend who was a *dysōnēs*, shopping impaired (literally, "a bad buyer").[88] Like the rest of Lynkeos's oeuvre, this manual treated mundane activities, especially food and eating—though, as almost all our knowledge of Lynkeos comes from Athenaeus, there is the possibility that his interests were wider.[89] In his manual, according to Athenaeus, Lynkeos was teaching a friend "what things he profitably ought to say to the murderous fish sellers."[90] To counter their steely glares (an embodied negotiating tactic) and refusals to lower the price,

Lynkeos suggested that his friend criticize the fish by quoting and adapting poetry, from, for example, Archestratus: "'The mormyre of the shore is a wretched fish, never good.' And 'Buy the bonito in fall'—but now it's spring. And 'The mullet is amazing when winter comes'—but now it's summer."[91] Such remarks, Lynkeos predicted, would put many customers to flight (and bystanders too!) and would force the seller to take your offer.[92]

Lynkeos's text presents a complicated layering. It evokes Archestratus's *Life of Pleasure*, which catalogued foods, especially fish, explaining where and when to get the best and how to prepare them exquisitely. Archestratus wrote this combination cookbook and lifestyle guide in epic verse, sometimes mimicking famous lines; his words about the mormyre echo Hesiod's description of his hometown, "bad in the winter, painful in the summer, never good."[93] Lynkeos snatches lines from a poem of praise and uses them to defame,[94] and he changes the context from fine dining to chaffering with fishmongers. The subtle and complicated humor seems to depend on these inversions, on the absurdity of quoting epic verse in a sordid situation, and on the idea that this might actually get a fish seller to lower his price. But beneath these literary layerings lies the practice of haggling. Insofar as it can be taken seriously (and even the humor depends on some serious content), Lynkeos's treatise offered buyers a superficial expertise, legitimated (if humorously) by its form in epic verse, to mitigate the asymmetry in information. Lynkeos assumes the discomfort of buyers at the haggling expertise of sellers and suggests that facility with conventional language, whether routine or altered, was an important resource in this situation.

Sellers might try to negotiate over more than the price. They might accept the buyer's price but attempt to dicker over the object or quantity. A character in a comedy of Alexis recounts this as a typical exchange: "If you ask, 'How much are you selling these two mullets for?' he says, 'Ten obols.' 'That's high. Would you take eight?' 'If you buy this other one.' 'My friend, don't be silly: take what I'm offering.' 'That much? Get out of here.'"[95] Or the Aesopic tale of Hermes, who took human form and came to earth to learn what people thought of him. In a statue-maker's workshop he saw a statue of Zeus and asked how much it cost. A drachma, the maker replied. Then he asked how much the statue of Hera cost. Even more, he answered. Then he saw his own statue, and figuring that as the messenger of the gods and the god of profit he would be highly valued, he asked the price. "If you buy the other two, I'll give you that one for free."[96]

Buyers, too, could haggle about the quantity or quality of goods. Among his anecdotes, Machon recounts the following:

Chaerephon was once buying some meat. They say that when the butcher cut off some meat that happened to have a lot of bone, he said, "Butcher, don't add on the weight of the bone." "But it's very sweet," the butcher said, "and you know what they say: the closer to the bone, the sweeter the meat." Chaerephon responded: "It may be sweet, my friend, but when it's added on, it hurts everywhere."[97]

Although the verbal sparring here concerns not the price but the goods, it shows similar tactics. The seller resorts to a common saying to justify his position, while the buyer had to counter this with some arch words of his own.

How buyers and sellers negotiated over a lagniappe—an extra tidbit or bonus—reveals the precarious nature of trust in such relationships. Millett has argued that merchants and customers might do things to introduce *philia* into the transactions.[98] He focuses on merchants extending credit, but offering a lagniappe could do the same thing, as illustrated by an anecdote from Theopompos: The agents of the tyrant Hieron of Syracuse bought gold from Architeles, a Corinthian, and after they'd bought as much as they wanted, Architeles "filled his hand with as much as it could hold and gave it to them in addition. In return Hieron sent from Sicily a ship of grain and other gifts."[99] Hieron requited Architeles' colossal lagniappe with an equally free (and tyrannically enormous) gift, establishing positive relations all around. But in ordinary market relationships, such gestures, instead of building trust, might get entangled in and trumped by the dynamics of distrust. People bickered over the lagniappe. Reciprocity, after all, could cut both ways. Theophrastus suggests that a person without shame would attempt to get his lagniappe by reminding the butcher of some past favor—or, if the butcher didn't give it to him, would grab some tripe from the table and leave with a laugh.[100] This anecdote also demonstrates that customers could come to expect a bonus—that is, that they understood it not as a free gift from a merchant, an inducement to trust, but as a rightful prerequisite. So you find stories of shoppers demanding—and sellers refusing—a lagniappe. One of Antiphanes' characters recounts a shopping expedition for a feast, including buying some fish (gobies). "When I asked the fish seller, that thief, to throw in a bonus, he said, 'I'll give you an extra: the news is, they're from Phaleron!'"[101] Or this character from Aristophanes: "And if someone asks for a free onion to spice his sardines, the vegetable lady gives him the fish eye and says, 'Are you asking for an onion because you want to be tyrant? Or maybe you think Athens grows spices as her tribute to you?'"[102] The fundamental asymmetry of market relationships generated a distrust resistant to compensatory tokens.

Haggling depended on verbal acuity. You had to perform the patter. Hesk has discussed the ways that traders used insults, metaphors, and innuendos in what he calls "combative capping."[103] Additionally, hagglers relied on conventional sayings. Bargainers used these in three related ways. First, pithy sayings provided a kind of justification by lending authority, as you can see in the passage from Euripides' *Cyclops* quoted at the opening of this chapter. Second, people used them to balk their rival. Note how the fruit seller in the following exchange deploys an aphorism ("The fair is everywhere rare . . .") to force the conversation on apples to a juncture:

Seller: Take these apples, my girl.

Girl: Beautiful!

Seller: Beautiful, yes, by the gods! You see, their seeds have just now arrived in Athens from the king.

Girl: By Artemis, I was thinking you were going to say that the golden apples were from the Hesperides, since there are just three.

Seller: The fair is everywhere rare—and costly.

Girl: I'll give you three obols for them, if that much. Here, I'll count it.

Seller: Or these pomegranates.

Girl: How fancy!

Seller: Fancy indeed, since they say that this was the only tree that Aphrodite planted in Cyprus.[104]

Third, no saying stood as the final word, if you could one-up your rival.[105] Lynkeos's treatise attempts to equip a shopper with clever and invincible sayings. This suggests that you could succeed not merely by adhering to convention, but also by a witty invention.

Enacting the Conflict of Exchange

The basic antagonism (as the Greeks perceived it) of economic exchange, as well as the form it took in haggling, sustains Herodas's seventh mime (third century BCE), in which a woman named Metro and some friends go to the cobbler Kerdon's shop to look at shoes. While on the surface Herodas's mimes are merely vignettes of daily life depicted through dialogue, they achieve a complexity and humor through ambiguity, layering, and conjunction with other mimes. In the seventh mime, Herodas encodes a psychosexual drama between Metro and Kerdon into the conventions of haggling, with surprising results.

Much of the previous scholarship on mime 7 has been limited in its approach and conclusions. Rightly situating this mime in the context of the Herodas's oeuvre (particularly in relation to mime 6), scholars have focused rather narrowly on the question whether the repetition of the names of two characters (Metro and Kerdon) means that the shoes they discuss in mime 7 stand in (either as euphemy in the conversation, or as a decoy in the box) for the *baubons* (dildos) discussed in mime 6.[106] In other words, the scholarly literature deals mainly with the question whether mime 7 is naughtier than it appears. Though an understandable reaction to the expurgations of earlier scholars, this focus has neglected both similarities with other mimes and differences from mime 6.

Reading mime 7 in juxtaposition with Herodas's other mimes raises two important points. First, a comparison to mime 6 shows some similarities but even more important differences. Indeed, mime 7 enacts a dramatic reversal from 6, the contrast between a desperate seller and a desperate buyer.[107] The reversal depends on many similarities.[108] Metro and Kerdon are characters in both, and each concerns (among other things) an unconsummated deal—for a dildo in mime 6 and for shoes (or, if you prefer, "shoes") in mime 7. But note the changes: The man who had spurned the offers of a fervid buyer has now become a desperate seller. Whereas the women had praised his wares, he now extols them himself.[109] And if the female buyers had been willing to have sex to complete the exchange, Kerdon himself now professes love, flirts, and (perhaps) implies intercourse.[110] Far from being a continuation of the sex-hungry women of mime 6 (as, for example, Finnegan 1992 assumes), Metro in mime 7 feeds on domination, spurning sex. This relates to my second point: like some other of Herodas's mimes, mime 7 depicts a sadistic woman. In mime 3 a mother has her slave whip her son "until [as she says] his worthless spirit is left barely on his lips" (lines 3–4), and in mime 5 a woman has her slave (and lover) bound and threatened with torture and tattooing, until she relents. In both, Herodas shows the victim crying and cowering at length. Kerdon, the seller in mime 7, is neither a minor nor a slave, and cannot be physically abused. Instead, Metro uses the conventions of haggling to berate and humiliate him.

In mime 7 the relationship between Metro and Kerdon is, formally at least, that of seller and buyer, as Kerdon labors to persuade Metro to purchase some shoes, though without success.[111] In this vignette, Metro, accompanied by some other women, goes to Kerdon's shop to examine his wares.[112] They converse at length through the conventions of haggling. As he shows the shoes, Kerdon extols his products (e.g., "It is not the case that some parts are well made and others not, but all the [handiwork] is equal"), reveals how much his materials cost, laments that he has a large family to feed, and predicts that the variety of his stock will satisfy every woman. Then the discussion of prices begins:

> Metro: For how much do you want to sell that pair which you lifted up before? But see you, don't put us to flight with louder thundering.

> Kerdon: Value it yourself if you wish and set what price it is worth. One who allows this does not readily cheat you....

Then an aside:

> Kerdon: O Hermes of profit and profiting Persuasion, if something does not now chance into the cast of our net, I do not know how the pot will fare better.

> Metro: Why are you muttering instead of having searched out the price with free tongue?[113]

> Kerdon: Lady, this pair is worth one mina, you may look up or down. Not the least shaving of a copper would come off [the price], if Athena herself were the customer.

Metro now answers obliquely and sarcastically. Although her statements do not mention the price or the pair of shoes in question, Kerdon treats them as a negotiating tactic and he continues to insist on his stated price:

> Metro: It's not surprising, Kerdon, that your little house is full of abundant lovely objects. Guard them [carefully] for yourself; for on the twentieth of Taureon Hecate holds the marriage of Artacene, and there is need of shoes; so, wretch (τάλης), perhaps with good luck, or rather certainly, they will rush to you. Have a sack stitched so that the cats won't plunder your minas.

> Kerdon: Whether Hecate comes, or Artacene, she will not get them for less than a mina; consider this, if you please.

Metro then mocks him—he has the good fortune to touch women's feet!—and calls him "an irritation and a wicked disgrace,"[114] and then she asks him how much he'll charge her friend for a different pair.

> Metro: Again blast out a word worthy of yourself.

> Kerdon: Five staters, by the gods, is what the harpists [Eu]eteris comes each day asking me to take, but I hate her, even if she promises me four Darics....

Because of the mutilation of the papyrus, Kerdon's next words are uncertain, but he seems to offer two pairs for seven Darics. Kerdon then proceeds to flirt with Metro, to put the shoes on the women's feet and to remark how well they fit, to affront a woman "cackling at the door more loudly than a horse," and finally to offer Metro a veiled invitation.

Metro exercises a sadistic dominance over the impotent Kerdon. The bulk of mime 7 reverses Kerdon's situation as recounted briefly in mime 6. There, Koritto and Metro, secluded in Koritto's home, discuss how Koritto could not get Kerdon to sell her a second dildo:

> Koritto: Metro, what did I not do? What persuasion did I not bring to bear on him? Kissing him, stroking his bald head, pouring him a sweet drink, calling him papa, almost giving him my body to use.
>
> Metro: But if he had asked for that too, you should have given it.
>
> Koritto: Yes, I should have....[115]

But mime 7's Kerdon is abject. He tries everything; he is, by turns, obsequious, pitiable, boasting, hurt, and flirtatious. He persistently endures Metro's abuse in the futile hope that he may yet sell some shoes. But no, by refusing to buy, Metro now has the power, and she humiliates Kerdon. Metro is unrelentingly self-confident, dismissive, aggressive, abusive.[116] She has brought her friends to watch her humiliate the cobbler. The woman snickering at the door seems to enjoy Kerdon's degradation.[117] Although Kerdon is above a slave—Herodas at least let him berate a servant at the beginning of the scene—Metro treats him like one, an insult most apparent in her line, "Why are you muttering instead of having searched out the price with free tongue?" (The word translated "muttering" was frequently used of slaves, as at 6.7.) In two other places she directly commands him how to speak to her. And twice she addresses him with insulting epithets.[118]

This mime works by appropriating haggling and leveraging it to create complex meanings. Herodas gives form to Metro's violence with the aggression latent in haggling. He reverses the usual asymmetry of roles: whereas normally sellers' knowledge gives them power over buyers, here the buyer's knowledge of her own indifference gives her the advantage over Kerdon. Both Kerdon and Metro engage in the verbal cleverness that constituted haggling. Shrewdly, Kerdon repeatedly switches his approach, tone, and register, attempting to keep his customer engaged. Metro, for her part, haggles by not haggling. Here the ambiguity of refusal aids her (and contributes to the complexity of the mime): if refusing to haggle can be a haggling tactic, she both does and doesn't haggle. She exhibits the evasiveness sometimes associated with slippery sellers. She cunningly keeps Kerdon engaged without fully engaging herself.

It is a complex scene. Herodas uses the conventions of haggling to stage a buyer's revenge fantasy. At the same time, because the buyer is a woman, we watch an act of awesome, uncontrolled female sadism. But finally, I should note, the scene makes the most sense if you understand Kerdon as a willing, even eager, participant in his own abasement, a man who enacts the haggling script not out of necessity (he says he's already refused another customer for personal reasons [lines 99–104]) but so that he can extend to Metro an enigmatic invitation to join him later. Naughty indeed.

Controlling Haggling

For each of the perceived asymmetries of power between buyers and sellers—with regard to information about the goods and competence at negotiating—you can imagine passing laws that attempt to rectify them. And, in fact, you can see many legal attempts to regulate both sellers' goods and the language they used.

Cities attempted to control the nature of commodities both through rudimentary quality norms and through mandating standard measurements for quantities. Alain Bresson has treated both of these (though he seems too generous in estimating their effectiveness), and I take them up in chapter 3. You can see both at work at Athens, for example, for which Aristotle lists the following market officials: *agoranomoi* (commissioners of the agora), *sitophylakes* (overseers of grain), *metronomoi* (custodians of measures and weights), and *emporiou epimeletai* (overseers of the wholesale market).[119] The *agoranomoi* were required to "oversee everything for sale so that it is all sold pure and unadulterated (*akibdela*)."[120] However much this vague and subjective norm attempts to regulate the quality of goods, it hardly constitutes a "standard," and it conforms to the general lack of objective quality standards in Greece. Most poleis mandated standardization of measurement, however (also the subject of chapter 3). Here I will anticipate only one of my conclusions: Athens, at least, required the use of standard measures *only* in retail contexts, where information asymmetries would be most extreme (since traders at the wholesale level would likely have more expertise in the commodities they traded). Insistence on standardized measures in retail contexts, then, seems to have responded to the distrust evoked by the structural asymmetry of information caused by coinage.

Other laws attempted to control the language through which buyers and sellers interacted. An Athenian law demanded truthtelling in the agora.[121] The issue of haggling, not simply of price, may lie behind other laws that limited the mark-up a merchant could make. Aristotle, for example, reports Athenian regulations linking the price of ground barley and wheat bread to the price of the unprocessed grain.[122] While you can see such regulations as expressing a notion of a just profit, they also have the effect of eliminating, or at least limiting, haggling.

Some people took the iterative verbal exchanges of haggling as fundamentally fraudulent. Plato's regulations of retail trade in *Laws*, book 11, offers a highly philosophical critique of haggling premised on the idea that things have real, objective, unchanging values. In presenting his laws about business transactions, he first offers a law about finding buried treasure (913a–14a). This peculiar beginning in fact illustrates his general rule: that people shouldn't touch others' property (913a). This general rule underpins all his economic regulations in the rest of the section. When Plato considers sellers, his overriding concern is the problem of *kibdeleia*, "adulteration" (916d). Although this initially suggests some sort of qualitative debasement of the product or the coin, his sense seems to be much wider. He proceeds to equate *kibdeleia*, lies, and trickery or fraud (*apate*) and to argue that all of them are like swearing a false oath to a god. And to deal with all this, he makes this law: "Whoever sells anything at all in the agora must never name two prices for what he's selling. When he names a single price, if he does not get it, he may bring his goods back again after he's taken them away. And let him not set a higher or lower price on the same day" (917b–c). Changing the price, therefore, is evidence of fraud, lies, and *kibdeleia* and violates the general rule against trying to get what's not yours because it misrepresents the real value of the object. (Both prices can't be the real price.) Indeed, he refers back to this law just a bit later, when he writes that the law "advised sellers not to set a price by attempting to impose more, but to do so in line with the essential value, and the law mandated the same of a contractor, since he is a craftsman who knows the value [of his work]."[123] Thus, Plato objects to the adulteration of the real value of an object through the practice of varying the price, as in haggling.

Plato's argument drew upon popular ideas about the relation of price to value. True, his critique of haggling conforms to his theory that the changeability of our world shows its unreality and inferiority, but others agreed with his critique of haggling. In one of Alexis's comedies, a character praises a law that would require fish sellers to name one irreducible price.[124] Such a law, he says, would make vendors happy to accept the fish's real value (ἀξία) and would enable everyone to buy reasonably (κατὰ τρόπον). The logic parallels Plato's: haggling shows that merchants attempt to get a price greater than the actual worth of the object. In fact, Plato's scheme of naming a single price was not mere philosophical speculation, nor was Alexis's pure comedy. On Delos in the late third century, the law required merchants selling firewood and charcoal to charge only the value they had declared for customs dues.[125] Such laws attempt to institute practices different from haggling for determining the price of an object. They depend on a distinction between haggled price and real value.[126] They do not explain how one knows the real value, though they presume that the seller (but perhaps not the buyer) does know it.

Precisely this context—attempts to circumscribe the haggling tactics of sellers—explains an important aspect of an Athenian law of 375/74, the law of Nikophon.[127] This law established two *dokimastai*, certifiers who examined and certified coins, one for the city of Athens, the other for its port, the Piraeus. Although you might assume that a law certifying coins worked to the benefit of sellers (who accepted coins), the law seems to have been written to check certain sellers' practices.

Scholars have disagreed about the context and causes of this law. It was passed some time during the Athenian year of 375/74 and presumes an earlier law, which might have been passed at any time in the previous quarter century, a period which began with Athens's abjection at the end of the Peloponnesian War and concluded with its revived imperial ambitions.[128] Nevertheless, most scholars situate the law in general political and economic contexts: Stroud, for example, argues that the law responds to a shortage of authentic Athenian coins; Alessandri argues that the law was part of Athens's attempts to rebuild its economy and currency after the ruinous Spartan defeat; Engen argues that the Athenians were attempting to maintain the international demand for their currency; and Ober argues that the law keeps transaction costs low by protecting the Athenian "brand" while carefully not imposing too many costs on transactors.[129] I don't want to deny the relevance of such broader contexts, but I would like to supplement them with an analysis of the particularities of this law and the local context it presumes.

The text of Nikophon's law specifies a mundane problem: sellers' behaviors in the marketplace.[130] The law's initial clause (lines 3–4) states a general principle: Athenian coinage must be accepted when it's found to be silver and has the public stamp. I infer that authentic Athenian coins were not always being accepted. The rest of the law, however, suggests that this was not a generalized problem, but a more precise one. Subsequent clauses designate particular locations, the various markets of Athens (including the Piraeus; lines 18–23), and stipulate a precise group of people, those who sell things (lines 17–18 and 30). Although these clauses of the law describe remedies, I infer that these were the proximate circumstances that prompted the law. Sellers—and no one else—were the problem.[131]

The law's provisions provide further evidence about sellers' behaviors.

The law instructed the *dokimastai* to destroy plated or fraudulent (*kibdelon*) coins and to return to the owner foreign silver coins that imitated the Athenian stamp (lines 8–13).[132] Presumably, in line with the general principle articulated at the beginning of the law and the following specific provisions, sellers were required to accept coins the *dokimastes* judged to be authentic Athenian ones. The imitation Athenian coins were not counterfeits (plated or base), but coins minted by foreign states in imitation of the Athenian brand, of variable but usually high silver content, and sometimes almost indistinguishable from authentic Athenian issues.[133] As Buttrey argues, the *dokimastes* did not determine the precise silver content of coins, but categorized them based on appearance, fabric, and certain rough tests.[134] These categorizations suggest that sellers' rejection of authentic Athenian coins had to do with the presence of counterfeits (which seem to have been rare) or imitations (which were more common). Although the wording of the law points in a particular direction, you need some imagination to go beyond this point.

It's likely that the law responded to, and attempted to control, sellers' bargaining tactics. Sellers, I suggest, tried to profit at buyers' expense by not accepting Athenian coins. Consider what it might mean to "not accept" a coin. Scholars usually take "not accepting" coins to mean a flatout rejection, and this is certainly possible. Merchants may have been refusing authentic Athenian coins out of an overabundance of caution, fearing counterfeits. But unless such suspicion was a generalized phenomenon— which is of course possible, though the law does not say so—it's unclear why Athens's entrepreneurial class should have been beset by fear of risk.[135] It may be, however, that sellers were not rejecting Athenian coins, but simply not accepting them *at full value*. (With legal tender, to demand a discount amounts to rejection.) As several scholars have recognized, the law still left imitations in circulation subject to possible discounting, their value determined by ad hoc bargaining.[136]

Scholars discredit the idea that people could trade in a world where coins (here, the imitations) fluctuated in value. T. V. Buttrey puts the case:

> The discount would itself be impossible to calculate, since the intrinsic value of the coin is indeterminable. Note too that each individual coin presents its own problem. Private dealing in such material would be perilous, for it would be based only on a wild guess as to its intrinsic value. For all practical purposes every such coin, individually evaluated, would cease to circulate as money and would become an object of barter.[137]

It seems unimaginable.

Consider, however, the United States from 1838 to 1863, the era of "free banking," a period during which the federal treasury minted coins but printed no paper currency. Instead, banks, thousands of them, issued debt obligations, which looked like paper currency and functioned as money. Both state-chartered and private banks issued such money[138]—as did city and county governments, railroads and other transportation companies, and even local stores.[139] In this welter of notes, discounting was common, for three reasons: transportation costs (to go to the place where the note was issued in order to redeem it), the risk of default by the issuing entity, and the possibility of counterfeits.[140] This gave rise both to an unsystematic expertise—there were knacks for assessing currencies[141]—and to privately published bulletins that listed the discount rates on various bank notes. Brokers appeared to exploit arbitrage opportunities.[142] Of course, there were important differences between this and the Greek world: American notes had no intrinsic value but were always supposedly redeemable for something else (specie, travel miles, tax payments, merchandise), and the procedures of redemption affected the discounting. The risk of default differed from the risk posed by an imitation Athenian coin: for debt obligations there was some small (and possibly unknown) risk of total loss, whereas imitation coins usually retained some intrinsic worth. The situation in the antebellum United States was extraordinarily complex (more so than I've described here), but people were able to buy and sell despite the intricacy and uncertainty.

However possible such discounting might have been, I must admit that there is not much direct evidence that it happened in Athens. As a presumed background, it would add trenchancy to the idea of the cynic Diogenes that in his ideal state, dice would be used instead of coins.[143] The most obvious parallel (for which good evidence does exist) would be the exchange of foreign currencies.[144] These were discounted. It would cost you money to exchange currencies, and the license to do so could be profitable.[145] Examples from inscriptions suggest that this fee could amount to 6 or 7 percent.[146] Of course this is not just a parallel, since imitation Athenian coins were, in effect, a different currency. What the spread would have been between authentic (*dokimon*) coins and imitations is unknown, but Androcles' report of a loan agreement suggests it was enough to make you stipulate repayment in the former.[147]

Sellers could have used the threat of discounting authentic Athenian coinage against buyers. After they had struck a deal—after the inquiries, the flattery, the hyping and knocking, the shifts and feints and responses, when they had agreed on an amount and a price, and perhaps even a lagniappe, when the customer presented their money, when the conflict was finally over—the merchant could still balk, complaining that these were not good Athenian coins but Egyptian knockoffs: who knows how much they're worth, but for you I'll accept them at a discount. The seller here took a calculated risk, that they buyer would not walk away from this sudden defiance. It was a game of chicken. Analyzed in terms of transaction costs, the seller threatened to impose the additional costs of renegotiating on both parties unless the buyer bought his way out (by accepting the discounting of his money).[148] In such negotiations, sellers held a cunning advantage: while they could argue that a coin was really worth less than its face value, customers could not seriously contend (by way of counterstrategy) that it was worth more. Sellers, that is, had room to compromise from their initial positions; buyers did not. A passage from Diphilos's comedy *The Busybody* points to the strategy of introducing the question of currency after the deal had been seemingly consummated. (The speaker is describing a particularly shifty fishmonger, apparently somewhere other than Athens.)

> If you ask how much the sea bass costs, this man answers ten obols without adding in what currency. When you pay him the money, he demands Aiginan coins. And if he owes you change, he gives it back in Athenian coins. Both ways he takes a cut.[149]

If the idea that sellers attempted to wrest even more from buyers by demanding a discount on authentic Athenian coins on the pretence they might be imitations remains hypothetical, it is still the best hypothesis to explain the emphasis in Nikophon's law on the culpability of sellers. If the law had the effect of protecting sellers from questionable currency, its explicit provisions predicate sellers alone as the problem. Note, too, that even if you consider the confiscation of a buyer's counterfeit currency as a punishment, the penalty for sellers refusing to accept a good Athenian coin was much greater (forfeiture of the day's entire stock, plus fifty lashes for merchants who were slaves). With the law of Nikophon, the community of buyers tried to limit sellers' haggling.

Conclusion

Like Lynkeos's friend, Greeks tended to think of themselves as buyers in need of help, exploited by sellers who knew more about the commodities, negotiated more adeptly, and had shadier characters. Of these three interrelated asymmetries, the second may have been the most galling, since the hope of learning the truth about the goods and the sellers depended to some extent on language itself—which was already implicated in the seller's superiority. Merchants' assurances about the goods or claims of trustworthiness for themselves were already suspect, dependent as they were on a manipulative, strategic use of language. If legal regulations provided some relief, total escape seemed utopian. Herodotus, however, provides just such an alluring vision:

> The Carthaginians also tell this story: There is a place in Libya beyond the Pillars of Heracles, and people inhabit it. Whenever the Carthaginians arrive there, they unload their cargoes and array them on the beach. Then they retreat to their ships and send up a smoke signal. When the inhabitants see the smoke, they come down to the sea and set out gold before [or, in exchange for] the goods. They then retreat inland, away from the cargoes. Then the Carthaginians disembark and look it over, and if the gold seems to them worth the goods, they pick it up and leave. But if it doesn't seem worth [the goods], they reboard their ships and wait. The natives come back and set out even more gold until they persuade them. And neither side (the Carthaginians say) wrongs the other, for the one group does not take the gold before estimating the value of the goods, while the other group does not take the goods before the Carthaginians take the gold.[150]

Whether such silent trade actually happened is impossible to verify; Herodotus does not endorse the veracity of this story himself; he simply repeats what he tells us the Carthaginians said.[151] But the story embodies the dissolution of the asymmetries of the agora: There is no certified coinage, only goods and gold, which both sides inspect and proportion. Neither side cheats the other, despite the obvious opportunities to do so. And the negotiations, even through multiple iterations, are not corrupted by manipulative language, by haggling. The whole transaction is profoundly, serenely impersonal. Unfortunately for the Greeks, trade without haggling was possible only at the edge of the world.[152]

CHAPTER 3

Measuring

In the early fourth century, a man charged a group of grain retailers in Athens with violating a law that prohibited anyone from buying up more than fifty phormoi of grain.[1] Because a phormos is usually understood to be a basket, scholars who have encountered the word in this prosecutor's speech and elsewhere when it seems to indicate an amount (commonly of grain)[2] have usually sought to determine exactly how capacious a phormos was. For weak, circumstantial reasons, they have mostly concluded that it was roughly or exactly equivalent to a medimnos, a measure of capacity that was both standardized (at Athens it held about 52 liters) and systematized (it equaled 6 hekteis, 48 choinikes, and 196 kotylai).[3] Here scholarly curiosity about the phormos ends. Virtually no one has wondered why a text would use two differently named but equivalent measures, or why it would use one word instead of another in any particular situation.[4]

But the distinction between a phormos and a medimnos points not to discrepant though interchangeable words or objects but to fundamentally different practices of quantifying grain and, more broadly still, to the extent and ways that Greeks used standardized measures.[5] Phormoi were containers usually associated with specific commodities and used in a particular practice—the long-distance trade in grain—which, because of the customs of this trade, people could use as practical units: they could see them, assess them, count them. As far as we know, they were never systematized (integrated with smaller or larger measures); nor were they ever officially standardized. The medimnos, on the other hand, was a systematized, standardized measure—which Greeks rarely used in actual measuring. It was, however, fundamental to the intellectual manipulation of quantities.

We live in a world so suffused with, and even constituted by, standardization—of weights and measures, of course, but of myriad other things from batteries to the dimensions of intermodal shipping containers—

that we rely on these systems without thinking. But Greeks could trust abstract systems of standardized measurement in only a few situations; more often they had to rely on personal trust in others and on their own expertise. With grain, they had to develop through experience a sense of how good any batch was and how much might be in any phormos, a kind of estimating or eyeballing that particularized every transaction.

This chapter, then, offers the history of practices, not objects; of measuring, not measures. Archaeologists and antiquarians have extensively documented the many standard measures from ancient Greece. The names and sizes of the standards might vary from city to city, but generally all cities had standards of length, volume, and weight, with different volume systems for liquid and dry substances. A few objects that had to be interchangeable were also standardized, especially bricks and roof tiles.[6] Greeks made coins, of course, in line with their systems of weights. But if many scholars have worked intensively to determine the objective *size* of standard measures, they have attended less to the practical ways in which Greeks *used* them—or did not use them.[7]

In this chapter I examine the trade in grain so as to understand when and how Greeks used standard measures and practical units. When handling grain, Greeks were likely to use practical units (phormoi) to quantify amounts. The absence of objective quality standards undercut the importance of precise standards of quantity, so that any method of quantifying grain—counting bags, measuring volume, or weighing—depended on an ineluctable element of personal expertise. Although standard measures had significant virtues, these were often realized in situations abstracted from the physical handling of things, such tasks as establishing ratios or unit prices, or describing large (but unmeasured) amounts. In two situations of endemic distrust, however, the polis intervened to enforce the use of standard measures: in retail trade in the agora and in transactions conducted by officials of the polis. I conclude with an examination of the trade in grain in Hellenistic and Roman Egypt, in part as a contrast to that of the classical period, in part to indicate the limitations of ancient practices when considered in light of modern systems of standardization.

The Standardized World

Disenthrall yourself of a world saturated with exact measuring and systems of standardization. It was not always so. Specific, idiosyncratic, and unstandardized measures have been common throughout history. Although today such measures persist in certain situations (for example, women's clothing sizes),[8] we live mostly in a world where abstract, standardized, universal measures are (or are thought to be) the norm. This has been a very recent—and very difficult—achievement. In his history of standard measures in Europe, Witold Kula (1986) makes it clear that whatever the drawbacks of local, peculiar, or unstandardized measures, many people defended them fiercely and abandoned them reluctantly, and then only under the relentless pressure of the modern nation-state. (Kula's book allows you to understand that charming time when the uniformity and abstraction of the metric system seemed as absurdly utopian and impractical as any of the *philosophes'* ideas.) In what follows, then, I hope to guard against assumptions that might arise from the modern prejudice in favor of standard measures, and, like Kula, I hope to explain situations of both the use and the absence of standard measures.

Unlike Kula, however, I will argue that any history of the standardization of quantities must also take into account variability of quality. A quantity of grain is not wholly independent of its quality. Here again it's necessary to understand contemporary systems of quality standardization so as not to fall into error. Consider an offhand comment by Pritchett, tucked into a footnote, which points out that that both Theophrastus and Pliny distinguished the density of wheat from different regions: "To the modern, wheat is wheat, but the ancient was acutely aware of differences."[9] The modern person's capacity to treat wheat as wheat, however, is not due to an inability to appreciate its variations (as Pritchett implies), but rather is made possible by a set of complex systems that have *created* uniformity in wheat and many other commodities. These systems of standardization of quality—grading, licensing, regulating, branding,[10] etc.— have a deep history. This chapter is not that history, but my argument here does depend on an awareness of it.

Wheat became wheat through a history of interrelated systems, which have affected all agricultural production. This history concerns the mechanization of growing, processing, and distributing agricultural products, modeled on the assembly line and needing interchangeable parts. It concerns the intensive breeding and genetic manipulation of plants and animals, which has aimed not only to make these more productive but to make the products more appealing to consumers (in color, shape, etc.) and more amenable to mechanized processing (through uniformity).[11] And it concerns the development of objective standards to classify the variations of quality that (even after all that manipulation) still occur. The history of the standardization of quality grades for wheat, in particular, includes the rise of the Chicago Board of Trade, a trade group of the grain merchants of the nineteenth century, a story Cronon tells thrillingly in *Nature's Metropolis.*[12] Because of the huge capital investment in railroads, their owners lost money when the cars sat idle as gangs of men loaded and unloaded grain in bags. To speed up the process, the railroad owners began using mechanized grain elevators. This required, however, that wheat, which had previously been shipped from the farm to its final destination in sacks, be shipped in bulk, and to prevent the mixing of inferior with superior wheat a system of grading had to be developed and adopted—and forced upon reluctant farmers, who feared that the rules of grading were skewed to the advantage of the grain elevator owners against the farmers.

In the United States today there are eight classes of wheat, six grades in each class. (For barley there are two classes, each with three subclasses.) Each grade has a minimum *test weight*, which is its weight per unit of volume with a standardized moisture content. Test weight is useful as a rough measure of the amount of energy in grain (hence its food potential). The test weight of any batch of wheat is determined empirically and independent of the moisture content. If the actual moisture content of a batch of wheat differs from the standard (13.5 percent for wheat, 14.5 percent for barley), the weight of the wheat is adjusted accordingly.[13] Finally, as you may remember from reading your cereal boxes closely, grain is measured and sold by weight, not volume. Except for determining how much space is needed for storage or transport, weight matters.

The highly articulated and differentiated distinctions of quality and quantity create fungibility—wheat of a specific class and grade is interchangeable. Thus wheat buyers can know the precise quality and quantity of the grain without ever seeing it. Indeed, traders in wheat can be completely ignorant of wheat itself. What they trade are abstract quantities of abstract qualities, and they trust not so much the seller as the systems that create fungibility. The operation of these systems consistently circumscribes and concentrates expertise: those who buy and sell wheat have become experts at assessing the market (forecasting, for example, the factors that affect supply and demand), not experts in the physical properties of wheat itself. And the assessment of the quality of wheat by graders depends not on their unfettered judgment but on the application of objective rules (about test weight, degree of adulteration, moisture content, etc.).[14] In our world, unlike the Greeks', the quantity and quality of grain can be specified with a high degree of precision.

The Classical Grain Trade

However great the aggregate trade in grain became during the classical period, it was arranged and undertaken not through large, durable organizations (firms or governments) but through many small enterprises reliant on personal trust and expertise more than on objective, impersonal systems.[15] Statements about the magnitude of this trade require circumspection, since there is little direct evidence and few inferences are uncontested. Nevertheless, despite these uncertainties, it seems fair to conclude that Athenians began consuming substantial amounts of imported grain during the Peloponnesian War[16] and that in the fourth century they purchased a lot of foreign grain, mostly wheat—on Garnsey's conservative estimate, perhaps half of the city's food supply.[17] Greeks in other cities, too, may have consumed significant amounts of imported grain.[18] Despite the amount of trade, grain traders operated in small groups.[19] Importers frequently sailed with their cargoes, sometimes in a ship they themselves owned. At other times they sent agents to travel with their goods, a practice that may have increased through the fourth century.[20] At no time did the scale of these relationships transcend the personal; the problem of delegated authority was dealt with through mechanisms of personal trust.[21] If you sent someone else with your cargo, it was either a business partner (with congruent interests) or a trusted subordinate, sometimes a slave or former slave.

In conducting trade in the classical period, merchants relied on personal trust and expertise; abstract systems tended to supplement, not replace, these, as evidenced by merchants' use of writing. Merchants wrote letters to distant business partners or agents directing them to do certain things, a practice that extended already existing relationships of trust.[22] Moreover, although Greeks kept lists of debts and copies of contracts, there is no evidence that they kept accounts of expenses. Bresson's claim that merchants kept accounts of routine expenses misapplies the evidence: Aristophanes' character Strepsiades did not record daily expenditures but did record his debts; the same was true of the trierarch Apollodoros.[23] Greeks did not use writing to construct and regulate abstract (economic) entities—firms, voyages, investments, and the like.[24]

As an illustration of how documents operated within relationships of trust, consider the case of Chrysippos, who had lent money to Phormio to ship a cargo to the Bosporos. When Chrysippos began to distrust Phormio, he tried to have him watched. In a subsequent Athenian trial, Chrysippos reported:

> So then Phormio came to the Bosporos, carrying letters from me, which I gave him to take to a slave of mine who was wintering there and to a business partner. I stated in this letter the money that I'd lent and the security, and I asked them, as soon as he [Phormio] unloaded the goods, to inspect them and shadow him. But, so that they wouldn't know what he was doing, he didn't deliver the letters he got from me.[25]

Chrysippos's letters extended the reach of his personal relationships over great distances but did not constitute an independent alternative. Chrysippos did not rely, for example, on a system of authenticating documents (bills of lading, invoices, receipts, etc.) or on a bureaucracy to make sure that the borrower did what he'd promised. Indeed, Chrysippos's plan ultimately failed because there was no impersonal system of moving documents (such as a post office), so that he had to rely for delivery of the letter on the very man he distrusted.

Nor did Greeks usually treat documents as things with an authority of their own, separate from the relationships that generated them. However much Greeks used written contracts, the witnesses to an agreement, not the document itself, remained essential in adjudicating disputes.[26] This was true even in Athens, where, after sometime around 350 BCE, merchants had to use written contracts to invoke special commercial legal procedures.[27] Nor, with some rather limited exceptions, were there authoritative official documents. Thus, while cities may have issued tokens, seals, or bronze plates as identification, we know of no systems of more complex official documents: licenses, permits, bills of lading, receipts, passports, and the like. Bresson has argued that such documents did exist, but whatever the strengths of the individual points he makes, he has not shown that there were *systems* of documentation.[28] Indeed, Bresson's argument overlooks the most obvious way that officials would have gathered information about merchants' home cities, destinations, or cargoes: not from documents but by oral inquiry, supplemented by oaths.[29] Greeks used writing to buttress, not to supplant, existing relationships of trust (or suspicion).

Phormoi

While the medimnos was an abstract measure, part of a system of measures, the phormos was a customary unit, part of the process of moving grain. The context of use distinguished them.[30] A medimnos was a measure of volume—abstract because its capacity was independent of the situations in which the grain (or any other commodity) was handled. It was not a container, and it often designated amounts that had not actually been measured. As a standardized measure, the medimnos's primary virtue was abstractness rather than precision. A phormos, on the other hand, was a specific, contextualized unit: phormoi were containers (probably sacks) used for shipping and storing produce, especially grain. Although phormoi had capacities, these were secondary characteristics, not what defined them. Their capacities were not officially standardized, which is why it's not possible to exactly specify how large they were; nor were they part of a system of ranked measures. However, the size of phormoi was, to some degree, defined by their weight. The technology for handling grain set an upper weight range, beyond which they would no longer be useful: the amount that humans could lift and carry in a sealed container. But a phormos was not a standardized weight either. Rather than being a measure of *volume* or of *weight*—both abstract qualities—the phormos was a *unit of grain* deeply rooted in the processes of moving large amounts of grain to distant markets.

The salient physical features of a phormos derived from its use, and two of these make it more like a "bag" than a "basket" (its received translation).[31] Containers that were used as practical units were often closely linked to particular substances, and Greeks typically associated phormoi with agricultural produce.[32] Two properties of phormoi, however, linked them to long-distance trade in grain: stackability and sealability. Unlike archetypical baskets, phormoi were easily stackable, which would seem to have depended on being flexible rather than rigid. Herodotus, Aeneas, and Polybius refer to a military use of phormoi: filling them with straw to fill trenches or with sand to build barricades or walls.[33] Open baskets of sand seem unwieldy in this situation, especially if, as Aineias recommends, they were piled to considerable heights.[34] Something like sandbags, flexible and sealed, seem more likely. Other evidence makes clear that phormoi could be sealed: Plutarch refers to a tyrant who killed a man and disposed of his body in the sea in a phormos.[35] As I understand it from the movies, putting the body in a phormos makes sense most if it could be sealed—with weights added. Aeschines said that Demosthenes sought to make the Athenians understand their constrained international position with a metaphor: "We are being sewn up like phormoi."[36] There were, indeed, special needles used for phormoi.[37] The fact that phormoi could be securely closed is an especially significant point: sealed containers, because spillage is not a problem, can be hoisted and carried more easily than open ones. The word *phormos*, then, could denote a range of woven, sealable containers, from a rigid basket to something like a burlap bag.[38]

As a unit of grain, the phormos was useful not because it had been officially standardized but because it was part of the practice of moving grain. Though little evidence shows directly how grain was transported, the use of phormoi seems the most likely method. In considering how Greeks moved grain in phormoi, you should consider three modes of transport: human, animal, and maritime.

Shipping grain by any means invariably involved human labor, that of porters and stevedores. Some of these laborers were probably slaves, others were likely free men earning money, and many must have found frequent work in the busy port of Athens, though ancient sources reveal little about these humble cogs.[39] One inference scholars have made from the need for human transport in a premechanized age is that a phormos must have been no larger than a reasonable burden for a man to carry—

though whether that meant it held about a medimnos or much more is entirely unknown.[40] The technology of sealing phormoi would increase the amount a person could carry.

Over more than the shortest distance on land, some form of animal power was employed, whether to pull a cart or to carry panniers.[41] In Athens, where the city lay five miles from the port, a considerable amount of grain had to be brought up.[42] Some of it, too, may have been imported by land; Thucydides reports that when the Spartans occupied Dekelea, grain from Euboea had to be shipped instead of brought overland.[43] Whether for short distances or long, it's reasonable to imagine much of this transported grain packed in sealed phormoi.

Greeks shipped a huge amount of grain across the Mediterranean, Aegean, and Black seas—though underwater archaeology shows almost no evidence of it. This is not only because grain is perishable, but also because when sodden it swells to the point of breaking a ship apart, dispersing the evidence of the wreck.[44] Parker's catalogue *Ancient Shipwrecks of the Mediterranean and the Roman Provinces* lists no more than a handful of wrecks with any trace of grain, out of hundreds known.[45] Only clusters of more durable objects—olive seeds or almonds—insinuate the presence of bags.[46] Still, the techniques of transport point toward bagged grain, against the likelihood of bulk shipping. First, in a time before mechanization, shipping grain loose in the hold would have increased labor costs because it would need to be put into and taken out of containers repeatedly just to be loaded and unloaded. Second, grain had to be held motionless in the hold (or it could capsize the ship), probably an easier matter with bagged cargo (which could be stabilized with ropes). Third, grain shipped by sea would also have to be moved at some point by humans and by animals, in containers. Thus, it seems likely that grain was shipped in some sort of container, and these were almost surely sacks.[47] (Amphoras were not used to ship grain.)[48]

The market in grain was primarily responsible for the need for transportable containers. Production for domestic consumption deployed containers differently. In what Sigaut has characterized as the "Mediterranean system" of agriculture, the system that prevailed in classical Greece, grain was harvested with a sickle (usually by men), sheaved, threshed by animals soon after the harvest, winnowed immediately, and stored.[49] In such domestic production, grain was moved from the fields in sheaves and then moved again from the threshing floor to the storage area. Since threshing floors seem to have been located near the places of storage and consumption—the house on the farmstead or the village[50]—the sheaf was the more important container for movement, and the grain (and chaff) could be moved to storage in ad hoc containers. Farmers could then use different containers for storage: bins or jars. They probably used phormoi too, at times, though, as I argue in chapter 4, the prevalence of phormoi as storage containers on the estates of the rich may relate to their distinct needs to move grain.

A phormos, then, was not, in the first instance, a standardized measure (a capacity defined by the state as part of a system of measures) but a customary object used in trade. For grain, which had to be transported over great distances and by different means, or had to change hands (physically or legally) multiple times, the phormos was the container of choice.

Practical Units and Systematization

There is no evidence that the phormos was ever standardized or integrated into a system of measures, and no need to assume that it was. The phormos belonged to that class of units where the container is the amount and the amount the container. Even today, we still use such unstandardized but practical units: When you plan a party, for example, you estimate the amount of potato chips you need, not in *ounces* but in *bags*, and beer in *bottles*, not *gallons*. Similarly, Greeks used *hamaksiaios*, "wagonload," as a unit of big, heavy things[51]—inexact from our perspective, but eminently practical for them.

Such practical units did not starkly oppose standardized measures— you can imagine there might be attempts to integrate or link such units to larger systems—but the unit remained essentially based in practice. With three such practical units you can see this interplay at work. Consider first one kind of basket, the *kalathos*. On the island of Delos, a *kalathos* was more than a basket; it was an amount of charcoal. Since Delos, a small island, uniquely had to import all its fuel, the *kalathos* may have been the customary container in which it was packaged.[52] Here the *hieropoioi* (the officials in charge of the temple of Apollo) bought charcoal for fires on the altar by the *kalathos*, but they also recorded purchasing fractional units: "half-*kalathos*" and "eighth-*kalathos*."[53] The *half* alone does not systematize a unit,[54] but in conjunction with the *eighth* it represents an attempt to do so. Note, however, that the Delians did not link the *kalathos* to a smaller unit, but merely fractionalized it. This suggests that the *kalathos*, however official it may have become, remained isolated from any more comprehensive, abstract system of volume measures and rooted in its role as the container in which charcoal was imported. Several decades later, a law regulating the sale of wood, timber, and charcoal at Delos indicated that the *agoranomoi* (market commissioners) kept the "scale (and) measures for charcoal," which all sellers had to use.[55] Thus at Delos the *kalathos*, a customary container for shipping charcoal, had been standardized but not systematized, remaining a unique measure for this one commodity.

The connection between containers as practical units and standardization appears as well with another kind of basket, the *kophinos*.[56] Several inscriptions from Boiotia and Thessaly show grain gauged by *kophinoi*: 1. In the third century BCE, the officials charged with selling subsidized grain to citizens of Chaironeia were instructed not to sell more than 30 *kophinoi* per day.[57] 2. During a grain shortage in Rome in the second century, Thessaly agreed to send 430,000 *kophinoi* of wheat to Rome.[58] 3. In the first century, a benefactor in Akraiphia gave 1 *kophinos* of grain to each person who attended a festival.[59] 4. In the first century CE, the tithes and rents from some sacred land in Chaironeia were quantified in *kophinoi*.[60] From these it emerges that the *kophinos* was a unit that could quantify grain, but it's less clear that it should be consistently systematized, standardized, and abstracted. Scholars have concluded that a *kophinos* was three sixteenths of a medimnos, though some dispute its absolute size.[61] I am reluctant to make the equation, which rests on a highly emended fragment of Strattis, an Athenian comic poet of the late fifth or early fourth centuries (fr. 13), especially on taking literally lines that look like a joke we don't understand, and arbitrarily rejecting some of the numbers in the passage while accepting others.[62] If these inscriptions provide some indirect evidence that the *kophinos* was a standardized measure,[63] it is unclear whether it was the same size over time and in different places; nor is there any evidence, except for the dubious passage in Strattis, that it was systematized with other measures or fractionalized. Nevertheless, *kophinoi* were common containers on farms,[64] and they seem to have been very strong since they were imagined as appropriate for hoisting stones or lowering men, as well as for hauling dung.[65] Indeed, the references to *kophinoi* show it as a household container for moving things rather than storing them. The *kophinos* seems to have had a customary capacity, so that Aristotle could use it as a measure of size that he anticipated his audience would understand, as could the writers of the New Testament story of the loaves and fishes.[66] These texts could rely on their audiences' comprehension, not because the capacity of the *kophinos* had been officially fixed by the government of Boeotia (or Athens, or Judea), but because its purpose—moving heavy objects on the farm—remained consistent. The use of the *kophinos* as a measure in the four inscriptions cited above should be understood against this background of household practice as much in the context of systemization of measures.

Finally, consider a third kind of basket, an *arsichos*, as it appears in a lease of sacred land in fourth-century Amorgos. This inscription delineates the duties of the farmer who takes up the lease, and among these it specifies: "Each year he will apply 150 measures of manure with a basket (*arsichos*) holding 1 medimnos and 4 half-hekteis. If he does not apply it he will pay a fine of three obols per *arsichos* shortfall. He will make a pledge to the temple administrators that he has applied the manure according to the lease agreement."[67] This lease invents a special measure for the occasion, the *arsichos*. The lease does not specify the total in abstract measures (200 medimnoi, which equals 150 *arsichoi* at 1.3 medimnoi each) but rather looks to ordinary practice—taking manure to the fields in *arsichoi*—and attempts to regulate and rationalize it. The measure here is the practical one, the basketful, but it's translated into abstract measures (the medimnos). Practice, however, remains primary. (Note, too, that as with many other situations where relationships were regulated by the use of measures, accountability resided not in an audit or in surveillance but in an oath.)

Like the phormos, these containers were not abstract but specific and contextualized units, whose usefulness as measures initially arose from practice. As practical, customary measures, they were confined to specific cities or areas and used for a restricted range of commodities. They depended upon and generated local knowledge, a kind of expertise. As Mahir noted of a West African grain market where people did not consistently rely on standard measures, "the ability to judge the quantity of product in a measure at a glance is one of the most fundamental skills required in trading."[68] Similarly, in classical Greece, farmers who sold some of their produce, or traders, retailers, and others who dealt in and moved large amounts of grain, could count phormoi and other nonstandardized units because they were part of the practical world of their expertise; lacking this expertise, we see them as inexact measures.[69]

Medimnoi

Unlike the phormos, the medimnos was an abstract, notional measure. It was commonly used in two particular contexts: to enumerate very large amounts of grain, and to commensurate grain by describing an abstract "price." In both contexts it was an imaginary measure because no grain was actually measured. Its work consisted not in its precision or exactness but in its abstraction, in allowing people to imagine an amount of grain that was not in any particular container or context. Its abstraction allowed for grain to be treated as fungible.

Used to describe large amounts of grain, the medimnos was notional because the quantities were probably guesses (however educated they may have been), not the result of actually measuring by medimnos. Just because a text records an amount of grain in medimnoi does not mean that it was measured. Take an inscription from Delphi in 361/60 that lists mostly money contributions toward rebuilding the temple, but also includes this in-kind gift:

> The Apollonians: three thousand Pheidonian medimnoi of barley. From this there was one thousand eight hundred seventy five Delphic medimnoi. The price of this was three thousand five hundred eighty seven drachmas, three obols, and a half obol. The Apollonians brought this to Delphi by sea at their own expense. Ainesidamos of Delphi [and] Aristokleidas the Apollonian brought the grain.[70]

Scholars have been trying to figure out how to get from the first number, 3,000 Pheidonian medimnoi, to the last, 3,587 drachmas and 3.5 obols. Assuming that the first figure represents the precise measurement of this shipment of barley, they have argued either that it was sold for 1 drachma and 5.5 obols per Delphic medimnos (which gets you pretty close, 3,593 drachmas and 4.5 obols, within about 6 drachmas of the price), or that it was sold for 2 drachmas for each Delphic medimnos, but there was a loss of grain (through handling, vermin, etc.) of 4.33 percent.[71]

Both theories misapprehend the two numbers. The inscription recorded the ostensible amount of the gift (as claimed by the donors) and the exact amount of money realized (for which the officials were accountable). How much grain was actually there didn't matter to these officials. The number of medimnoi was recorded to honor the donors, not as part of the officials' accountability. Three thousand was a common number for benefactors to choose—but the unit could vary (different medimnoi, drachmas too).[72] The fact that the grain was recorded in Pheidonian measures and mathematically converted to the local system shows that if the barley was measured at all, it was done back in Apollonia and not at Delphi.[73] The price was all that mattered to the Delphic officials. The inscription reveals nothing about how the grain was sold off (in batches or all at once?), so you can't know whether the buyers measured it or not. But even if the buyers did measure out the amount of grain exactly, the officials felt no need to record this amount. The exact amount of grain was not as important for the officials' record as either the amount claimed by the donors (honoring them would require, it seems, accepting their claim at face value) or the exact amount of money realized from the sale (for which the officials would be accountable). Positing an arbitrary loss is unnecessary.[74] In this honorary inscription, then, the unit of measure, the medimnos, may bear some relation to the amount of grain, but it is not a relation established in any immediate sense through measuring.[75]

The medimnos also allowed Greeks to create abstract prices, which did not pertain to any particular transaction but were generalized. An average price would be an example of an abstract price. The fact that an average price may be a price that *no person actually paid* shows how abstracted such prices are from individual and specific transactions. Greeks, too, referred to abstract prices. For example, a merchant involved in an Athenian legal suit noted that at a time of shortage, the price of grain reached 16 drachmas (per medimnos).[76] There are, however, two important things to note about abstract prices in Greece.

First, the relation of any ancient particular price to an abstract price (whether modern or ancient) differs from the relation of modern particular prices to abstract prices. Modern abstract prices depend on fungibility, an objective qualitative equivalence that allows for interchangeability.[77] As I noted above, complex systems of grading and branding create the modern possibilities of fungibility—systems entirely absent in the ancient world. In the case of antiquity, you should not assume a qualitative commensurability of goods, even when they are described with the same word. Rather, you should understand particular prices—the outcome of negotiation, bargaining, haggling—as reflecting both the quantitative *and* the qualitative uniqueness of the thing purchased. Thus, abstract prices for antiquity must smooth over both the qualitative diversity of commodities and the effect these had on particular prices. To put it differently, because of qualitative disparities in goods, ancient particular prices have a less direct relation to any abstract price than modern particular prices do.

Thus, some caution is in order when studying ancient prices. One thing modern scholars have tried to study are ancient price fluctuations, an enterprise that depends on average prices.[78] But they have not paid enough attention to the ways that average prices may obscure qualitative variations. For example, more than one scholar has used a papyrus account-log of purchases for workers in a record office in Tebtynis, Egypt, in September and October 45 CE (*P. Mich.* 2.127) to show the degree to which wheat prices could fluctuate over the short term. Duncan-Jones uses this document to confirm the idea that wheat prices could vary by a factor of two around harvest time, Rathbone says it shows the effects of excessive flooding on the Nile, and Drexhage (followed by Reger) uses it to demonstrate that prices could fluctuate even during a single day.[79] But given that the quality of "wheat" in antiquity could vary much more than that of *No. 1 hard winter red wheat* today, you should expect particular prices to reflect the qualitative variability of individual batches. While it would be unwarranted, on the one hand, to attribute all variations in particular prices to qualitative variability, it is also unwarranted to leave this out of the equation entirely.[80] Indeed, the evidence that Duncan-Jones relies on suggests that qualitative variations could play a significant role in deviation of particular prices from average ones. He also cites two other papyri that provide a series of prices over time, each a record of sales by producers. In both of these, the variation in particular prices is only about 10 percent, far less than the 93 percent recorded in *P. Mich.* 2.127. Duncan-Jones concludes from these three documents that prices could vary significantly with the seasons but did not necessarily do so. If you assume, however, that the wheat sold by a single producer over a period of weeks was qualitatively more consistent than that bought by a single purchaser (since the former came from a single source, the latter probably not), then the larger deviation from the average in the prices for wheat in Tebtynis may for the most part have reflected the qualitative variability of the grain. This would suggest that average prices over time were not as volatile as sometimes claimed, though particular prices could be. My point here is not that abstract or average prices cannot be useful historical tools, but that they can obscure the greater particularity of ancient transactions.

Second, while modern and ancient abstract prices may look the same, they have been created by very different mechanisms. Modern abstract prices are usually the result of empirical and statistical procedures: sampling, weighting, averaging, and so forth. There is scant reason to assume, however, that ancients relied on even a simple statistical methodology. Thus, it would be wrong to refer to the price stated in Dem. 34 as an "average" price, though, since it's not the price of a particular transaction, it is an abstract price. But if modern scholars have often shown circumspection by refraining from calling ancient abstract prices statistical averages, merely treating them as *not statistical* fails to come to grips with the complex intellectual mechanisms by which they were generated. If money allows for the commensuration of goods, the commensuration of prices still requires a second-order abstraction. That is, to generate a single "price" from a series of discrete transactions—x amount for this batch of grain, y amount for another, z for a third, and so on—requires another tool of abstraction, one that makes not the quantities but the qualities equal. That mechanism was the medimnos. If the exact number of medimnoi in any particular transaction was not usually measured, the medimnos was a tool not of *precision* but of *abstraction*. (After all, every transaction was already precise: an exact amount of money for a particular load of grain.) Grain of very different qualities, therefore, could be treated as fungible for the purposes of an abstract price.

Measuring with Standard Measures

Although standard measures like the medimnos were powerful tools of abstraction, Greeks did measure with them at times, especially in two particular contexts of distrust: the delegation of authority within the polis, and retail sales.

The many mechanisms of accountability in Athenian democracy are well known, from the preliminary and retrospective reviews of office-holders to the inscription of government inventories and audits.[81] In all these cases, the delegation of authority entailed an accountability linked to the absence of personal trust. The practices of accountability for those officials responsible for handling grain or other objects or commodities required them to measure (or weigh) these things. (Those officials whose primary responsibility was monetary but who may have handled com-modities simply in order to sell them—the *poletai* in the Attic Stelai or the officials at Delphi seem to have been accountable only in terms of money, and did not take care to accurately measure what they sold.) Officials' use of measures highlights the relation between trust and measuring, and the inscriptional evidence reveals more about the details of the practice of measuring than other sources, especially its limits and imprecisions.

The account of the *epistatai* of Eleusis from 329/28 gives the most de-tailed description of measuring.[82] The section that describes measuring grain (lines 253–99) first briefly accounts for barley paid as in-kind rent on leased land and then, in much more detail, the returns for the yearly first-fruits offerings to the Two Goddesses (a tithing called the *aparche*). These are listed by Athenian tribe and several Athenian colonies, with en-tries for both barley and wheat. The accounts then list the allocations of this grain to various ritual purposes, the costs associated with handling it, and the proceeds from selling the remainder. There's one last entry for a colony, Imbros, which sent in its offering late, including the handling costs and sale price.

The inscription makes clear the costs associated with measuring. The *epistatai* did not themselves measure the grain but hired a *prometretes*, who may have been either an official or the public slave of officials and who was apparently an expert at measuring.[83] They paid him 1 drachma and 1.5 obols per 100 medimnoi measured (lines 291, 299). Since daily wages in this inscription ranged from one to two drachmas,[84] measuring a hundred medimnoi of grain may have taken between half and a whole day.[85] Porters were paid 4 obols per hundred medimnoi to bring the grain out (apparently to be measured) (lines 292–93, 299). And to keep track of all these figures, the officials spent 52 drachmas on fourteen writing tablets, including the cost of the writing (line 292). The expenses of measuring and recording amounted to about 2 percent of the price the grain fetched when sold.[86]

This inscription also shows that there was some imprecision in measur-ing and accounting. The accounts do not balance. Although not all the individual contributions of tribes and colonies are fully preserved, if you add them all up, even allowing for what may be missing, the contributions for both barley and wheat do not seem to equal the total amounts the *epistatai* reported.[87] This suggests that when the *epistatai* received the contributions, they wrote down the reported amount of each, but did their own measuring only when they had all the grain together. (Thus, the porters had to bring out the grain because it had already been stowed.) But then the *epistatai* reported how much grain they sold, and for both barley and wheat they sold more than the total amount that they had earlier measured (after deductions). (The difference for barley is a small percentage, about 4.5 medimnoi or less than 0.5 percent, while for wheat it's larger, nearly 6 medimnoi or almost 8 percent.) The *epistatai* may have measured the grain again when they sold it (so that these numbers may be the results of imprecise measuring), or they may have added some (measured) excess grain from other (unrecorded) sources. In any case, trying to precisely balance the figures in the accounts seems hopeless.

The imprecision of measuring raises the problem of compacting, the degree to which the grain settles in the measuring vessel. Compacting is a critical issue in measuring—it's why today everything from raw wheat to breakfast cereal is sold by weight, not volume—because the degree of compacting can change significantly the volume of the grain. (This is also why you should not tamp down flour when measuring it for a cake.) There's a peculiar feature of some of the reported amounts in this inscription: three times an amount of grain is described as having an *epibole* (lines 285 and 298 [twice]) and three other times as having *epimetra* (lines 254, 281, and 285), in all cases with a measured amount named. Both words are a bit mysterious here, and there are no other texts that use them in clearly similar ways, but the *epi-* prefix seems to indicate something added on. Some scholars infer, therefore, that the Athenians sometimes added on a bonus to compensate for lack of compacting.[88]

For a number of reasons, however, this supposition cannot be right.[89] Indeed, for philological reasons it is unsound to link the words. First, two different words ought to designate two different things. Second, they differ grammatically. *Epimetra* exist in the nominative with the amount to which they relate in the dative; *epibolai* are attached to an amount paratactically, by "and" or the participle "having." *Epimetra* seem to be an addition to an amount, whereas *epibolai* seem to be a part of an amount. Third, they are in fact used in different contexts: *epimetra* occur in market transactions (sales or leases), whereas *epibolai* happen in nonmarket transfers of grain between officials. So it seems better to try to determine what these were separately, not together.

I see two possible meanings for *epibole* in this inscription. First, it could be taken in its common meaning of a fine. Two of the transfers with *epi-*

bolai are explicitly said to be late, and a penalty may have been assessed. Nothing indicates, however, that the third transfer with an *epibole* violated any rule. There is a second possibility. All three *epibolai* however are attached to amounts that are whole medimnoi but are themselves fractional; the *epibole* could then be the amount left over that is less than a medimnos, a kind of remainder.[90] But I remain doubtful about what this word means.

With *epimetra* it's possible to be more certain: *epimetra* were inducements to consummate a sale. Here's what the *epistatai* reported about the barley they had collected: The total amount was 1,108 medimnoi, 4 half-hekteis, and 2 choinikes, and they handed over for ritual use 3 choinikes less than 17 medimnoi. (They don't report it at this point, but that leaves 1,091 medimnoi, 5 half-hekteis, and 1 choinix. This number will become important.) They then report:

> We sold 1,027 medimnoi, one hekteus, and five half-choinikes and *epimetra* to these, 64 medimnoi, a hekteus, and five half-choinikes. Total price of the barley 3,082 drachmas and 3 obols, which was sold for 3 drachmas for each medimnos as the demos ordered. (Lines 281–83)

Follow this backwards: the Assembly (demos) ordered the barley to be sold at 3 drachmas a medimnos, and the *epistatai* sold 1,027 medimnoi, one hekteus, and five half-choinix at this price. (The total price is low by a couple obols.) Then they added on the *epimetra* of 64 medimnoi, a hekteus, and five half-choinikes (note that they charged nothing for this), for a total amount sold of 1,091 medimnoi, 3 half-hekteis, and 1 choinix—almost exactly the amount they had to dispose of. (It's low by 2 half-hekteis.) The *epimetra* was the bonus to get the buyer to accept the price set by the Assembly. The buyer seems to have offered a bid on the whole amount of less than 3 drachmas a medimnos (about 2 drachmas 5 obols), which the *epistatai* then, by an accounting trick, made equal to 3 drachmas a medimnos. The math with the wheat works more or less the same way, with two differences. First, the *epistatai* must have come up with some extra wheat because they gave over for sale more than the total received (minus deductions). Second, they divided the wheat into two batches, and they sold a batch of ten medimnoi for only 50 drachmas, less than the price of 6 drachmas a medimnos, which the Assembly mandated. This confirms what the analysis of the *epimetra* implies: the price mandated by the Assembly was above the current market price.[91]

The third *epimetra* in the account looks to have operated similarly. The *epistatai* recorded: "From (Hypereides) we took a lease payment of [619] medimnoi [of barley, during the] four [years], there were 2,476 medimnoi. *Epimetra* to the grain measured out: 256. Total medimnoi: 2,732" (lines 253–55). If you assume that the lease payment had been administratively fixed at 619 drachmas per year—public leases were commonly auctioned, but an administratively set price is not unknown[92]—then Hypereides' extra payment (*epimetra*) could have been the premium he offered to secure the lease for himself.[93] There is no independent evidence that this happened in this instance, but the facts conform to the interpretation I've offered.

The *epimetra* therefore was one of the practices that developed around situations where an administratively fixed price differed from the current market price, the problem of the gap, a problem that can manifest itself two ways. Take first the situation in which the fixed price was lower than the market price. This would create incentives to profit from the difference, focused most powerfully, perhaps, on those who determined who got the stuff at the lower, fixed price. Since prices act as allocating mechanisms, setting a fixed price—that is, disabling the market allocation mechanism—requires instituting an alternative way of deciding who gets stuff. The temptation would arise, then, for those with the power of allocating to sell access, that is, to capture for themselves part of the gap between the administratively set price and the market price. Greek cities rarely provided subsidized grain to citizens,[94] but when they did, this problem arose. Consider, in this light, the detailed mechanisms the city of Samos instituted in the second century to control a modest system of grain subsidies. (In this case, the subsidy amounted to the entire price— they were giving it away for free.)

> [The *meledonoi*] will measure out to the citizens who are in residence by *chiliastys* (a political division of the citizen body) all the grain that has been imported, measuring to each person each month a gift of two measures. They will begin the measuring out in the month of Pelusion and will keep measuring. . . . They will not measure out to someone on another's behalf unless that person is sick. They will make the distribution from the new moon until the tenth, and until the thirtieth for those who are not in residence if they come back. They will render an account each month of what was distributed, depositing it in the *exetasterion*, writing by *chiliastys* and putting down the name of those who received a distribution.[95]

The extraordinary detailed directions for the *meledonoi*—who gets the grain (and who does not), when (and when not) to distribute it, and the requirement for a monthly written account—attempt not only to guarantee that all citizens would receive their share but, more fundamentally, to prevent the *meledonoi* from capitalizing on the gap between the market price of grain and the subsidized price—whether through kickbacks, bribes, gifts, or reciprocal favors. Possibilities like these may underlie the concern at Athens that many officials (not just those who handled great matters) might be tempted with gifts.[96] Now back to the *epistatai* at Eleusis: Hypereides' *epimetra* of 256 medimnoi of barley, then, represented (at least part of) the difference between the administratively set price and the price he was willing to pay for renting the land, a difference the honest officials did not pocket for themselves but turned over to the cult renting the land.

Alternatively, an administratively set price might be higher than the market price. The issue here would not be corruption but the fact that no one would make a deal at such a price. The solution was to offer an inducement of some sort. This is precisely what the *epistatai* did: while maintaining the fiction of the price set by the Assembly, they added a bonus, which had the practical effect of lowering the unit price.[97] The peculiar features of the accounts of the *epistatai* of Eleusis, the *epibole* and the *epimetra*, reflect challenges in polis administration, price setting, and accounting, not exigencies of measuring.[98]

The accounts of the *epistatai* show that measuring was a protracted, costly, and probably inexact process. Officials measured because the law required them to and they would have to submit accounts.[99] If the information gained from measuring was far from costless, Greeks probably didn't measure without a compelling reason.

Measuring in Retail Trade

Greeks also used standardized measures in retail trade to overcome personal distrust. Many showed suspicion of *kapeloi*, sellers in the agora.[100] Such suspicion arose, I argued in chapter 2, not merely (or even mostly) from the adversarial nature of the buyer-seller relationship, but also from the use of coinage, which created asymmetric transaction costs: while sellers knew exactly what they were getting (coins), there was no compensating information for buyers. Neither the government nor the mechanics of mass production guaranteed the consistency of commodities. In every transaction, buyers had to worry if they were getting what they paid for. In retail settings especially, coinage conferred a significant advantage of information on sellers.

The political imposition of standard measures on retail trade can thus be seen as an attempt to endow buyers with advantages similar to those of sellers. The size of most extant official standard measures suggests that they were used only for small amounts. In Lang's catalogue of official dry measures found in the Athenian agora, the largest of the 69 identifiable measures was a half-hekteus.[101] An Athenian inscription of 222/21 points in

the same direction.[102] Erected by the *metronomoi*, the inspectors of weights
and measures, the inscription inventories the equipment they conveyed
to their successors, itemized as follows (lines 10–12): "They handed over
these measures and weights: 12 bronze half-hekteis for grain; two choinikes; [some number of] half-choinikes ..." (the rest of the inscription
is lost). Converted to fractions of a medimnos, these measures would be
one twelfth, one forty-eighth, one ninety-sixth (roughly, in contemporary units, 4 liters, 1 liter, and one half liter). The fact that they are listed
in descending order suggests that the largest standard grain measure the
metronomoi possessed was a half-hekteus, one twelfth of a medimnos.[103] At
Olympia and Heraclea (in Italy) in the fourth century, evidence likewise
suggests that official measures were relatively small.[104] Some Greek cities
required standard measures only in retail trade. An Athenian decree of the
late second century makes this explicit:

> The officials whom the laws order, from the provided patterns will have
> authorized versions (*sekomata*) made for the wet (measures) and the dry
> (measures) and the weights and will compel those who sell anything in
> the agora, or in the workshops, or the retail shops, or wineshops, or
> [storehouses] to use these measures and weights, measuring everything
> liquid with this same measure.[105]

The law compelled the use of standard measures only for those who sold
from retail locations.[106]

Similarly, some cities tried to guarantee the quality of certain retail
goods. Suspicion of vendors focused not only on the ways they measured
but also on whether they had adulterated their goods. Thus Thasos legislated against diluted wine, and in Athens the *agoranomoi* were responsible
for making sure that commodities were pure and unadulterated.[107]

Cities did not, however, require the use of standard measures in larger
transactions, away from the agora. Nor did they intervene in trade in
ways that might have indirectly promoted the use of standard measures.
In particular, cities taxed trade not based on volume or weight but on
value. Many cities imposed taxes on goods that entered, left, or passed
through their territory. The most commonly attested name for such a
duty, the *pentekoste* ("fiftieth"), referred to a proportional tax of 2 percent
assessed on the value of the goods.[108] The ways this tax was assessed and
collected probably varied over time and across cities—many cities had
customs officials, but some, like Athens, sold the right to collect duties.
Although historians often refer casually to measuring grain for duties, the
central problem was not measuring cargoes but affixing a money value to
them.[109] I discuss the practice of assigning money values outside market
exchanges in detail in chapter 5; here I will note that although the amount

of the goods would affect the valuation, there's no evidence that tax collectors established values precisely by measuring. Indeed, the valuation depended not (for example) on measuring and a schedule of values but on a declaration by the importer, a declaration that might have included a statement of the cargo and its origin (as at Athens for grain).[110] The organization of the grain trade did not rely on abstract systems; nor were such systems fostered by external pressures.

Cities intervened in trade to require measuring with standard measures only in the agora. This claim is consonant with the one possible broad attempt to impose standards, the "Coinage Decree" that Athens promulgated in the fifth century. Although most of the preserved sections of this decree concerned coinage, it also mentioned weights and measures in an oath it prescribed for the Boule (italicized figures enclosed in curly brackets indicate the approximate number of missing letters in the gaps):

> "The secretary of the [Boule ... {*10*}] will add to the oath of the Boule [the] following: If someone strikes silver coin in the ci[ties] and does not use co[ins of] Athe[ni]ans or weights or mea[sures ... {*26*}] and weights and [m]easures [... {*32*}] decree which Klearch[os proposed ... {*19*}]."[111]

Unfortunately, so many variables, uncertainties, and imponderables attach to any interpretation of this decree, particularly as it concerns measures and weights, that I think it's better to remain agnostic about its purpose and effects.[112] But in whatever way the law required the adoption of Athenian standards, this preserved section did not require the use of standard measures in situations where they had not been used before.

Weighing Grain

Today grain is quantified by weight rather than volume. Although Greeks sometimes weighed grain, they did so less to quantify by weight than to render a notional volume.

An Athenian grain tax law of 374/73 shows that at least sometimes both the polis and merchants weighed grain.[113] This law modified the procedures for purchasing the right to collect the tax on grain in certain Athenian colonies (the very colonies mentioned later in the Eleusis inscription, above). Tax collectors had previously paid for this right in cash, but now they had to pay in batches of grain (both barley and wheat). (Its purpose was to get more grain into the city.) It specified how these in-kind payments were to be processed:

> The buyer (of the right to collect the tax) will weigh out the wheat at a weight of a talent for five *hekteis*, and the barley at a weight of a talent

for a medimnos, dry and clean of darnel, arranging the standard weight (*sekoma*) on the balance, just as the other merchants.[114]

The law outlines a procedure for quantifying the volume of grain by weighing it.[115]

You can imagine good reasons for weighing rather than measuring grain: it would avoid the problem of compacting and would probably take a lot less time for grain already in phormoi (especially if phormoi were sewn shut). But challenges persisted and meant that expertise remained essential to even this operation. Greek practices of weighing grain had five limitations.

1. Greek balances may not have been particularly accurate.[116]

2. Although Greeks were aware that moisture affected the weight of grain (note that the grain tax law required the grain to be dry), there is no evidence that they had any technology to calibrate the moisture content. Moisture content is an objective number; "dry" is a subjective—or, rather, expert—assessment.

3. Greeks apparently never quantified grain directly by weight, though they sometimes used weight as a means of determining a volume measure. This meant that the conversion formula was critical.

4. The evidence suggests that while they had conventional formulas for converting weight to volume, they did not empirically determine the formula for any particular batch of grain. The Roman Pliny gives several formulas for converting the weight of different grains from different locations into volume, and Rathbone interprets these conversion methods as evidence that grain was commonly weighed to determine volume throughout the Roman empire.[117] Such shorthand formulas, however, even if they allowed that grain from different regions would vary in density, were not the same as actually determining the density of each batch of grain, and may have been adopted "not so much for [their] accuracy as the neatness and convenience of the basic formula."[118] Thus in the Athenian grain tax law, the ready formula that a talent of wheat is 5 hekteis, as Rhodes and Osborne observe, probably undercounted significantly the volume of wheat.[119] The volumes determined through such procedures may have borne little relation to the actual volume of the grain.

5. During the classical period, at least, Greeks did not usually quantify density, as today with the test weight of grain; rather, they assessed it subjectively. Theophrastus's discussion of the density of grain[120] suggests that Greeks usually understood it relatively, not in terms of objective (even if conventional) numbers. Theophrastus says that Pontic wheat is the lightest, Sicilian heavier than most, and Boeotian the heaviest of

all. By way of evidence for this last claim he reports: "They say that athletes in Boeotia consume not quite three half-choinikes, but that when
they come to Athens they easily consume five half-choinikes."[121] Thus by
"light" and "heavy" Theophrastus meant density (weight per unit of volume), which he understood as correlating to the nutritional content. His
scheme for describing density, however, is not quantitative but relative:
light, heavier, heaviest. Such relative rankings could have been achieved
objectively through the comparative weighing of two equal quantities of
different kinds of wheat, though Theophrastus's anecdote about athletes
does not point to such a procedure. Indeed, this anecdote provides the
only quantitative information in his discussion, in contrast to Pliny, who
gave specific, quantified weights. The absence of quantitative standards of
density during the classical period suggests that the normal way to judge
the relative density of a single batch of wheat was through expertise.

Except for the Athenian grain tax law, there's little evidence that
Greeks regularly weighed grain. Weighing was merely a quick way to
determine a volume measure—and not a particularly accurate one as the
Greeks did it—and it was not part of a procedure to empirically determine density. However often it may have been done, weighing did not
obviate expertise but required even more of it.

Standardized Systems in Hellenistic Egypt

The use of measurement in Hellenistic Egypt, particularly in the distribution of grain, provides a useful comparison to that of Greece—as
much for the differences in practice as for the similarities. Economic life
in Hellenistic Egypt was organized on a much larger scale than in classical Greece. While there were small-scale merchants in many commodities
in Hellenistic Egypt, there were also extremely large estates (e.g., that of
Apollonios, known from the papers of his administrator, Zenon), and the
state intervened extensively in the production and distribution of many
agricultural commodities, both through the cultivation of royal land and
through the collection of rent and taxes in kind. Moreover, the growth
of an international market for Egyptian commodities, first among Greek
states, ultimately at Rome, promoted large-scale enterprises.[122] One of
the characteristics of personal trust is that it limits scalability: because of
the investment of time and attention such relationships require, you can
only maintain a limited number. Large Egyptian estates and, even more
importantly, royal administration of economic functions were on such a
scale that personal relationships of trust alone could not organize them.

In a situation where authority had to be extensively delegated, Hellenistic Egyptians relied less on personal trust than on systems—objective, impersonal mechanisms of coordinating action. A receipt from 251 BCE (*P. Hib.* 98) illustrates these mechanisms:

> In the 34th year of the reign of Ptolemy the son of Ptolemy Soter, the priest of Alexander and the gods Adelphi being Neoptolemus son of Phrixius, the canephorus of Arsinoë Philadelphus being Arsinoë daughter of Ncolaus, the 24th of the month Mesore. Dionysius, captain, acknowledges that he has embarked upon the boat of Xenodocus and Alexander, the pilot on which is Ecteuris son of Pasis, of Memphis, through Nechthembes the agent of the basilicogrammateis, for transport to the royal granary at Alexandria, with a sample, 4800 artabae of barley, being pure, unadulterated, and sifted grain, by the measure and smoothing-rod which he himself brought from Alexandria, with just measurement, and I make no complaint.[123]

I note five mechanisms:

1. Quantities of grain were measured exactly. While many large, round numbers can be found, there are also instances where the specificity of the quantity suggests that it is the result of exact measurement. Moreover, many papyri explicitly state that the quantity was actually measured. Many receipts, too, specify the measure and mode of measuring used.[124] In these cases, standardized measures seem to have been used on even large quantities.

2. There was a rudimentary attempt to develop standardized qualities. This seems to have not gotten much beyond specifying that a particular shipment of grain was "pure, unadulterated, and sifted."[125] Although this categorization does not take into account the natural qualitative variations in the grain itself, those who handled grain were able to make subtle distinctions within the limited rubric.

3. Grain shipments were frequently accompanied by samples (*deigmata*) under seal.[126] These were intended to deter qualitative adulteration in transit.

4. Shipments were sometimes accompanied by guards.[127] (This is the one mechanism not provided for in *P. Hib.* 98, above.)

5. There was extensive written documentation of the distribution of grain, including accounts and reports to superiors and also receipts issued when the grain changed hands.[128]

The practices for handling grain in classical Greece and in Hellenistic Egypt differed substantially. Because of the scale of organization involved in the production and distribution of commodities in Egypt, something more than personal trust was required. The alternative was a system of objective relationships where trust was invested more in the system than in individuals. Contrast Xenophon's treatise on estate management from the classical period, the *Oikonomikos*, with the extensive evidence for Zenon's direction of Apollonios's estate in Egypt a century later. While Xenophon emphasized certain abstract principles of management,[129] he saw these as executed through personal relationships of trust. Thus, one of his main concerns was in the training of the estate manager's two main subordinates, his wife and his overseer. While hierarchical and delegatory, the relationships within the oikos remained personal and did not depend on objective mechanisms. Indeed, Xenophon's treatise is effectively a manual in micromanagement. On the other hand, Zenon's direction of Apollonios's estate—if for no other reason than its sheer scale—required him to deal with people more superficially. While Zenon certainly had to deal with myriad mundane details, these often concerned problems that were brought before him rather than difficulties he ferreted out. Indeed, much of his administration took place through written queries and directives— the evidence that has been preserved for us. Nevertheless, the papyri demonstrate that personal relationships remained important, as for example in the use of patronage. Systems of patronage attempt to make personal trust scalable: A personally trusts B, and B personally trusts C, so (C or B might claim) A should trust C. In practice there are limits to the scalability of such a system (A might trust C, but should he trust D, or E, or F?), limits that are often compensated for by the addition of impersonal systems (e.g., written accounts, auditors, etc.).

For all its dependence on abstract systems, however, procedures for shipping grain in Egypt were far from equivalent to modern ones. The limits of the Egyptian system can be best appreciated by examining a document that shows how officials actually used receipts and samples. Although this document, *P. Oxy.* 708, dates from the Roman period (188 CE), well beyond the date of this study, it's still useful because it's unlikely that the procedures during the Hellenistic period were more sophisticated.[130] So it can be taken to represent the apogee of system development.

> Antonius Aelianus to the *strategos* of the Diosplite nome in the Thebaid, greeting. Since the cargo dispatched from the nome under you in charge of [–]ausis of Sipos and his companions, amounting to 2,000 artabas of wheat, appeared at the *arsis* of the samples to be impure, I ordered that the amount of barley and earth in half an artaba of it should be ascertained, and it proved to be under measure by 2 percent of barley and likewise ½ percent of earth. Accordingly, exact at your own risk from the *sitologoi* who shipped the wheat the difference on the whole amount of grain, 50¾ artabas of wheat, and the extra payments and other expenses, and when you have added this total to the account of the procurator let me know.[131]

This document reveals a highly developed hierarchy and an articulated division of labor and responsibility. It also shows a precise and discriminating quantification of impurities. Nevertheless, it deploys this quantification not to objectify the grain but to mediate relationships between people. Note the sequence of events. When the grain arrived, the samples that accompanied it were subjected to an *arsis*, which revealed it was adulterated. There is no good parallel for the meaning of *arsis* here; it literally means "lifting," but the context shows that it must have been some kind of inspection.[132] Presumably the receipts accompanying this shipment had described the wheat as "pure and unadulterated" (as above), and an expert's inspection revealed otherwise. Antonius Aelianus then ordered a closer scrutiny, the point of which was to determine not whether the grain was adulterated but by how much. This greater scrutiny involved dissecting a half artaba (around 20 liters), sifting out the barley and dirt, and then determining their proportions. (The document doesn't say how this was done, but weighing seems most likely.) Antonius Aelianus then demanded that the *sitologoi* who had shipped the grain (and vouched for it) compensate him for the proportion of the shipment that wasn't wheat. As Mayerson pointed out, this document raises many questions about what next happened to the shipment of wheat, and everything we know about the economy of Roman wheat suggests it was treated indiscriminately with all the other wheat bound for Rome.[133]

This document, then, reveals some of the limitations of abstract systems in the ancient world. Even here, expertise remained fundamental to the system: Only an expert's judgment initiated the exceptional quantification of adulteration. Moreover, this quantification resulted not in the reclassification of the grain but in the demand for certain officials to compensate for the contamination. The system did not allow for the creation and manipulation of abstract entities (grain of various grades), but required the accountability of individuals.

Conclusion

The trade in grain in classical Greece reveals two spheres of practice: the intellectual manipulation of grain, which relied on the abstract measure of the medimnos, and the physical handling of the stuff, which frequently required people to eyeball phormoi and use their accumulated expertise to gauge the quality and quantity of the grain. Measuring grain was imprecise, slow, and costly (running about 2 percent of the value of the grain), and still required a subjective quality assessment; the evidence suggests that merchants often estimated with practical units rather than measuring with standardized ones. Nevertheless, poleis mandated the use of standardized measures in two situations: where the polis delegated authority to deal with grain to some of its officials, and in the retail marketplace. Both seem to have been attempts to solve problems of trust: of delegation and accountability in the first case, and of unequal access to information in the second. Indeed, in both situations standardized measuring attempted to compensate the amateur for the professional's superior expertise.

The history of measuring—of an abstract system understood as a practice—is not the same as the history of measures. Because the practice relates to the particular characteristics of any commodity, I would not claim that the trade in grain shows that Greeks didn't measure other commodities. But I would argue that it oppugns a presumption of measuring and prompts inquiry into how objects like phormoi or medimnoi were actually used.

CHAPTER 4

Keeping Track

King Midas, you may recall, by his mere touch turned anything to gold, a power that ultimately caused him to starve to death.[1] Aristotle, the earliest writer to report this legend, embeds it in a discussion of wealth-getting, which contrasts the unending pursuit of money, as through trade, to the limited and therefore natural pursuit of wealth through household management. For those suspicious of the effects of trade, as Aristotle reports it, the story illustrates the artificial and distorting nature of a primary mechanism of commerce, money, of which, like Midas's gold, a man may have a great supply and yet, hypothetically, go hungry. But I might suggest that the myth also holds a lesson about domestic economy: To think only about production or acquisition and not at all about consumption risks ruin. Modern scholars, too, might learn this lesson, since accounts of Greek households as economic entities tend to focus on questions of production. Yet, for Greek farm families, the problem of having enough was not only one of *producing* enough, but also of *organizing consumption*; it wouldn't matter how much you produced if you couldn't make it last for the whole year, that is, allocate it out over time. In addition to focusing on production, scholars' discussions about the economic rationality of the Greeks often take modernity as their implicit model. So, for example, some have debated whether and how Greeks calculated rates of return on investments, and, more particularly, the role of accounting in this activity, especially double-entry bookkeeping.[2] The debate about accounting, however, encourages a history that is less about the Greeks than about the genealogy of certain modern techniques and ideas, and even then fails to recognize the ways that modern methods of accounting evolve and are contested.[3] Instead of asking whether Greeks used written accounting, therefore, I want to ask how they kept track of stuff in households and, specifically, how they organized consumption.

By asking this, I aim to find the rationality inherent in the practices of such organization. I begin by considering the evidence for the limited use of systems of measurement and written accounts on Greek farms. Because comparative studies suggest that farmers typically adopt such expensive techniques only under pressure from the state, I examine the larger political economy in which Greek farmers operated, in particular the ways that landlords or (more often) the polis imposed financial burdens on farmers. Three case studies will show that these burdens did not require farmers to keep written records of production or supplies or even to precisely measure agricultural production. Instead, Greek farmers exercised strategic and rationalized control over stuff through what I will call containerizing. They divided supplies into batches, putting them in containers that they could manipulate physically and intellectually. Thus, they rationalized the dispensing of supplies through an art of allocating based not on measuring, written accounting, and mathematical calculations but on an expertise in gauging the fullness of containers and flexibly accommodating need, pleasure, and supplies. Finally, I examine how these practices constituted and affected social relationships of trust (and distrust) between husbands and wives and between masters and slaves. For spouses, arrangements for control over storage space significantly determined the degree of trust or distrust in the relationship. The feeding of slaves, curiously enough, provides the strongest evidence for measuring in Greek households. Slave owners sometimes mediated the personal distrust of this relationship by using impersonal systems like measuring.

The Limits of Measuring on Greek Farms

Greek households of the archaic and classical periods did not typically rely on standardized and systematized measures, measuring, or writing to keep track of supplies. Greeks were, however, generally familiar with systems of measures, as illustrated by a joke in Aristophanes: When Socrates asks the dull-witted Strepsiades what he thinks of the "four measure" (a kind of poetic meter), Strepsiades mistakenly discusses the half-hekteus, a measure of capacity which contains four choinikes.[4]

The evidence suggests four ways in which Greeks used measures intellectually: First, they used the language of standardized systems as ways of referring to rough amounts—as when one of Aristophanes' characters tells his wife to roast three choinikes of beans and mix in barley.[5] The character isn't directing his wife to measure the beans exactly; rather, since a choinix was commonly thought to be a day's rations, he's saying something like, "Whip up a triple serving!" Second, farmers might do simple calculations with a measure, adding or subtracting units of the same size. A farmer in a play says that he planted twenty medimnoi but reaped not quite thirteen, which meant seven were missing.[6] Neither of these uses relies on *systematized* measures. Third, Greeks relied on the different sizes of measures to indicate relative orders of magnitude: say, the difference between medimnoi and choinikes.[7] Fourth, Greeks used systems of measures to indicate proportions. As I note below, they did not describe a particular ratio as "one six-hundredth" (as we might), but as "one hekteus from a hundred medimnoi." Comedy provides evidence for these uses but does not show ordinary Greeks using systems for complex calculations, even for adding up smaller units into larger ones. Inscriptions show that officials made such calculations frequently, and ordinary people were probably capable of making them, even if laboriously (quick: how many cups does 24 tablespoons make?), but, in contrast to the four ways just mentioned, there's no positive evidence that they often did so.

Even if ordinary Greeks knew how to use systems of measures, however, you should not assume that the actual vessels they had were gauged to standard sizes. Indeed, a passage from Plato suggests that the utensils on a farm, even those used for measuring, would likely be jumbled. Plato's characters are imagining legislation for an ideal city, and one suggests the following. (I have paraphrased this long passage.)

> The division into twelve parts (which can be further subdivided down to 5,040 parts) will be the basis of many social institutions: politics, the military, coinage, and weights and measures. All of these must be made measured and harmonious. [Legislators] should not be afraid of a reputation for hair-splitting if they require that all utensils conform to the system of measurement. Indeed, the division and compounding of numbers is useful across applications, so that the legislator should order all citizens to strive to achieve systemization. The study of numbers is highly educational for household management, government, and other sciences; but only if you remove slavishness and love of money from the souls of those who study will the lessons be beautiful and proper.[8]

Plato wants to promote facility with complex calculations—the phrase I've rendered as "the division and compounding of numbers" indicates this—by instituting a universal *system* of ordered subdivisions (starting with 12, going all the way down to 5,040, which can be divided by all numbers up to 12 except 11)[9] common to all aspects of life. He requires that all vessels (σκεύη) fit this standard system, but anticipates that most people would think such standardization is mere hairsplitting (σμικρολογίαν). This suggests that the utensils most people used were sized quite inconsistently; the jar called a choinix at one farm was not the same as at another, and even at the same farm the kotyle filled four times might not make exactly one choinix. Plato worries here about systemization of measuring equipment, but the absence of systemization means they cannot have been standardized either. Indeed, to the degree that people measured things on a farm, they might often have relied on containers that were not standard measures—buckets, for example[10]—or on a measure that was the "standard" for that farm alone.[11] Thus, there is little evidence that Greeks did much actual measuring inside the household.

Beyond this, Athenian households do not seem to have used writing to organize or rationalize their consumption or production of things. It's likely that most members of the household were barely able to read and write or, at best, had limited skills (especially women and slaves, who often handled stuff most).[12] Evidence shows that Athenians wrote documents for some affairs—contracts, wills, loans—but only to regulate the household's external relationships, not to organize its internal processes.[13] In two prosperous Athenian households, those of Demosthenes and Diogeiton, each with multiple enterprises, there were written wills and written lists of loans and debts, but not even simple accounting records.[14] The fact that Athenians might use writing to record such external transactions does not, however, require that they were all comfortably literate. They referred to such records only infrequently, and could easily rely on others to help read them. Indeed Greeks often read (whether in the narrow sense of deciphering the text or the broader of interpreting it) in groups.[15] When Epicrates, for example, agreed to a written contract, it was read to him for his assent, and, when he sought to investigate in detail what it said and implied, he called together a group of friends and they read it together.[16] The procedures used here to read the written contract would work whether Epicrates was literate or not. Such a mode of literacy, however, if productive for the occasional document, seems ill suited to frequently updated written ledgers.

External Pressures to Measure

The claim that Greeks understood systems of standardized measures but neither possessed many standardized vessels nor did much measuring may seem curious but can be justified. Both vessels and measuring involve costs. Historically, the spread of measuring and of standard measures has tended to result from the degree to which households have been integrated into larger systems. More specifically, standard measures usually spread when authorities compel others to use them.[17]

During the archaic and classical periods, few external pressures on households would have compelled them to measure their production precisely with standard measures. Households that rented land almost always paid their rent in coin not produce.[18] If "sixth-parters" (*hektemeroi*) were common in Athens in the seventh century, sharecropping arrangements

were unusual in Greece of the classical period.[19] It's harder to generalize about taxes. Although Greeks are commonly said not to have regularly imposed "direct" taxes on citizens, several scholars have argued that
the exceptions invalidate the generalization.[20] And although money taxes
seem to have been more common, some taxes were collected in kind: the
Attic tax of a "tenth" (or "twentieth") associated with Pisistratus in the
sixth century, for example, or the tax at Kolophon early in the third.[21]
However, even for taxes assessed as a fraction of production and collected
in kind, there is little evidence that Greek farmers had to measure their
production.

To test this conclusion, consider three historical situations where you
might imagine that an external reason compelled the measurement of
production: tithes of produce for the gods, the Athenian grain tax of the
fourth century, and the Solonian classes in Athens. In fact, none of these
cases provide strong evidence of a need to measure.

Tithes. The legally mandated offering of *aparchai*, firstfruits, to Demeter
and Kore, goddesses whose cult was centered at Eleusis, on the outskirts
of Attica, might seem to require the measuring of crops. An Athenian decree from the third quarter of the fifth century obliged both Athenians
and their allies to offer firstfruits, and it invited other Greeks cities to
bring them too. It prescribed the following procedure:

> Let firstfruits be offered by Athenians to the two goddesses from the
> crops according to tradition and the oracle in Delphi: from a hundred
> medimnoi of barley not less than a hekteus, and of wheat from a hun
> dred medimnoi not less than a half-hekteus.[22] If someone produces
> more crops than this, or less, let firstfruits be offered in the same ratio.
> Let the demarchs collect deme by deme and hand it over in Eleusis to
> the *hieropoioi* from Eleusis.... Let the allies offer the *aparche* in the same
> way.... After writing on boards the measure of the crops (those from
> the demarchs according to each deme and those from the cities accord
> ing to each city) let [the *hieropoioi*] place [the lists] in the Eleusinion in
> Eleusis and the Bouleterion.[23]

The decree's specification of a sixth or half-sixth per one hundred medimnoi would seem to indicate exact measuring.

Part of a continuing program of making Athens the cultural and religious center of the Delian League, the empire it controlled in the fifth
century, and indeed of the Greek world generally,[24] the Athenian decree
intervened in and formalized a common religious practice. Offering firstfruits—not just the offering of initial agricultural products, but of food
before eating, or of any kind of income or gain—was widespread. People

commonly made a firstfruits offering to Demeter in their own home.[25] Such an offering of firstfruits did not constitute a set percentage of the crops, which is why they could be offered at the beginning of the harvest before most of it had been brought in.[26] Whatever the previous tradition had been, this decree attempted to promote widespread participation in the offering of firstfruits at Eleusis.

The decree did not, however, require farmers to measure their produce. If you assume that it did (and this would have to be an assumption, since the decree does not say so), then it also required a challenging mathematical operation, the comparison of proportions; on a hypothetical production of 71 medimnoi, for example, you'd have to solve for x in this equation: 100 medimnoi/1 hekteus = 71 medimnoi/x hektea—and to do so without writing.[27] This all seems needlessly complex, especially for a small amount of grain offered to divinities as a gift. Rather than using abstract mathematical numbers like "one six-hundredth" and "one twelve-hundredth" (translating it this way misleads), the decree specified two definite and imaginable amounts of grain, from which farmers could figure their *aparchai* by estimation and division, maybe even generous eyeballing.[28] The decree did require some measuring, but note by whom: not by farmers, nor by the demarchs who collected the offerings, but by the *hieropoioi* at Eleusis. (As I noted in chapter 3, the *epistatai* of Eleusis, the officials who oversaw the collection and use of the firstfruits in the fourth century, hired a professional measurer and recorded exact and small amounts of grain in *IG* II² 1672.) The decree required that grain be measured and recorded *only* by the *hieropoioi*. This inscription confirms that the polis, not the household, measured and kept written accounts.

The Athenian grain tax. In the early fourth century, the Athenians reformed the collection of taxes from some islands they controlled. The inscription of this law announces its subject at the beginning: "Law about the twelfth of the grain of the islands." Then its aim and primary action: "So that there may be grain publicly for the demos, sell the twelfth in Lemnos, Imbros, and Skyros, and the fiftieth, for grain."[29] The law does not define the twelfth or the fiftieth, but immediately launches into the minutiae of its implementation: "Each share will be 500 medimnoi, 100 of wheat and 400 of barley." You might expect that the law would next explain the use of these shares; instead, it switches subject: "The buyer will convey the grain to the Piraeus at his own risk," and the next twenty-one lines define the buyer's obligations in depositing the grain with the city. Then, suddenly, the law changes again: "The share for a *symmoria*, six men, will be 3,000 medimnoi." The law imposes collective liability on the men in a *symmoria*, and then turns to the duties of the officials who oversee this process, receiving and ultimately selling the grain in Athens (twenty lines). The law concludes with a difficult passage, which seems designed to transition from the old system to this new one (since it mentions the previous year and the future).

An inspiration to scholarly ingenuity, this law has so far largely thwarted consensus. There are several reasons for this. One relates to the dynamics of the discipline: It was first published only in 1998,[30] allowing little time for the apparatus of scholarship to generate a consensus. But two relate to the law itself. First, its drafting is complex, if not chaotic.[31] Second, the law did not inaugurate a new procedure but changed an old one; consequently, it describes only changes, leaving the substance of the procedures implicit. So, for example, the law does not define "the twelfth" and "the fiftieth," though they seem to be taxes.[32] Without reviewing the details of various scholars' interpretations of the law, I would say that each has its virtues and its difficulties.[33]

For the purposes of my argument here, the law provides no evidence of a state mandate that would make people exactly measure production. The tax was collected in kind, as grain,[34] and the tax collectors may have measured how much they received, since the city accounted for how much it got. But it's not clear that this would compel farmers to adopt measuring practices more widely. On Moreno's interpretation, farmers owed a set amount, however large their harvest.[35] But if "the twelfth" was a proportion of production, it's possible to imagine that the tax collectors insisted that all farmers measure out their produce with standard measures and mathematically calculate an exact proportion. But it's also possible that they would have approved measuring with nonstandard, ad-hoc measures (since the ratio mattered, not a absolute amount), or that they would have collected their share by physically dividing heaps of grain, or that they would have estimated and negotiated their payments.

Comparative evidence suggests, however, that farmers simply declared their production and that if the tax collector disagreed with a particular assessment, there was some mechanism for him to pursue his dispute.[36] Hellenistic Egypt offers the most detailed comparison.[37] The "Revenue Laws" of Ptolemy II, a compilation of regulations concerned (in the part preserved) with the collection of taxes on the produce of vineyards and orchards and the enforcement of the state monopoly on oil, offer three procedures. For wine, grape cultivators had to give the tax collector the chance to inspect the grapes before harvest; after harvest, when they made the wine, they had to summon the tax collector and measure it out with approved measures.[38] For the fruit of orchards, the cultivator made a declaration of an estimate (*timesis*) of his produce, from which the tax of a sixth was determined.[39] For oil crops, first the contractor visited the farms and made an assessment (*suntimesato*). Then the cultivators had to give a declaration on oath of their land and crops including an estimate (*timesis*).

For comparison with tax procedures of the classical period, note four aspects of the methods of taxation described in the Ptolemaic laws. First, the procedures usually relied on estimates. Although *timesis* (and its cognate verbs) usually refers to making a valuation in terms of money, in these documents it can refer to an estimate of produce as well.[40] This could refer to an estimate not only of harvested crops but to a forecast of production.[41] Such estimates were used instead of measuring in the case of orchard products, and possibly also in the case of oil crops.[42] Second, oaths were used to guarantee farmers' compliance and honesty, both in their estimates[43] and when they declared that they had disclosed their full crop.[44] Third, the laws reveal two procedures for dealing with disputes. On the one hand, a tax collector who doubted that a farmer had disclosed all his crops or had estimated them accurately could appeal to the authorities for adjudication.[45] On the other hand, when a tax collector believed that a farmer had underestimated his orchard crop, he could seize it and sell it himself, keeping the excess beyond the estimate but liable to any deficit as well.[46] This procedure did not require the intervention of authorities, and created incentives for an owner to estimate amply by allowing the tax collector the opportunity to profit on the difference between his and the owner's estimate. Fourth, tax collectors could rely on the state's extensive records to corroborate both estimates and measurements of production; indeed, some taxes were based on a rolling three-year average.[47] Because even the much more bureaucratized tax system of the Ptolemies relied on estimates and oaths, it is not unreasonable to argue that the Greek cities of the classical period—with much weaker central authority and comparatively insignificant reliance on written records— could have done so as well.

Solonian classes. In the early sixth century the Athenians authorized Solon to reform the laws, calm political unrest, and fix an increasingly polarized economic situation. Aristotle says that Solon allocated political rights proportionally to four classes, with the name of the highest, the Pentakosiomedimnoi (five-hundred-medimnoi men), referring explicitly to the agricultural production on which the classes were based. The evidence for Solon's reforms, however, is poetic, late, unreliable, or confused, and while there are prevailing scholarly views on many points, none is without worthy alternatives. I hope to stay away from this morass, except to comment on how these classes may have affected the use of standard measures in agricultural production.

The most detailed evidence concerning Solon's classes, Aristotle's *Athenian Constitution*, dates from two and a half centuries later. Aristotle says that Solon

> arranged the constitution in this manner: He divided it into four classes by valuation (*timemati*), just as it had been previously divided: Pentakosiomedimnoi, Hippeis, Zeugetai, and Thetes. He assigned them from the Pentakosiomedimnoi, Hippeis, and Zeugetai to hold the higher offices ..., giving each office to each in proportion to the size of the valuation.... Whoever made from his estate five hundred measures, wet and dry together, had to be in the class of Pentakosiomedimnoi. Those who made three hundred were Hippeis—though some say that those who could maintain a horse constituted this class.... However, it seems more reasonable that they were distinguished by the measures, just like the Pentakosiomedimnoi.[48]

Scholars have noted difficulties with this evidence: By Aristotle's day, people evidently disagreed about the original basis of the classes; indeed, some think that Aristotle had no direct evidence for how the classes had been determined, so he inferred it from the name of the highest.[49] It's not clear how different products—not just wet and dry, but different types of each (i.e., wheat and barley)—were to be added up to the requisite five hundred medimnoi. I will add one more: With reference to taxes at Athens, *timema* usually referred to the value of a person's whole property, not the amount of its produce.

But if you accept the value of this evidence (and scholars tend to rectify rather than reject it), there is still the question of how the production of each farmer was assessed. A hundred years ago, scholars imagined exhaustive land surveys and complicated tax schedules;[50] today the consensus is that farmers assessed and declared their production themselves. "One also wonders if the farmer really measured the crops accurately. A modern farmer is able to evaluate a particular heap of grain quite precisely by sight and so could of course his ancient colleague."[51] In Robert Connor's ingenious theory, farmers revealed their production in the offering of firstfruits, which as a religious practice was monitored and maintained socially and informally, not by law.[52] Some such guess is probably right: Even in the classical period, when the institutions of the polis were much more highly articulated than in Solon's time, much of the tax system was regulated by private individuals. The difficulties of the evidence, and the likely conclusions when these are resolved, provide no sound basis for arguing that the Solonian class system required farmers to measure their production.

When transferring wealth, Greek households normally integrated into larger economic and political systems, through money and coinage rather than through technologies of measuring. But even in those situations where the state defined its relationship to households through amounts of produce, there is no evidence that these compelled scrupulous measuring.

Containerization

Greek farmers used physical manipulation of containers to calculate and account for their supplies. It was neither in writing nor even in memory that they kept knowledge of the extent of their supplies, but in the physical disposition of objects. Anthropologists have show that people in many cultures (including our own) often calculate not with abstract numbers but in contextually specific ways.[53] Indeed, Greeks, as Reviel Netz has argued, calculated not with symbols (written numbers) but with counters.[54] Accounting on the farm proceeded by the same principle: the physical manipulation of the objects themselves constituted the calculations. There were two steps to this process. First, supplies were divided into batches meant to last a specific length of time (usually a month or a year); the batches might well be the same as the amount a specific container would hold. Second, each batch was allocated out over the period. Neither step required any form of standardized measurement, and if the containers' capacities were roughly understood, they would probably have been thought of in terms of time (e.g., a month's supply of wine) as well as of volume. Such techniques constituted an accounting of supplies and a rationalization of their use.[55] The first step, then, was containerization.

A unique set of documents, known as the Attic Stelai, which record the sales of the property of men condemned for impiety in 415, reveals the prevalence of containerization.[56] Just before the Athenians launched their invasion of Sicily, a religious scandal took place: first, statues of Hermes all over the city were defaced one night, and then rumors circulated that people had been mocking the mysteries of Demeter and Kore. Religious hysteria may be too strong a characterization, but the extent of the attack on the Hermes statues certainly shocked the Athenians, who took extraordinary steps to investigate. Eventually dozens of men were condemned (including the famous Alcibiades, then a general) and their property confiscated and sold at auction.

Found in fragments in the Athenian agora, pieced back together, and published in the middle of the twentieth century, the ten Attic Stelai are accounts of the items, sale prices, and taxes—long lists of everything from worn clothes and damaged jars to furniture and food, to slaves, houses, and land. As David Lewis has shown, the officials who auctioned the property (probably the *poletai*) did not do so all at once but over the course of many months, beginning with what was easiest to process and sell, moveable and nearby items, and proceeding to land and more distant things.[57] Although fragmentary, the lists take you into the world of the Athenian rich: Kephisodoros the metic, who owned at least sixteen slaves (total value over 2,500 drachmas); Oinonos, whose land in Euboea sold for over 81 talents; and of course the glittering Alcibiades.

Athenian households organized agricultural produce essentially through containers. The *poletai* sold off almost all the produce in the containers it was stored in: phormoi (wheat, lentils, vetch, figs, almonds, coriander seed, and barley), half-full phormoi (salt), half-full sacks (unwashed sesame, millet, and Italian millet), baskets (carbonate of soda), and jars (barley). Sometimes they sold crops without containers: unharvested crops, of course, had not yet been packaged.[58] And in only two instances did they sell something by the medimnos, which would seem to indicate that it was either loose (dumped in a storeroom) or in a container that couldn't be moved (e.g., a built-in bin or jar in the ground).[59] The predominant impression from the lists is of an orderliness rationalized by containers.

These lists reveal the practices of using containers in households, but most scholars have understood them differently. One tradition, which goes back to antiquity, is lexigraphical. In this tradition, the problem these lists pose is figuring out the meaning of the words, which is taken to be a description or definition of the objects they refer to. Much of the commentary first published with the inscriptions was highly lexigraphical.[60] As I have argued in this book, however, what matter are not so much the objects themselves but the ways people used them. A second approach, also found in the original commentaries, does treat the words as revealing a practice, the process of selling off the stuff.. As such, the words for containers describe "measures" rather than physical objects on the implicit assumption that what was auctioned was measured in objective, standardized capacities for sale.

There are several reasons these containers should not be treated as "measures" in any strict sense of the term. First, as the lexigraphical analysis shows, their names refer to containers, but, except for phormoi, they have otherwise never been thought to be measures. And, as I argued in chapter 3, phormoi were primarily containers, not measures. Second, that phormoi were containers (discrete, physical objects), not measures, is suggested by the fact that they could be sold either collectively (422.93 lists "15 phormoi of wheat") or individually (421.126–36 lists "one phormos of wheat" fourteen times in a row). Third, in systems of measures, you'd expect smaller units within the larger ones, as the medimnos was composed of 6 hekteis, 48 choinikes, and 192 kotylai. There's no evidence that any of the containers in these lists fit into such systems. (The terms *hemisakion* ["half-sack"] and *hemiphormia* ["half-phormos"] are not smaller units; they indicate, rather, that the *poletai* found a bag of millet that had been partially emptied.) Fourth, the auctioneers showed no concern for precise measuring: none of the entries includes fractions of units. (What are the odds that every time they measured out some commodity, it came to a whole number of a very large measure?) Fifth, if a phormos was a measure equivalent to a medimnos, the *poletai* switched between them arbitrarily and inexplicably.

Treating these objects as measures misapprehends the inscriptions and the process of selling. The *poletai*, after all, were not primarily making an inventory of property but were precisely listing the money they collected at sale. For the purposes of an auction, it was enough to point to a bag (or batch of bags) and ask for bids. This was, as I argued before, a world where people were used to eyeballing amounts, and where you should assume the absence of exact measurement unless it was required. For the *poletai*, the only exact measurement that mattered was the monetary one. These words on the Attic Stelai, then, do not reflect measurement in the process of selling but containerization in the process of storing and keeping track of agricultural produce.

But if these texts reveal the depths of practices of putting stuff in containers, they were nevertheless in this case the practices of the rich. What made the rich different, however, was not just the quantity of stuff they had, but how they organized it. The fact that most produce was in transportable containers, phormoi most of all, may be significant. It may represent the visible effects of the hand of the market within the household, whether the things packed in phormoi and other movable containers had been bought in the agora or had been produced on site and packaged to be sold there. But it may also reflect the lifestyle of the rich and the ways they organized production and consumption across space. Fragmentary as they are, the stelai reveal that some rich men owned several properties: Euphiletos of Kydathenaion owned three houses (one with a farm) and two other farm plots (426.79; 430.14–18); Polystratos of Ankyle owned two houses (one with a garden plot) and a farm (426.65–71; 424.5–8); someone whose name is not preserved owed farms in Thria and Athmonon (421.20–23); and Adeimantos of Skambonidai owned a house with various appurtenances, a productive farm, as well as a house and farm far away in Thasos (430.1–2; 430.10–11; 426.45–46). Indeed, four of the properties sold were outside Attica: in Thasos, Euboea, and Abydos (426.45, 143; 424.18–20; 427.77). The sites of production were scattered.[61] For the rich to concentrate or consume their wealth, it had to be made portable, either packed in movable containers and sold for easily transportable cash (which then may still have entailed portable packaging for sale), or converted to

self-moving packages (animals). But for the rich, the sites of consumption were sometimes multiple as well: the rich may have moved between
houses in the city and in the country,[62] or moved in the summer to escape
the heat.[63] The rich differed from other farmers less in their use of containers than in their extensive reliance on transportable containers.

Accounting and Allocating

The Attic Stelai demonstrate the fact of containerization but not how
Greeks used these containers to keep track of stuff and rationalize consumption. Three accounts of Greek farms reveal the relevant details.

Hesiod's *Works and Days* portrays a farm of the early archaic period,
where farmers did not use measuring to keep track of or allocate food.
Instead, they rationalized the consumption of supplies by physically manipulating them: dividing them up, putting them in batches (in containers), and then dispensing them by an art of allocation.

The organization of supplies within the oikos proceeded by dividing
space and time. Hesiod repeatedly insists that produce should be put in
containers (*aggeiai*),[64] thus be divided into discrete batches, which farmers
could manipulate both physically and mentally. Hesiod's system also depended on synchronizing the consumption of batches with the observable
divisions of the year, months, the parts of which could either be observed
in the moon or counted as days.[65] He advises that jars (*pithoi*) of wine
should be opened on a particular day of the month.[66] Dispensing from the
pithos throughout the month proceeded not by mathematical calculation
and measuring, but by an art of allocating:

> When the *pithos* is begun and when it's coming to an end have your fill,
> But in the middle be sparing. Thrift is miserable at the bottom.[67]

Hesiod's art of allocating relies on containerization to relate consumption
and time through the relative fullness of the vessel. As a general rule, this
art depends on "thrift," a term that should be understood relationally:
to be sparing or thrifty is to distribute less than the amount which might
drain the *pithos* in exactly one month—that is, to make sure the jar's contents will last by accumulating a surplus. When you almost reach the bottom, however, when it's clear that you've parceled out the wine so that it
will last the month, then you can (and should) abandon thrift and drink
to satisfaction. Continuing to scrimp at this point would impose needless
miserliness. This art of allocating, then, while recognizing the scarcity of
supplies, aims as well at satisfaction, at pleasure. So Hesiod's advice is to
drink more amply when the jar is opened, just when the wine would be
freshest.

Hesiod recommends a similar art for dispensing food to slaves. Rations should be apportioned monthly.[68] In winter, however, he advises cutting the rations to animals in half, while free men should get most (but not all) of their usual allotment.[69] Nothing here indicates that Hesiod imagined measuring any of these. Unlike Roman agricultural writers, for example, he did not specify whole or partial rations by standard measures, and the verb used for distributing them (δατέασθαι) indicates a practice of dividing, not measuring.

Nonetheless, Hesiod does suggest one situation where a prudent farmer would actually measure: when supplies are lent to others and paid back (lines 349–50, 397). When Hesiod discusses lending to a neighbor and his decision to no longer lend to his slacker brother, he uses a form of the verb meaning to measure.[70] In these cases, however, the farmer measures not to account for his own supplies but to account for the debt (as line 350 makes clear). Measurement here stands as a technique for attempting to regulate and control social relationships *outside* the oikos.

The estate represented in Xenophon's *Oikonomikos*, Ischomachus's farm of the classical period, though evidently larger, wealthier, and more monetized than Hesiod's, hardly measures more. Ischomachus offers three systems of keeping track. For common tools and utensils, he stores them in determined (and, apparently, readily accessible) places where they can easily be found and their absence noted.[71] For things used only occasionally (as at festivals), he requires the housekeeper to memorize their places, while he keeps a written inventory for himself.[72] And for things used up (food supplies and money), he divides them into monthly or yearly batches: "We separated out the things which are used up by the month, and stored up separately the things calculated for the year. In this way it's more noticeable how it will turn out in the end."[73] Ischomachus here describes an art of allocating not unlike Hesiod's: he puts supplies in monthly or yearly batches and then visually monitors the relations between the progress of the month or year and the diminution of the supplies, regulating consumption so that the batch will last to the end of the period. Ischomachus assigns to his wife the job of overseeing all this, including making sure that the money laid aside for the year's expenses isn't used up in a month.[74] He likens her job to that of a queen bee, who must fairly divvy up portions of the supplies for each worker.[75] Specifically, he directs his wife to stand by the housekeeper as she measures out.[76]

An early Hellenistic text, book 1 of the *Oikonomika*, which draws on Xenophon's account, elaborates this art of allocating:

> But in large estates, when the staples have been divided up by the month and for the year, and similarly for the equipment used daily and seldom,

these things ought to be given over to the stewards. Additionally an inspection should be made of them from time to time, so that what is preserved and what is deficient can be observed.[77]

But in contrast to this system, which it calls "Persian" or "Lakonian," the text also explicates a different strategy, which it names "Attic."[78] Instead of storing their produce in containers, farmers with small estates might convert their crops to cash: "First they sell and later they buy, and the placing in the storeroom isn't necessary in the smaller regimes of management."[79] This system may seem quite different from the one I've just described—more modern, more rationalized—but it may well have followed similar principles. There is little evidence to link this system to literacy, and it doesn't require written accounts any more than the other. While there is evidence that people used written memoranda when lending or borrowing, there is scant indication of their use in other circumstances of household management involving money.[80] Thus, most farmers would not have kept accounts of their money separate from the money itself; they managed it, rather, by counting and division into batches. Indeed, the description in Xenophon of grouping things into yearly and monthly batches seems to apply both to supplies and to money.

Scholars disagree on the degree to which ordinary Greek farmers sold and bought agricultural produce. It's probably best to understand this as an important strategy to control risk, which most farmers used to a greater or lesser extent depending on preferences and circumstances.[81] Thus Phainippos, a very wealthy man, reported that he sold off some of his grain and kept some at home.[82] Though more easily quantified than produce, money seems to have been treated the same way as other "things that are used up" (to use Xenophon's phrase). Many households, too, would have had periodic money income (e.g., from state pay or other occasional paid labor, the sale of seasonal produce, the renting of a slave, etc.). There is little evidence of the way families incorporated such income into an overall budget; the evidence of comedy suggests it may have been spent on whatever need, desire, or whim was most immediate.[83]

Although neither Hesiod nor Xenophon describe reality unproblematically,[84] and although neither of the farms they write about would have been typical for the time (both being among the more prosperous, Ischomachus's especially), it's possible to infer the methods of accounting in Greek households and the role of measurement among these techniques. I would note that these farmers made little use of writing. You wouldn't suppose an eighth-century farmer to have employed it, but if anyone were going to use writing, you'd expect it to be Ischomachus, a very wealthy man by

Greek standards. Yet in his household, writing was employed *only* to keep track of infrequently used items, as a method of auditing the housekeeper.[85] Other than this, there's no indication that his farm relied on writing at all.[86] Indeed, although Aristotle noted that literacy could have been useful for managing an estate,[87] it was far from necessary. So most Greek farmers didn't keep records, receipts, registers, or logs of what they produced or consumed. I would therefore be wary of assuming that they needed to measure—that is, turn into an abstract and calculable number—their crops and supplies.

Keeping Track and Trust

Containerizing functioned effectively within households as a kind of accounting—minimizing the need to measure with standard measures or to rely on written records—in part because access to containers could be controlled. Greeks developed techniques to control access to space, not merely by closing containers[88] but also by sealing or locking them. Locking seems to have been the less common of these techniques, perhaps because Greek locks were relatively simple devices and were probably more expensive than seals. Locks could be applied to chests and to doors. More commonly Greeks used signets (often on rings) to impress a pattern on a softer material (e.g., clay or wax) that had been applied over an opening or onto a draw string around the opening. The weakness of such seals, of course, was that they did not prevent someone from opening the storeroom or the container or indicate what might have been removed; they only made it clear that someone had pried in.[89] Seals were probably most useful when there was a limited and known group of people who might have opened the container—as within a household. The evidence suggests that the primary things Greeks put under seal and lock were easily moved valuables: money and women's clothes.[90] There is evidence that they were concerned about the security of stored food supplies,[91] but it is less clear how often access to these was restricted.[92] Indeed, Xenophon implies that the security of the food storeroom should be guaranteed by its location in the house more than by any external mechanism.[93]

Such storage techniques also served to mediate relationships between people in households. Examine, then, two of the most important: the one between husbands and wives and the one between masters and slaves.

Techniques of accounting for things by organizing and manipulating their spatial arrangement constituted a primary way in which husbands and wives related, and that relationship could be one of distrust or of trust.[94] A woman in one Aristophanes' plays captures the duality, casting

it, fancifully, as a historical evolution triggered by the playwright Euripides, whose dramas of independent women inspired (or terrified) Athenian men to monitor their wives more closely:

> What was our concern before, managing on our own and removing
> things on our own initiative—barley meal, olive oil, wine—all that's no
> longer possible because our husbands now carry concealed keys, heart-
> less Spartan things with three teeth. Before it was possible to open up
> the door using a cheap seal ring. But now this house slave, Euripides, has
> taught them to use intricate seal rings, which they keep to themselves.[95]

Although the technical aspect of the difference concerns the use of keys
and unreproducible seals, what matters is the difference in trust. The husbands' new distrust is signaled less by new technologies (there were seals
even before) than by the fact that they reserve these for themselves, keeping the keys and seals secure on their persons.[96]

Technologies for exerting greater control over space, however, did not
cause or require husbands to distrust their wives; indeed, they could also
be the basis of fostering trust. Wives and husbands might share responsibility for locking, sealing, and bolting spaces,[97] becoming, like Ischomachus and his wife in Xenophon's treatise, joint rulers of the household.
The cleverness of the Xenophontine system is that the wife is liberated *into*
the role of master; especially through the presence of slaves, she comes
to align her interests with those of her husband. In a patriarchal household, there was always the possibility that the wife would identify more
closely with the slaves than with her husband—a possibility which, from
the husband's point of view, would probably end badly, whether he were
cuckolded or killed. Technologies of closing containers allowed husbands
to deploy trust tactically, to their wives alone.

Masters used some of these technologies of keeping track of stuff, especially the control of space, to frame their relationships with slaves. As
the previous paragraph makes clear, locks and seals were directed more
against slaves than against wives. Additionally, although doors between
rooms seem to have been unusual in Greek houses,[98] doors with bolts
were sometimes installed to the "women's rooms."[99] The purpose of locks
on doors on the "women's rooms" was apparently to control slaves, especially their sexual activity.[100] It was also possible to entrust one slave with
the control of others, as Xenophon allowed with the overseer and head
housekeeper. But insofar as the strategy of trust depended on aligning the
single slave's interests with those of the master rather than with those of
the other slaves, it was unlikely to be pursued extensively.

Masters, however, also relied on a different practice to regulate and
structure their relationships with slaves: measuring. Slaves often got ra-

tions (*epitedeia*) of ground barley meal, and these rations could be measured.[101] Measuring objectified and focused the conflict in these relationships, but it also transformed them. To understand how, remember this: slaves' rations were not measured as part of a comprehensive system of accounting. As a point of comparison, imagine a situation of ideal slavery, where a master has total and unfettered control over his slaves and feeds them however much he wants. In some Greek households, in contrast, this relationship could be regularized, almost contractual, so that both parties could become quite persnickety about the proper techniques of measuring. On the one side, then, Theophrastus says that a tightwad master would measure out provisions (*epitedeia*) to those in his household using a miserly[102] measure with its bottom knocked in but leveling the top very exactly.[103] Measuring made the master a stingy retailer. On the other side, Herodas's character Koritto addresses her slave, whom she berates for taking no initiative: "You are some stone lying in the house, not a slave. But when I measure the barley meal, you count out the crumbs, and if anything should fall to the floor, the walls won't suffer you as you mutter and seethe the whole day."[104] It would overstate the power of slaves to call this relationship fully contractual; slaves had no legal recourse, and if unsatisfied with the way their masters measured their food, all they could do was complain. At the same time, however, masters seem to have behaved *as if* bound by a contract: Theophrastus's tightwad engaged in the kind of legalistic finickiness of someone bound by an agreement but trying to give as little as possible. To get the slaves to act as if bound by the agreement, masters themselves had to act as if it bound them.

Conclusion

Greek households relied on abstract systems in limited though complex ways. Externally, money frequently linked households to the larger political economy through the payments of rents and taxes and through acceptance of pay for public service. In addition, householders often kept written records of others' or their own monetary debts (though not, it would seem, records of income or expenses), memorials of continuing relationships of trust (or, perhaps, distrust) rather than receipts for concluded transactions. Internally, however, there is little evidence that households kept written accounts or used standard measures. The strongest evidence for the reliance on such abstract systems concerns the relationship between masters and slaves. It's tempting to understand the precise measurement of domestic slaves' rations as reflecting slaves' difference and duality: as members of the household they had a claim on its resources but only a limited one, which was completed with the filling of the measure. But to stop at this would be to miss the reciprocal way that measuring caused the master (and his wife, too, insofar as she supervised the process, as Xenophon imagines) to appear not as a serene lord but as a finicky huckster, dickering over crumbs. As with marketplace transactions, the use of measuring transformed a generalized conflict into a specific form, and so defined the parties themselves. Otherwise, Greeks organized economic activities in households without abstract systems. Instead, to manage consumption they relied on local expertise, especially the knacks of eyeballing and thrift. Both of these depended on divvying stuff up in batches corresponding to periods of time, storing it in containers of recognized (but not standardized) sizes, and allocating it out by continually adjusting, through sight, the depletion of the container to the passage of time. To the degree that the patriarch willingly shared his control of these containers—with his wife, especially, but possibly also with a slave or two—he could cultivate relationships of trust within the oikos.

CHAPTER 5

Valuing

Just as chapter 2 considered the establishment of prices in the agora, haggling, as an interpersonal activity, so this chapter treats the attribution of money values in nonmarket contexts, especially in the civic domain, as an essentially social practice. It wasn't just objects bought and sold in the market that Greeks routinely valued, but seemingly anything and everything: religious offerings, dowries, people, friendship, freedom, punishments, honorary rewards, citizenship. Practices of valuing mediated the relations between the polis and citizens, especially when establishing liability for taxes or liturgies, eligibility for office, or qualification for citizenship. Greeks usually described the process of valuing with a set of related words: *time* (honor, of course, but also worth or value), *temesis* (a valuation or assessment), or *timema* (estimate or valuation, but also a class based on such an estimate). This chapter offers a history of these *timemata*, civic valuings.

I approach civic valuing as social not only because the outcome of these practices configured the relations between individuals and the city, but also because, in the classical period at least, individuals declared values freely and unilaterally, a radically subjective declaration, which was not checked against a number established empirically or statistically but was balanced (potentially or actually) against someone else's equally subjective countervaluation. Such declarations were entirely ad hoc: no comprehensive system existed to value generally; instead, people declared values at just the moment they were needed. Later, in the Hellenistic period, under the influence of large-scale kingdoms, some cities attempted to institute more objective methods of valuing. For qualifying citizens, they instituted more comprehensive practices, censuses, which relied more explicitly on money values. The greater use of money values, however, did not create the objectivity of these new processes; instead, reliance on disinterested (though amateur) commissions to assign values gutted the radical subjectivity of practices that relied on trust in particular, interested individuals.

As in the rest of the book, this chapter prioritizes practices (valuing), rather than things (money). It draws on Netz's analysis of counting and coinage. Netz has made a compelling case for augmenting the analysis of the abstract category of "coinage" with consideration of the specific ways that people used coins and other tokens in actual practices of counting. People performed complex calculations, he argues, by manipulating pebbles on an abacus, results that might be recorded in (but were not performed through) written numbers.[1] But in the case of using money values outside market exchanges, money was purely notional, and no physical counting took place. An analysis of counting, therefore, must be complemented by an analysis of valuing. This focus on the uses of money also attempts to thwart a determinism that can attribute profound effects to a mere object. Even in the modern world, the context of money's use determines the degree of its abstracting power, as the work of Viviana Zelizer shows.[2] Thus, as I will argue, what matters is not (or not only) money but the particular practices by which people attribute value.

To follow my argument, you should put aside preconceptions about what money "does." Money doesn't necessarily objectify or depersonalize. In the classical period, the practices of assigning money values, *timemata*, were radically subjective. Greeks placed trust in autonomous individuals to value their own stuff; to the degree that such declarations were accountable, it was not to an impersonal system (e.g., through verification by written records) but to a particular individual who might challenge them. Conflicts over valuing could create and intensify personal relationships. Nor did money automatically commensurate. While commensuration through money enabled exchange in the market, in other settings it sometimes created *quantified incomparables*, not by using a continuous scale of values but by setting an absolute threshold.

Unilateral Valuing

In contrast to the bilateral negotiations of market prices, the basic act in most *timemata* was a statement of value by the owner. Such statements had three characteristics: they were unilateral, they were unverified (though they might be challenged), and they were ad hoc.

Many situations of official valuation confirm the fundamental importance of the unilateral declaration of value.[3] The *pentekoste*, a customs duty of one fiftieth the value of goods imported or exported, a duty common to many Greek states,[4] relied on the owner or shipper of goods to state their value. While tax collectors would inspect goods, the shippers valued them. Thus Aineias tells this story: plotters planned to capture an unnamed city by smuggling in weapons hidden underneath clothing in containers. "The tax collectors (the *ellimenistai*) opened them and saw what appeared to be only clothes and then sealed them until the importers put a value on them."[5] There's no evidence here or elsewhere that the valuation relied on written documents; rather, as Aineias reports, the shipper simply declared it. A law from the island of Delos from the late third century shows that shippers stated the value at their own discretion. This law, the beginning of which is lost, aimed to regulate the local market for wood and charcoal.[6] It required the use of public measures in sales, prohibited resale, and attempted to eliminate haggling by requiring importers to sell wood and charcoal for the price that they'd valued it at for the *pentekoste*. Although such a law would undoubtedly have affected the behavior of importers (by creating a counterinducement to low valuing their merchandise for tax purposes, since this was the price they had to sell it for), it simply relied on the already existing tax mechanisms. Thus importers seem to have been free to value their wares at whatever value they wished; they were not constrained by documentation of previous prices or valuations. (Additionally, in this law the *agoranomoi*, the officials in charge of maintaining the price in the marketplace, did not rely on the initial declaration to the *pentekostologoi*, the customs officials; rather, they solicited from the importers a second declaration, which named the value they'd stated in the first declaration.) An inscription from Kyparissia in the Peloponnese from the fourth or third century confirms this general picture, as well as giving a sense of the tax collectors' role in approving the valuation.

> God.
>
> If anyone imports to the territory of the Kyparissians, when he has taken out his goods, let him register before the *pentekostologoi* and pay the fiftieth, before bringing up anything or selling it. If he doesn't, let him pay ten times.
>
> Whatever someone exports by sea, when he has registered before the *pentekostologoi* and paid the fiftieth, let him load, summoning the *pentekostologos*, and let him not load before this. If he doesn't, let him pay ten times the fiftieth according to the writing. If someone values insufficiently, the *pentekostologos* will confiscate what he lacks according the writing.[7]

Although virtually complete, the brevity of this text, as well as its use of unusual or unique words, leaves its meaning uncertain in some places.[8] Nevertheless, the law seems to give the *pentekostologoi* the power to enforce registration and payment through a tenfold fine in the event of noncompliance and to assure sufficient valuation through seizure of goods to make up the amount.[9] Responsibility for the valuation rested with shippers; thus they registered and paid even before a *pentekostologos* inspected the cargo. The *pentekostologos*, however, might challenge shippers' valuation of their cargo. Against what baseline the *pentekostologoi* compared shippers' valuation is unknown: it could have been their own knowledge of current wholesale or resale market prices or (what they might have known even better) recent valuations of similar cargoes.

In other fiscal contexts you find a similar use of unilateral declarations of value. The Revenue Laws of Ptolemy II (discussed in chapter 4), for instance, relied in certain instances on such unilateral valuations. As well, Antimemes of Rhodes, one of Alexander's officials, allowed people to insure their slaves in the army camp by registering them at whatever value they wished.[10]

Timemata for Offices

Greeks used unilateral *timemata* not only for fiscal reasons but also for political ones. Inscriptions provide several examples of money values used to set qualifications for particular offices in different cities. In chronological order:

- In Erythrai (465–52 BCE) judges in certain trials had to have a worth (*axia*) of 30 staters.[11]
- At Samos (260 BCE), the two men elected to oversee the grain supply had to "have property (*ousia*) of not less than three talents each" (lines 41–42) while the grain buyer had to "have property of not less than two talents" (lines 46–47).[12]
- In Corcyra (before 229 BCE), to oversee a foundation the Boule chose three officials who should be "the most powerful in wealth."[13]
- A treaty between Teos and Kyrbissos (third century BCE) stipulated that *phrourachs* (garrison commanders) were to be appointed for Kyrbissos, men not younger than thirty and having a *timema* of land and house free (from debt) of 4 talents.[14]
- In Andania (92 BCE) a law regulating religious celebrations required the financial officials to have a *timema* of not less than a talent.[15]
- At Minoa on Amorgos (first century BCE), the two *epimenioi* had to have a *timema* of not less than 200 drachmas each.[16]

These inscriptions show a use of money-based *timemata* for offices distributed across space and time. (Although the evidence clusters late, mostly in the Hellenistic period, the case of Erythrai shows that Greeks used definite money criteria for office at least as early as the fifth century.) Although the requirement on Amorgos was low, the others set rather high standards.[17]

Literary evidence confirms that cities used *timemata* for some offices, providing several specific instances. The reconciliation agreement in Athens after the expulsion of the Thirty, for example, required those who held office under the oligarchy and wished to remain in Athens to submit to a review before a court of people who met a *timema*.[18] An early fourth-century source reports that the Thebans allowed only those citizens "who possessed some quantity of property" to serve on the four Boulai.[19] (Some time later, Aristotle described a different arrangement: Thebes allowed craftsmen to share in the government if they had abandoned manual work for ten years.)[20] Aristotle's *Politics* provides further evidence, offering four specific instances of cities with wealth-related *timemata*:

- Thurii required a high *timema* for the highest offices. Aristotle does not explain how they assessed this *timema*, though the subsequent lacunose passage concerns land ownership, which may imply this was the basis (1307a27–29).
- Ambracia had a *timema* so small that eventually men with nothing held office, since, Aristotle notes, "small" is hardly or not at all different from "none" (1303a21–25).
- Leukas repealed the law that required the preservation of the original land allotments, which decision, Aristotle claims, made the constitution excessively democratic since "it no longer happened that they entered into the offices from the prescribed *timemata*" (1266b21–24). It would seem that ownership of the original allotments was the basis of citizenship, and that they became subdivided, allowing more men to meet the *timemata*—not a wealth but a (special) land requirement.
- Aphytis promoted agriculture among its citizens (although there were many of them, and only a small amount of land)—Aristotle relates this in a difficult, obscure passage—not by assessing the whole of their possessions but by dividing (the land) among themselves into such parts that even the poor could exceed in the *timemata*.[21] (This would seem to be the same phenomenon as at Leucas, but analyzed in terms of a different effect.)

Unlike the inscriptions, where the *timemata* used money to qualify people for office, the literary sources' description of these remains vague. With Aristotle, the first three cases concern qualification only for office; the last one is uncertain. (It might concern citizenship, a subject I consider below, rather than office.) Aristotle also does not reveal whether these *timemata* were figured in money values; the first two could have been, but the last two explicitly used land ownership.[22] Nevertheless, the evidence of the inscriptions and of other sources indicates that even as early as the fifth century some Greek cities used *timemata*, possibly figured in terms of money values, to qualify citizens for some offices. But none of this shows *how* they determined a potential official's worth.

The case of Athens, however, does, and it shows that *timemata* were occasional and unilateral. Aristotle's *Constitution of the Athenians* reports that the Athenians used the Solonian classes as the basis of allocating offices.[23] According to this text, Solon "made a division into four classes based on *timema*"—named, in descending order, the Pentakosiomedimnoi, the Hippeis, the Zeugetai, and the Thetes—and "he gave each office to each of them in proportion to the size of the *timema*."[24] (Aristotle imagines that Solon assessed the *timemata* not as money but as an amount of agricultural produce.) Over the course of 250 years, the Athenians had loosened or removed most of these qualifications,[25] so that the only office Aristotle mentions as still being restricted in his time was the Treasurers of Athena.[26] At least three other laws in the classical period made reference to these classes for other purposes.[27] Modern scholars have many disagreements about the classes, especially about their original basis and about how this may have changed.[28] Instead of examining how the Athenians determined the classes in Solon's time, a precarious and uncertain enterprise, I want to examine how they did so in the period of Aristotle. I offer two conclusions.

First, no law defined these classes. Aristotle reports debate about whether Solon defined the Hippeis, the second-highest class, by service in the cavalry (as the name would imply) or, as Aristotle thought more likely, by an estate which produced 300 medimnoi of produce, on analogy, it seems, with the name of the highest class, the Pentakosiomedimnoi (or "five-hundred-measure men").[29] As several historians have noted, this argument suggests that neither Aristotle nor those who held the contrary view could find a law defining the Hippeis—which implies that there was no law defining *any* of the classes.[30] This is turn implies that Aristotle's definition of the Pentakosiomedimnoi was based on etymology (not on any legal or historical text), and that this name served as the basis of his quantification of the other classes.[31] Though Aristotle was trying to discover how Solon had defined the classes 250 years earlier, contemporary legal definitions would have been useful indications, but apparently there weren't any. Whether this was because Solon presumed the definitions found in previous laws (and so didn't put them in his), or because the law defining the classes had somehow disappeared (a conspicuously convenient assumption), or because Solon never formally defined the classes in a law (apparently an inconceivable possibility)[32]—what matters for my analysis is that the Athenians continued to use the classes in the fourth century without reference to formal, legal definitions.[33] To some, this may seem entirely unworkable, but it seems in keeping with the ways that

Greeks sometimes did things—for example, with the fact that Athenians frequently named but didn't define crimes in their laws. What matters is not so much a formal definition as the processes in which the categories were invoked, used, and sometimes contested.

Second, membership in a class was determined only when necessary and by self-declaration.[34] As I mentioned in chapter 4, there's no evidence of a census in Solon's time—or in the fourth century, either. (The Athenian state did keep some centralized records—lists of those liable for military service, for example—but nothing suggests that these were ever put to use to value and classify Athenians.) Instead of an objective status, class membership was something that Athenians declared at the moment it became pertinent. This is clear with regard to offices, a primary purpose of the classes. Aristotle says that Solon did not allow the lowest class, the Thetes, into office, and then remarks that "even today when someone who's about to be randomly assigned to an office is asked in what class he's classified, no one would say in the Thetes."[35] The other situations that invoked classes similarly point to self-declaration. Thus, an Athenian law attempted to compel wealthy relatives to marry or dower poor girls whose fathers had died:

> Regarding heiresses who are classed as Thetes. If the nearest relative does not wish to have her, let him take responsibility for marrying her to someone else. In addition, if he's a Pentakosiomedimnos, let him give a dowry of 500 drachmas, if a Hippeus 300, if a Zeugetes 150—all in addition to what she has.... If the nearest relative neither marries her nor takes responsibility for marrying her to someone else, let the archon force him either to marry her or to take responsibility for marrying her to someone else. If the archon does not force him, let the archon be fined 1,000 drachmas, to be dedicated to Hera. Let whoever so wishes denounce to the archon the man who does not do these things.[36]

Despite the precise quantification of the dowries, there is no need to assume a preexisting catalogue of citizens by class. Whether the heiress was classed as a Thete is not a straightforward question, for women were not put into Solonian classes, and even if an heiress's classification reflected the amount of property left to her by her father, that amount would not necessarily correspond to his class (since two daughters of a Zeugetes might both be poor when they split the property). So it comes down to the question of whether the heiress had been left "unprovided," as one litigant paraphrased the crux of the law.[37] The status of the heiress and her nearest relative could have been determined by the parties involved (which might include a potential husband, a potential volunteer prosecutor, and the archon); should these negotiations have broken down, it would have been a matter for a court to determine. I would note, finally, that all theories for an objective determination of Solonian classes would have to allow for just these ad-hoc determinations if the law was to have the effect of protecting poor women who had rich relatives. If any time elapsed between the objective assessment and the man's death, he may have fallen (or risen) in class standing. In fact, in every instance there would need to be a verification of the status of the heiress, rendering superfluous any previous objective determination.[38]

The Athenian classes may provide a parallel for other cities. Aristotle called these classes *timemata*, even though he believed that Solon had defined them not by money but by amounts of produce, which may suggest they were analogous to money-based classes. The *timema* was the result not of an objective process (a census, an inventory, or an audit of receipts) but of a self-declaration at the moment it was relevant.[39] Declarations would have been verified by the ability of others to challenge them, and competing claims would have been settled rhetorically through adjudication.

A final indication of the fundamental importance of unilateral statements of value is the procedure used when a man wished to decline an office because it was too burdensome or expensive.[40] In the Hellenistic period, offices often entailed an expenditure, a liturgical burden, and some men might want to be excused, claiming insufficient worth. An inscription from the Macedonian town of Beroia from early in the second century required those selected to serve as *lampadarchs* to supply oil for ten days to the boys in the gymnasium; if such service was too burdensome, they had to swear an oath to this effect.[41] In the classical period, too, those appointed to office might swear off if they could not undertake it (e.g., because of illness).[42] In the case of service in the Athenian cavalry, which could be expensive despite stipends to support horse ownership, a man who felt he was too poor could simply swear off: Aristotle notes that "if anyone swears that he is unable to serve in the cavalry because of his body or his wealth, the Boule releases him."[43] The act of swearing off was unilateral and unverified.[44]

Valuing and Subjectivity

Allowing people to value their own property would seem to create a situation open to abuse: intentional misvaluing to serve the owner's interests. For Greeks, however, the primary problem seems to have been full disclosure, not undervaluing. Recognizing the possibility of both, they made unilateral declarations of value accountable not by verifying them against objective records but by making them (actually or potentially) contestable within specific social relationships.

The ancient evidence suggests overwhelmingly that the primary concern about unilateral declarations for taxes was full disclosure of assets, not their valuation. Some of the evidence, it's true, is ambiguous: Participants in an Athenian *antidosis* did have to swear "to declare [their] property rightly and justly,"[45] and it's unclear whether this was meant to guarantee full disclosure or proper valuing (or both). But while modern scholars may lump the problems of disclosure and accurate valuation together,[46] litigants in the Athenian courts focused on the former: some denounced their opponents for hiding assets to avoid taxes (among other reasons), but none accused them of undervaluing them.[47] Even an instance that some have taken to refer to undervaluing turns out to refer to concealment: Thrasyllos remarked about Pronapes, the husband of the woman with whom (in the 350s) he was contesting an inheritance: "Pronapes registered a small *timema*, but, as if he belonged to the knightly class, he thought himself worthy to serve in these offices."[48] Though some have taken the "small *timema*" to refer to undervaluing of property,[49] the language rather plays on the disjunction between a *timema* for other purposes and the use of classes as the basis of qualification to office, and it would seem to allude to the fact that such declarations of worth for office weren't verified at the time—for example, by comparing them with a *timema* for taxes. Thrasyllos went on to contrast Pronapes' small *timema* with the behavior of his own adoptive father, who "made his property visible for you." This contrast hinged on full disclosure, not on correct valuing.

The idea that Greeks may have undervalued their property assumes an objective value against which their declarations could be compared, but in most situations no such objective value existed. Exceptionally, the customs law from Kyparissia (quoted above) raised the possibility of undervaluation, but in this situation the tax collectors would have known, I imagine, either recent prices for the very items in question or taxes recently paid on similar commodities (or both); that is, there would have been comparative cases against which to judge *timemata*. (Note, too, that even this law emphasized the risk of concealment over undervaluation: it punished failure to declare with a tenfold fine but merely compensated for undervaluation.) Generally, however, Greeks treated *timemata* not as right or wrong, as under- or overvalued, but as contestable. For Greeks, valuing was not an empirical problem (for example, by an appeal to receipts or other documents, or witnesses); instead, it was a social matter, with two people hashing it out. The unilateral declaration of value, which was the fundamental act in a *temesis*, did not necessarily go unanswered: declarations of value may not have been objectively verified, but they could be challenged.

In general, Greeks socialized the problem of valuing in two ways: by relying on or constituting specific social relationships where the parties' interests conflicted on the question of valuing, or by making it possible for anyone to challenge a valuation. This distinction tended to correspond to the difference between the typical fiscal practice of valuing along a continuous scale and the political practice of valuing at a threshold. In most political contexts, the question was not what the man was worth but whether his worth was enough to qualify. While fiscal declarations of value were negotiated along a continuum by two interested parties (a tax payer and a tax collector), political valuations were subject to challenge through litigation with an all or none verdict.

The first method of dealing with the problem of valuation involved creating a relationship with multiple parties whose interests in the amount of the valuation conflicted. This method is most clearly exemplified by taxes like the *pentekoste*. In most cases, the relevant tax collectors were in fact private individuals who had bought the right to collect taxes and who therefore had personal financial interests in valuations as high as possible. The Athenians devised an even more ingenious way of situating unilateral declarations of value within social relationships. Matthew Christ (2007) argues that the Athenians restructured the *eisphora*, a special and intermittent war tax, in 378/77. Whereas previously all men who met a certain high level of wealth paid an equal amount, the reforms of this year distributed the burden more proportionally. The new system divided the 1,500 wealthiest Athenians into one hundred groups (*symmories*); each group paid the same amount, but within each group the burden was distributed in relation to wealth. These *symmories* were, then, the administrative apparatus not just for collecting the *eisphora* but for soliciting and scrutinizing *timemata*, which served as the means for proportionalizing the burden within the *symmory*. Christ emphasizes the ways that these *symmories* created "mutual scrutiny" of the members' declarations of value.[50] The Athenians embedded these declarations within enduring social relationships, since *symmories* were relatively small and stable in membership.

Within such relationships, disputes about values could result in litigation, but Greeks seem to have favored private negotiation. A lengthy inscription from Ephesos in the third century exemplifies this preference.[51] Here warfare had devastated the land and farm buildings,[52] many of which had been used as security for loans. The problem with the devastation was not simply that it had lowered land values, but that it had interrupted the flows in the system of credit in two ways: it deprived borrowers of income, and it made credit scarce.[53] Borrowers, whom the law calls "farmers," could not pay either the interest (from their farm income) or the principal when it came due (because they couldn't get a new loan). When a borrower defaulted, the lender typically took possession of the security. The law addressed a situation, then, where default had become endemic, giving lenders a windfall.[54] Its solution was to partition the land of a defaulter, giving the lender a part in proportion to the amount of the loan in relation to the value of the land at the time the loan was contracted. This required procedures to determine what that value of the land would have been:

> It is allowed for the judges, if the business doesn't appear to them to be adjudicatable [*dikastikon*], but the farmer has valued it more and the lender less, it is allowed to them to value however much as seems good. Of the debt there will be no countervaluing. If the valuing is agreed while the loan is disputed, or the loan is agreed while the valuing is contested, let there be judgment [*krisis*] about what is disputed.
>
> What the jurors judge, when the *eisagoges* have registered these on a whitened board, and decisions of the arbitrators, with respect to which they agreed in the court, let them hand them over to the Supervisors of the Common War. When the Supervisors of the Common War have received the judgments and the arbitration settlements, let them select by lot, from the thirty chosen by the demos for each five-day time frame, five men as dividers of properties, and select by lot as well the places, recording these. Those randomly chosen will make the divisions, each taking the places which have been allotted.[55]

The law set out a two-stage process: first the valuing, then the division. In both stages, only if the parties have not settled the matter themselves or with the help of an arbitrator did the judges make a judgment (*krisis*). In its subsequent provisions, the law repeatedly says that judgment happens only if private settlement has failed.[56] This attempt to promote private settlement explains a peculiarity of the first line: the provision that the judges give a judgment only if the matter isn't "adjudicatable" (*dikastikon*). The editors of *IJur* cited the laws of Gortyn as a parallel: these laws distinguish two ways a judge decides, "give judgment" (δικάδδεν) and "decide on oath" (ὀμνύντα κρίνεν).[57] In the former, the judge ratified a claim given (or denied) under oath; in the latter, he investigated, weighed facts, used his discretion, and took an oath himself. At Ephesos, then, the editors argued, the judges had complete freedom to value the land, but had to accept the loan value.[58] Although the parallel to Gortyn is apt, however, the editors have misapplied it. I would argue, on the contrary, that for the matter to be "adjudicatable" the parties must already have come to an agreement. The "adjudication," then, consisted of the judges formally approving the parties' private agreement—as, indeed, the law required the parties to confirm the arbitrator's decision "before the court."[59] This parallels the law's provision that privately agreed divisions of land must be publicly registered (lines 24–25). This law's many provisions reflect a preference for private settlement over litigation.

The practice of valuing was socialized in a second way: While tax valuations often relied on negotiations within specific relationships with conflicting interests, valuations in political settings seem to have generally left it open to anyone to challenge a *timemata*. There is little direct evidence for this, but it would conform to the principle of the institution of the volunteer prosecutor, common throughout Greek cities.[60] At Athens the routine questions asked of potential officeholders—who their parents were, whether they treated them well, whether they had served in the military and paid their taxes[61]—seem to have been separate from the question about the potential officeholder's *timema*. But just as it was possible for anyone who wished to accuse a man standing for office after he had answered the earlier questions,[62] so it seems reasonable that there would have been an opportunity to challenge his *timema*. Such a challenge would have probably resulted in a form of a legal hearing.

Calculating Values

In the classical period, one person declared a value, a declaration which, if challenged by another person, produced interpersonal negotiations or perhaps litigation. Yet an important question remains: what sort of reference point did Greeks use in assigning a money value to things outside market exchanges?

David Schaps argues that by the fourth century, Greeks thought of value as predominantly, even exclusively, exchange or market value.[63] And, indeed, you can find many passages that document such thought, as when Xenophon has Kritoboulos and Socrates discuss who's richer:

> And with a laugh Kritoboulos said: "By the gods, Socrates, how much do you think your property would get if it were sold, and how much mine?"
>
> "I think," Socrates said, "that if I could find a good buyer, my whole estate, along with the house, would easily get me 5 minai. I know accurately, however, that yours would get more than a hundred times as much as that."[64]

But even if Greeks thought in terms of "market values," it still matters by what methods, other than exchange, they established such values. In this case, the value of the estates is established by *imagining* a sale to a "good buyer." It's unclear what the force of the qualification "good" is: for a seller (Socrates here) to maximize his income, what he'd want was a *bad* buyer. In this case Socrates may be imagining a *morally good* buyer who would pay the true worth of the property, or maybe he means "good [*for me*]"—in fact, someone bad at bargaining. But Socrates' five minai constitute a "market" value only in a secondary sense; primarily it's an imaginary value. Note the procedures Socrates does not undertake: comparing his estate to similar estates that recently sold, considering its appraised value for a loan, or consulting its assessed value for tax purposes. There's no way to judge the accuracy of Socrates' statement—no way, that is, to engage in procedures more accurate than imagination—though his famous irony may have protected him from the common fault of homeowners: overvaluing their house.[65]

In fact, despite Socrates' professed certainty to know the value of Kritoboulos' estate "accurately" (*akribos*), it's unclear how he—or anyone else—could determine this. Several factors would have made it difficult. Not so important from the perspective of my argument would be the tendency of some Athenians to hold some of their property secretly.[66] More to the point, there is little evidence of the mechanisms needed to generate even basic statistical knowledge of both individual properties and of the market as a whole. Athens had no central land register, though each of the 139 demes may have maintained one. This is important because if you imagine a functioning land market, prices could fluctuate significantly in response to events,[67] and these changes would need to be tracked. Nor is there evidence that land in Athens had been accurately surveyed to determine its area—an important basis for comparing properties. And even this is not enough: you would need to know the particular features and condition of each piece of land to evaluate its potential market price. Two sources suggest that significant investment in agricultural land could double its value.[68] (I'm certainly not arguing that particular negotiated prices could not have reflected such elements;[69] rather, I'm suggesting that Athenians did not have the mechanisms to abstract and aggregate such prices into what we would consider accurate "market values," or to separate out the various characteristics of a piece of property that would increase or lower its market value.) It is not enough, then, to use a reference to an imaginary sale to describe something as a market value; what we need to know are the mechanisms through which particular values were generated.

One speech from the Athenian courts offers a detailed illustration of the way Greeks thought about valuing estates in terms of money (Dem. 42). The speaker, whose name we don't know, had been assigned a particular liturgy, in this case prepaying the special war tax (the *eisphora*) and then collecting it from a group of wealthy men.[70] (At Athens, the wealthiest men were assigned to do certain state functions like equipping and manning a warship for a year or producing a play for a dramatic festival, burdens called liturgies.) The Athenian generals assigned liturgies based on reports from the demes about wealthy men, but if one of the men picked felt that another man was wealthier than he, he could challenge that man either to take over the liturgy or to exchange property. If he refused both, the case went to court. There is some obscurity about how this procedure, called an *antidosis*, worked: it looks as though Athenians thought that two men might actually exchange property, but it's more likely that negotiations occurred or, if these broke down, litigation over who should undertake the liturgy. The general rule was that the richer man was supposed to undertake the liturgy.[71] In this particular case the speaker had challenged a man named Phainippos to exchange property; in the ensuing legal case, he aimed to show that Phainippos was the wealthier of the two.

Initially, then, this man's speech (we don't have Phainippos's plea) would seem to offer a particularly good instance to examine how Athenians went about valuing. As with most Athenian legal speeches, however, reader beware: the speaker may have been trying only to obscure the issue and confuse the jurors, so that what we have is not a straightforward discussion of valuing but a fog of lies and disinformation.[72] G. E. M. de Ste. Croix offers a trenchant analysis of this problem, focusing on a single issue: the speaker's claim of the physical size of Phainippos's estate. At one point the litigant said that the farm was more than 40 stades in circumference, a number some scholars have used to figure the area of the farm.[73] As de Ste. Croix notes, however, we have no idea what the shape of the parcel was, and unless this farm was twice the area of the next largest-known Attic farm, it couldn't have been anything like a regular rectangle.[74] "Why," de Ste. Croix asks, "should land be described in this extraordinary way, by giving its circumference, unless such a description, without being too greatly exaggerated, was likely to mislead the dicasts [jurors] into thinking the area much greater than it was?"[75] De Ste. Croix rightly criticizes earlier scholars for trying to convert this linear number into an area, but he errs, I think, in accusing the speaker of obfuscation, and for two reasons. First, Greeks often described the magnitude of a space by its perimeter as opposed to its area, especially if the perimeter was irregular. Herodotus, for example, did this with lakes and islands.[76] Polybius noted that "most people infer the size of [cities] from their circumference," though he recognized that a city with a smaller area than another could have the larger circuit.[77] Nevertheless, despite this awareness, even Polybius often gave the magnitudes of cities by their circumference.[78] Two factors probably account for this practice. Estimating the area of irregular shapes is not easy,[79] and landholdings had clearly defined boundaries around which people could (and frequently did) walk. Thus giving the size of an area by its circumference was not necessarily "extraordinary." The second reason de Ste. Croix judges the speaker too harshly is that the speaker was not describing the size of the farm, but indicating his scrupulousness in walking its boundaries:

> After notifying Phainippos of my suit, I invited some of my relatives and friends and walked to Kytherus to the edge of his farm. First I led them round the extremity, which was more than 40 stades in circumference, and I showed them, and called them to witness in Phainippos's presence that there were no debt markers (*horoi*) on the boundary of the farm.[80]

The speaker here was arguing that the debts that Phainippos subsequently claimed to owe were fictitious, since creditors often marked mortgaged property by posting *horoi* on its boundaries, and in this case the speaker claims to have found none.[81] The speaker made no inference from, or even further reference to, the size of Phainippos's farm.

I have lingered on this one case because it delineates the larger challenge: when an Athenian litigant said things that don't make sense to us (like describing a farm by its circumference), was it because he was trying to bamboozle the jurors (assuming they think like us) or because he and the jurors in fact thought differently than we do? In this instance, the context would seem to require the seemingly strange number (though, of course, the speaker himself constructed that context, so that he still might have done so in order to give as large a number as possible). Nevertheless, even if he sought to mislead, he did so in a way that made sense to the audience—by describing the size of an irregular area by its circuit. Even effective bamboozling takes the form of coherent thought.

The speaker, attempting to persuade the jurors that Phainippos was wealthier than he (*plousioteron*, §§3, 4), did not proceed as you might expect. His primary argument had nothing to do with valuing: Phainippos had repeatedly violated the legal procedures for an *antidosis* case. The speaker began with this claim (§§1–2), organized his speech around its particulars, and offered it as the fundamental reason the jurors should vote in his favor (§30). You might suspect that in failing to directly address the main question of wealth, the speaker was obfuscating the facts, or compensating for the facts being against him. On the other hand, the strategy allowed him to tell a story (of Phainippos's perfidy) as opposed to merely offering an accountant's report, a story that also allowed him to cast his opponent as a violator of the law.[82] As I argue in chapter 8, both of these were important rhetorical resources of litigants. What the speaker had to say about valuing, then, was embedded in and subordinated to the rhetorical context, and must be ferreted out.

In fact, the speaker had very little to say about the money value of his or Phainippos's estate. Both parties had submitted inventories of property, which the speaker had the clerk read to the jurors (§§16, 25), but

these lists did not include valuations.[83] The speaker made one reference
to the total money value of his estate—years earlier when he inherited it:
"My father left behind property of only 45 minai for each of us, for my
brother and for me," which he then compared to his opponent's inheritance by noting that both Phainippos's biological and adoptive fathers had
been wealthy enough to win choral victories in the Dionysia (§22). At no
point did the speaker provide a money value for Phainippos's whole estate, either now or in the past. Nor did he ever put a value on the land or
the houses of either estate.

Although the speaker avoided talking about the present capital value
of the estates—the numbers we would expect to be compared in this situation—he did speak repeatedly about the money value of two immediate, verifiable things: debt and income.

This case seems to have been a contest to see who could show greater
debt. Phainippos in his declaration of property had listed at least four
debts, which totaled more than three talents (§27–28). The speaker argued that two of these were fictitious: "You fabricate nothing other than
that you have private debts to the same amount as my debts to the city."
(§29) Indeed, the speaker's own accounting relied heavily on a debt of
three talents he owed the city for a mining venture that had gone bad: this
was the first and last money value he mentioned to the jurors (§§3, 32).

He also referred to income: Phainippos's estate, he claimed, produced
wood for the market at a rate of 12 drachmas a day (§7), which had accumulated to 30 minai since the case began (§30), and he sold off more
than a thousand medimnoi of grain and eight hundred measures of wine
at 18 and 12 drachmas per unit respectively, very high prices (§20).[84] The
speaker, it's true, was evasive about his own income, saying only that
while he had formerly profited greatly from the silver mines, he had now
lost almost everything (§20).

A similar absence of abstract capital values may be found in other legal speeches. In one, an invalid defended his right to a state pension for
disability before the Boule (Lys. 24). In Athens any man who could not
work and who possessed less than 3 minai was eligible to receive support
of one obol a day.[85] Someone accused this man of being able-bodied and
capable of a trade, so that he could live without the pension (§5). He responded that he inherited nothing from his father, he had long supported
his mother, he had no children to support him, and his trade gave him
little help, so that the pension was his only income (§6). His accounting, such as it was, mostly concerned income and expenses. His only arguments about his wealth *as capital* were that his father bequeathed him
nothing and that his accuser would rather undertake ten liturgies than exchange property with him (§9).

Or read Isocrates' *Antidosis*, a pamphlet in the form of a speech in an *antidosis* suit. Keeping with the fiction of the suit, he responds to the charge that he "possesses a multitudinous estate."[86] He argues that no other sophist was particularly wealthy, and that Gorgias, the richest of them, left at his death only a thousand staters. You shouldn't think, he says, that the earnings (*tas ergasias*) of sophists are equal to those of theater actors, but rather you should recognize that people have property (*ousia*) equal to their professional peers.[87] Like the speaker of Dem. 42, Isocrates conflates what we would distinguish, capital and income. He also gives a comprehensive money value for an estate only at the point of inheritance.

From these speeches, several related patterns emerge in the ways Greeks valued. In general I might say that when it came to wealth, Greeks preferred the immediate to the abstract. Thus, the question of "wealth" concerned not only capital (to use our term) but also—and especially—income. Compare this to Xenophon's analysis at the beginning of his *Oikonomikos* that only that which brings an advantage counts as wealth.[88] I am arguing, of course, not that Greeks could not distinguish capital from income,[89] but that the evaluation of what persons were worth could hinge more on how much monetary income they actually had as opposed to a hypothetical price they might realize if they sold their property. In fact, the reliance on exchange values—not just prices in sales but values set in other kinds of property transactions, as when a man valued his estate in his will or when a lender assessed its worth in using it as security for a loan—the reliance on these exchange values seems to have militated against speculating on an abstract capital value. Thus, the speaker of Dem. 42 attributed specific monetary values to items that had been valued in transactions: debts (including dowries), produce sold, and inheritances. Of course, you can question the speaker's knowledge of how much wood or produce Phainippos sold, or the price he got for these, but the speaker invented prices and amounts (if he did invent) only in the context of exchanges. The speakers in all three speeches imagined the moment of inheritance as the time when someone would value an estate.[90] Greeks did not seem to imagine that estates had monetary values; rather, there were particular moments when someone might attribute a value to them. Moreover, except for valuations in inheritances (which were unilateral and unverified), the value of land (what we would call its capital value) seems to have been uncertain. As a commodity that changed hands infrequently and was unstandardized,[91] land in general or specific parcels of it were rarely associated with market value. Perhaps the best indication of the value of land would have been the income derived from it.[92]

Of course, Greeks conceptualized value in many ways—as you would expect in a world without standard accounting rules. Thus it's only fair to acknowledge that in his suit against his guardians over their management of his inheritance, Demosthenes put something like an abstract capital value on all his property.[93] Although from our perspective Demosthenes' accounting is, to put it generously, a bit wonky, the way he categorized his property conformed to the general idea of distinguishing immediate value, items that brought a regular and predictable income (*energia*), from those that did not.[94] While Demosthenes assigned a value to all of these items, the broad distinction seems to recognize that assets producing income denominated in money constitute a more immediate form of wealth than those that require subsequent actions to liquidate.

Desocializing Valuing

In the Hellenistic period, perhaps for the first time, Greeks used two alternatives or supplements to unilateral declarations of value: fixed tariffs and independent commissions. Both alternatives objectified valuing by removing it from parties with immediate interests in the value, and both eliminated or subordinated the processes that depended upon these interested parties: unilateral declaration and negotiation.

The state could abolish unilateral declarations of value by owners by simply decreeing a value for certain things—establishing, that is, a tariff. At least two decrees supply evidence of states doing this with confiscated property. An inscription from Eretria in the late fourth or early third century records a contract for draining a marsh. Although much of the right-hand side of the stone is lost, lines 19 and 20 seem to allow the contractor, Chairephanes, to dig a conduit through private land at a certain price per foot.[95] A roughly contemporary inscription from Tegea provides a more detailed description of the use of fixed compensation.[96] The text, an edict (*diagramma*) from a Macedonian king, probably Alexander, required the city to readmit exiles and restore at least some of their property. Each exile was to have one house (*oikia*) plus a garden. The edict continues:

> For the price [*tima*] of the *oikiai*, let him recover two *minas* for each *oikos*, and the assessment [*timasia*] of the *oikiai* is to be whatever the city decides; but let him receive double the legal value [*timama*] of the gardens.[97]

Scholars have disagreed about who receives the money (the exiles for the houses they lost, or the present owners for the houses they must give up), whether the meanings of the three *tim-* words differ (and if so, how), and whether *oikos* means the same as *oikia* ("house"), or indicates a "room" (so that the compensation corresponded to the number of rooms in the building).[98] The settlement of these issues, however, is not critical to the main point I would like to make: in this case the problem of reintegrating exiles and restoring their property was dealt with through a single, fixed price (whether per house or per room). Similarly, tariffs—which skip the process of valuation and simply impose a set amount—are known from the Hellenistic and Roman periods, but not the classical.[99]

The second way to replace unilateral declarations of value was to use an independent commission. Such commissions achieved a kind of objectivity less through expertise than through disinterestedness; their hallmark was, ideally at least, the absence of social relationships with those whose property was being valued. Again, the Hellenistic period provides more evidence of such practices. In 303, with regard to compensation for property, King Antigonos I sent two letters to the people of Teos offering advice on their *synoikismos*, their unification, with the people of Lebedos.[100] Although forced movements of scattered populations into single cities was a favorite project of Hellenistic kings, the courteous tone of these letters and a recent earthquake in the area may mean, as R. A. Billows has argued, that the citizens of the two towns sought the king's help in a voluntary unification.[101] In either case, the king advised the people of Lebedos to abandon their town and move to Teos; they were to be compensated for their houses (the demolition of which Billows attributes to the earthquake), and a group of valuers from an independent city, Kos, was to set the amount of compensation.[102] Similarly, in the late third or early second century, the Boeotian city of Tangara decided to build a temple to Demeter and Kore. The decree authorized some permanent officials and a special commission to determine where to situate the new temple, allowing that "if anyone's land or house is needed for the construction of the sanctuary, the polemarchs will convene the people and designate eleven valuers, according to the common law of the Boeotians."[103]

The History of Valuing Citizens: Athens

In the Hellenistic period, censuses came to supplement unilateral declarations of value—especially for determining citizenship. At the same time, money came to be used as a criterion of citizenship. Although it's commonly said that many Greek states, especially oligarchies, had property qualifications for citizenship, there is little evidence that Greek cities used wealth evaluated in terms of money as a criterion for citizenship until late in the fourth century. All Greek states determined citizenship in the first instance by descent: only the children of citizens could themselves become citizens. At Athens, for example, before 451/50 a person needed one parent of citizen status to inherit citizen status; after this date, both parents had to be citizens. Within this framework, however, some states imposed additional criteria to restrict the proportion of citizens. Historians usually characterize these as "property qualifications," following Aristotle's famous insight that oligarchy is only accidentally the rule of the few, but is essentially the rule of the rich. This insight, however, is limited in two ways, as I showed above: first because Aristotle provides no explicit evidence of a city that used wealth in its most abstract form, money, as the basis of citizenship, and second because his examples show instead a concern for the activities a citizen could undertake. Despite being based on a broad view of many Greek cities, Aristotle's *Politics* provides little evidence for the use of money values as a mechanism for qualifying citizens.

You can trace the history of these changes in qualifications for citizenship—from unilateral declarations to comprehensive, objective censuses, from qualifying activities to a pure wealth qualification—most fully in Athens, the city, ironically, most famous for its commitment to unqualified citizenship. Several times over three hundred years the city is reported to have qualified (or considered qualifying) citizenship:

- In the time of Drakon (c. 621), Aristotle reports, "citizenship [*politeia*] was given to those who provided arms," treasurers and archons were picked from those who had property worth at least 10 minai (without debts), and generals and cavalry commanders had to have at least 100 minai of property.[104]
- In 411, under the stress of the Peloponnesian War, the Athenians voted to abolish their democracy, and put the government in the hands of a council of Four Hundred, while restricting the franchise to a group called the Five Thousand, understood as "those who could most powerfully aid the state with their bodies and property."[105] The ancient sources disagree about whether this group was to be arbitrarily limited to only five thousand,[106] or was meant to include all who served as hoplites.[107] Either way, the ostensible criterion was a man's military function, not his wealth. Still, the criteria of enrollment seem to have left considerable room for interpretation, at least according to the son of one of the Four Hundred, whose father, "when he was registrar (*katalogeus*), registered nine thousand, so that none of his demesmen could be at odds with him, but he wrote down the name of whoever wanted him to, and he accommodated even those who were not eligible."[108]
- When Sparta defeated Athens in the Peloponnesian War (404), it imposed a government by committee known as the Thirty. It hardly makes sense to speak of "citizens" under the Thirty, who acted not

from any authorization from Athenians but because of the presence of the Spartan army. But the Thirty did enroll a broader group in their government, the Three Thousand, people with greater rights than others. The criteria of selection remained mysterious even at the time; indeed, it was said that the Thirty kept delaying publishing the list as they added and subtracted names.[109] One of the Thirty, Theramenes, objected to the process, because three thousand was an arbitrary number if they wanted to enroll "the best of the citizens."[110] Although the size of the body was objectively defined, the criteria of inclusion were moral;[111] Theramenes himself experienced the subjectivity of this when Critias, the leader of the Thirty, unilaterally struck his name from the list.[112] (The essentially subjective nature of the criteria of inclusion is reflected in the other list the Thirty kept, the notorious "Lysander's list," a catalogue of enemies, which seems to have been compiled, in part, from voluntary denunciations and was remembered afterwards as a tool of personal retaliation.)[113]

- Just after the Athenians expelled the Thirty, in 403, "Phormisios, one of those who had returned with the demos, brought forward a suggestion that the exiles be allowed to return, but that they offer the *politeia* not to all but to those who owned land. The Spartans also supported this idea."[114] This suggestion was much more inclusive than the qualifications under the Five Thousand or the Thirty, and more objective as well, though the Athenians chose to return to their previous democratic practice of unqualified citizenship.

- In 322, Antipater defeated Athens, which had revolted from Macedonian rule after the death of Alexander. Diodorus reports that Antipater "changed the *politeia* from democracy and ordered that the citizen body (*politeuma*) be constituted from a valuation: those having more than 2,000 drachmas would be in charge of the government and of the elections, while he expelled all those below the valuation from the *politeia*, alleging that they were troublemakers and militaristic (though he offered land in a colony in Thrace to any volunteers). More than twelve thousand were removed from their fatherland, but those who possessed the determined valuation (around nine thousand) were appointed to control the city and the land, and they ran the government according to the laws of Solon."[115]

- In 318 Cassander, Antipater's son and successor, again imposed terms on Athens, insisting that the *politeuma* be administered with an assessment of at least 10 minai (1,000 drachmas).[116]

The evidence for each of these is problematic, and scholars continue to debate their particulars. An essential document, Aristotle's *Constitution of*

the Athenians, has many limitations. In particular, many scholars believe
that the document and its sources incorporate visions of the past colored
by the fierce debates about oligarchy and democracy of the late fifth and
fourth centuries. For example, many scholars have denied the veracity or
authenticity of the chapters about Drakon, which seem to fit awkwardly
into the design of the whole and report suspiciously anachronistic details. Although the treatise structures its history in terms of the evolution
of Athenian democracy, it tends to represent the polis, even at its earliest stages, as fully articulated and institutionalized. It is, for example, unlikely that in the seventh century there was a formal rule defining "citizenship" (*politeia*), even if certain customs prevailed. Nevertheless, several
patterns emerge.[117]

First, diverse criteria were proposed or used for limiting citizenship:
functional (service as a hoplite), moral ("the best citizens"), territorial
(land ownership), or monetary. If in practice all of these criteria included
a majority of the wealthy and excluded a majority of the poor, however,
it is misleading to lump them together as "property qualifications" and
treat oligarchy (literally, rule by few) as though it were simply and essentially rule by the wealthy (as Aristotle does). To do so obscures the historical specificity of each of these definitions: the program to restrict the
Five Thousand to those best able to aid or serve the state seems related to
the military difficulties confronting Athens at that stage of the Peloponnesian War, while Phormisios's idea of restricting citizenship to landown-
ers compromised between a narrow oligarchy and the traditional democracy, a compromise that also eliminated the subjective moral criteria so
abused by the Thirty.

Second, money (which is to say, wealth in its most abstract form) came
to be used as a criterion of citizenship only late in the period. Earlier criteria articulated specific activities that linked citizens and the polis: military service, land ownership, whatever virtues made the best citizens.
(The Solonian classes, too, if they derived from agricultural production,
defined citizen rights in terms of a primary activity, farming, linked to the
territory of the polis.) As a criterion of citizenship, money was unteth-
ered from the polis as a place: there was no requirement that it be generated or spent in Attica. Money detached citizenship from the city.

The Process of Valuing Citizens: Cyrene

By the late fourth century, some cities were beginning to determine citizen status and rights by using monetary values, which were assessed
through increasingly objective and comprehensive procedures. The best
evidence for this use comes from an inscription from the North African

city of Cyrene—though it is a complicated text. Dating from 321, this
edict (*diagramma*) records a "constitution" imposed on the Greek city by
Ptolemy I.[118] Two problems have thwarted scholars. First, the stone is so
abraded that some parts of it are unreadable. The earliest text, that of Ferri
(1925, reproduced in Cary 1928), left many lacunae. Oliverio's subsequent
edition (1928) filled many of these gaps, often with letters marked with a
dot to indicate uncertainty. One might normally prefer the later edition.
But when Fraser (1956–58) examined the stone again, he concluded that
many of Oliverio's readings not only made no sense but couldn't be seen
on the stone at all. Unfortunately, *Supplementum Epigraphicum Graecum*
(*SEG* 9.1 [1938]), had reprinted Oliverio's text without even his marks
of doubt. I have opted for the conservative course, following Fraser consistently or, where he offers no guidance, Ferri.[119] The second problem is
that the language and grammar of the inscription are frequently ambiguous; the imprecision suggests that a straightforward or literal reading is
not always sufficient, but how often this should be supplemented with an
inferred or expanded meaning is contestable.

I offer the following somewhat literal translation of the lines that bear
directly on the question of money values used to qualify citizenship:

7 Let the citizen body be the Ten Thousand. They (the Ten Thousand)
   will be the exiles who fled to Egypt

8 whom Ptolemy indicates and (those) for whom the *timema* of their
   "deathless" property

9 with that of their wife is (worth) 20 Alexandrian minai, which
   (*timema*) the assessors

10 will estimate as free (from debt), and (those) however many to whom
   it is owed 20 Alexandrian minai

11 with the "deathless" (things) of his wife if they have been valued not
   less than

12 the debt and the interest. Let those who owe make a counterdenial on
   oath, if the neighbors do not

13 have the *time*. These too will be established of the Ten Thousand if
   not younger than thirty.

14 The elders will chose the assessors from the Ten Thousand, sixty
   men not younger than

15 thirty who have sworn a legal oath. Those chosen will assess value as
   much as

16 it writes in the laws. In the first year, they will be active citizens out
   of the earlier *timemata*.[120]

The inscription outlines the criteria and procedures for determining who
could exercise full citizen rights.[121] Although the *diagramma* grammati-

cally defines four distinct groups of men who qualify as citizens, I will argue that it actually refers to four procedures—which could be used singly or in combination—for qualifying citizens.

The first procedure is clear (lines 7–8): Ptolemy designated as citizens some number of the exiles who had fled to him and whom he was restoring as he imposed this *diagramma*. After this, however, understanding the procedures becomes less straightforward. If read literally, the inscription would indicate that the Ten Thousand should consist of those exiles Ptolemy designated who *also* met certain wealth levels. Nevertheless, as Pagliaro has argued, the inscription is elliptical here, and that the relative pronouns in lines 8 and 10 refer not to the exiles but to the Cyreneans who had remained.[122] This gives a second and third procedure for determining full citizens.

In the second procedure described by the *diagramma* (lines 8–10), the assessors value the property of a man, along with his wife's, and if it amounts to more than 20 minai, he too qualifies as a citizen. This property must be "deathless," a word that probably indicates material, debt-free assets, as opposed to credits.[123]

The third procedure allows those owed a certain amount of money to qualify for citizenship (lines 10–12). The *diagramma* here defines a group of men whose assets consist of credits, as long as their wife's material property reaches a certain level. Scholars debate whether these men must hold 40 minai of wealth (20 of their own credits and 20 of their wife's material property) or only 20 (10 plus 10). For my purposes, however, the procedure is more important than the criteria. Here, unlike the previous procedure, the assessors are not said to do any valuing. The sometimes elliptical inscription may simply be implying this, but in fact there would be little need to assess the value of a credit since this was already set in money terms. Similarly, the inscription refers to the wife's assets in the past perfect ("have been valued") not because the assessors evaluate them, but because they had already been evaluated in money terms in a marriage contract.[124] The assessors did not have to value credits and dowries.

The next two clauses establish a fourth procedure for qualifying citizens, taking account of their debts (lines 12–13). The clauses, however, are somewhat obscure: "Let those who owe make a counterdenial on oath, if the neighbors do not have the *time*. These too will be established of the Ten Thousand if not younger than thirty." It's not immediately clear who "those who owe" are, what the swearing is about, or why the neighbors should get involved. Because the grammar shifts—it's a full sentence with a stated subject ("those who owe") as opposed to a relative clause with an implied antecedent (like the second and third procedures)—some scholars infer that the inscription is no longer defining who should be citizens. Instead, they take the subject as those who owe the creditors of the previous clause, and argue that this sentence establishes the procedure for verifying their credits. The debtors, on this reading, must swear (presumably to the amount of the debt, which constitutes the creditor's asset), but only if the neighbors of the creditor don't meet the property qualification for citizenship.

Such interpretations of these clauses are not satisfactory. Pagliaro took them to mean that for potential citizens who have lent money (those described in lines 10–12) there must be testimony verifying the loan, from the debtors if for movable property, from the neighbors if for land—or, if the neighbors didn't meet the property qualification, from other citizens over thirty years old.[125] This depends on an alterative restoration in line 12, [κ]ἄν instead of [ἐ]άν ("and the neighbors" instead of "if the neighbors"). Fraser reported nothing on this letter in his reexamination of the stone, so the better restoration depends on which gives better sense. Pagliaro's interpretation has one advantage: it explains the thirty-year age minimum, which is awkwardly placed and phrased if it's meant to apply to all citizens. However, several factors tell against his reading. First, it subjects the text to suspicious amounts of supplementation, justified by the fact that it's elliptical.[126] In general, sensible shorter supplements should be preferred over convoluted longer ones. Second, it creates grammatical anomalies, especially in line 13 where καὶ becomes superfluous and οὗτοι refers not to either of the nouns of the previous clauses (*those who owe*, or *the neighbors*), but to an imagined group in an imagined clause, *those called to swear instead of the neighbors*.

A better understanding is possible. My interpretation starts back in line 10, which, if read plainly, would seem to indicate that those who had debts of any amount could not become citizens; their *timemata* had to be "free (from debt)." However, I argue, lines 12–13 established procedures for people with some debt—for "those who owe"—to become citizens too. For them, the assessors didn't just value their property. In addition, to discover the full extent of the debt, they asked the neighbors. They questioned the neighbors because they were the people most likely to know about a debt that the potential citizen had failed to disclose. But if the neighbors weren't citizens (that is, if they didn't have the *time* to qualify), the debtor was put under oath, presumably to swear not just to the value of the debts but also to the fact that he had revealed them all. The primary problem with debts was that people would fail to disclose them and would qualify for citizenship without the requisite worth. (If all you had was 10 minai worth of property, you could borrow another 10 and fail to disclose the debt, thus appearing to be worth 20.)[127] This procedure was intended less to guarantee the valuation than to ensure the full disclosure of the debt as part of the valuation.

The law thus set out four procedures for determining citizens: designation by Ptolemy, valuation of property by the assessors, valuation of property in previous contracts (business or marriage), and verification of debt by neighbors or by self-declaration. This seems to me a more appropriate way to understand the text, since many citizens must have failed to fit into a single "group"—if Cyrene was like other cities, many wealthy men must have had some debts—while some would have been wealthy enough to qualify through a combination of procedures.

Elisabetta Poddighe has argued that the constitution put one further condition on full citizenship: in line with Aristotle's strictures, citizens could not engage in trades or manual labor.[128] This seems unlikely for two reasons. First, Poddighe relies without comment on Oliverio's speculative and unreliable text; she does not cite Fraser, whose more conservative text offers less support for her argument.[129] Thus, although the legible parts of lines 47 and the following mention working and trades and engaging in lawsuits and some group of people being "in *atimia*," Poddighe's unequivocal claim that the constitution excludes all manual workers (*banausoi*) from even passive citizenship (*politeia*)[130] depends on speculative restorations of missing words. Second, as part of her argument, Poddighe claims that the constitution prohibited the Ten Thousand from engaging in paid professions. There are two problems with this claim. Only Oliverio's version of the text prohibits professionals from holding offices of the Ten Thousand; Ferri's, however, keeps them out of *hetairiai*, which Cary argues may have been military groupings.[131] Second, whatever it prohibited, the law did not affect all paid professionals but merely those the city itself employed: "Whoever from the active citizens publicly (*demosiai*) acts as a doctor or as a gymnastic trainer or teaches how to shoot with a bow or ride a horse or fight in armor or acts as herald in the town hall, he may not...."[132] The key word here is *demosiai*, which indicates that the city employed these people. Placed at the beginning of the list, the adverb modifies all the occupations; indeed, the list consists of exactly the kinds of professionals that cities employed in the Hellenistic period.

The novelty of this constitution derives from its use of monetary values in conjunction with something like a comprehensive census. The clearly extant parts of the document did address some people's occupations, although in what ways remains unclear. But even if Poddighe is correct that the constitution formalized an elite prejudice against manual labor, prohibiting *banausoi* from being citizens—a stipulation for which Thebes provided a precedent—the deeper innovation of this document lies elsewhere: in using monetary values as the criterion for citizenship, and in establishing a process of assessment that was systematic, objective, and at least somewhat comprehensive. The number of assessors, sixty, attests to the magnitude of this undertaking. In many ways, it's unclear exactly how they worked. In particular, the inscription does not say whether they assessed every potential citizen or only those who petitioned for inclusion, but certainly they evaluated every active citizen, a group large enough to be called the Ten Thousand. It's clear, however, that the assessors did the valuing. Contrast this to the procedures for determining *timemata* for office in Athens, which were self-declared only at the moment of allocation to office. Like the virtually contemporary constitution Antipater imposed on Athens (322 BCE),[133] Ptolemy's constitution for Cyrene is the earliest specific evidence for abstract money values used to qualify citizens.

Commensuration and Incomparability

Greeks used money in two ways in their practices of valuing: to commensurate and to create incomparables. These correspond to creating a continuous scale of values and to setting a threshold. The use of money to commensurate is well known—it corresponds to the common idea of money as a means of exchange—and I discussed some practices of commensurating through prices in chapter 2. But Greeks also used money to create incomparable objects or categories, things that could not (or should not) be exchanged or equated. The most obvious way to do this was to assert that something was altogether outside the system of quantification, that it existed in contrast to it—that it was *priceless*—asserting an incommensurability.[134] But Greeks sometimes assigned specific monetary values to things, not to indicate their potential exchangeability, but to quantify their incomparability. This, it seems to me, is the implication of one of the few situations in the Homeric poems that use money values: The Greek Diomedes exchanges armor with the Trojan Glaukos— and Zeus must have deranged Glaukos, Homer says, because he traded his gold armor worth a hundred heads of cattle for bronze armor worth nine.[135] An initial form of commensuration—armor quantified through a form of money, here not drachmas but cattle—establishes the ultimate *incomparability* of the objects. The point here is not that Glaukos should have haggled, asking for another ten sets of bronze arms (and perhaps a lagniappe, too), but that the exchange should not have happened at all.[136] Similarly, on an occasion when the Athenians encouraged trierarchs to get their ships ready quickly, granting to the first to do so a crown of 500 drachmas, to the second one of 300, and to the third one of 200,[137] it seems unlikely that the second- and third-place finishers were somehow collectively equal to the winner. Rather, quantification here seems to have established a hierarchy of incomparables.

Valuing may distinguish as much as it equates. Greek debates over the best form of government often involved references to quantification and ratios. In chapter 7, I will discuss the question of arithmetic versus geometric proportions as analogies—or formulas—for democracy and oligarchy. Many uses of quantification relied on simple dichotomies, like property qualifications for office, for example: either you had enough or you didn't. Quantified rules of discrimination did not require an exhaustive accounting; rather, they required only enough information to determine whether a person met a threshold. Systems of classes melded the two: the classes were hierarchical, but there was no attempt to distinguish people within a class. Such incremental hierarchies—the difference between active and passive citizens at Cyrene, or the Solonian classes at Athens—probably recognized the limits and uncertainties of information; it's difficult to imagine that there could have been a Forbes list of the five hundred richest Athenians ranked in order of wealth. Rather, what the Athenians had were discrete classes, say, the three hundred wealthy enough to pay the *proeisphora*.

These procedures suggest that among various forms of quantification, monetary values had important roles in structuring relations between citizens. Money was one way to indulge the impulse to quantify. At Athens the person most often associated with that impulse was Solon.[138] In his own poems he spoke of the ten periods of humans' lives,[139] but later tradition attributed to him increasingly complex acts of quantification, starting with Herodotus, who makes him multiply the number of years a person might live by the number of months per year and days per month (adding intercalary days) to get the total expected lifespan in days.[140] At the later end of the ancient tradition, Plutarch attributed to Solon laws that quantified not just values of sacrifices and penalties for crimes,[141] but also the maximum number of funeral garments, the minimum distance trees should be planted from boundaries, or bee hives located from other hives—seventeen different quantifications in all.[142] Greeks associated Solon not merely with valuing but, more broadly, with quantifying. Later writers associated him with ratios, in particular 5:3:2:0. According to Aristotle, Solon defined his classes by amount of produce: 500:300:200:less than 200.[143] Then, he says, they elected archons from the top three classes in proportions 5:3:2.[144] A law attributed to Solon in the manuscript of one of Demosthenes' speeches specifies minimum dowries for orphaned girls whose relatives came from the top three classes as 500, 300, or 150 drachmas.[145] And Solon was said to reward victors at games with crowns of 500 drachmas for the Olympic, 100 for the Isthmean, and in proportion for the rest.[146] Ratios, I would argue, are more important than isolated numbers because they are quantities that are explicitly commensurated—in many cases, so as to create incomparables.[147]

Conclusion

As procedures for determining values, *timemata*, that is, valuations in political contexts, differed from haggling. First, *timemata* were unilateral. During the classical period, people valued their own stuff, though there was a growing tendency to have independent valuers do the job. Such valuations could be challenged, which would require an opposing party, as in haggling. Yet there was a second important difference even here: unlike market negotiations, which might fail to reach an agreement, a challenge to a *timema* had to have an outcome. And this points to a third difference: the challenge to a *timema* often introduced a third party as a final decider, typically a judge or a jury. Moreover, insofar as large juries adjudicated disputed *timemata*, rhetoric transformed the conflict, a subject I take up in chapter 8. Finally, although in fiscal contexts (as with taxes like the *pentekoste* or the Athenian *eisphora*) valuations were aimed at enabling equivalences, in political contexts they were often aimed at creating quantified incomparables, thresholds that distinguished absolute differences (as between those who could hold an office and those who could not). *Timemata* put money to very different uses than bargaining.

Valuing in political contexts looks more like measuring. Over the fifth and fourth centuries, there was a general trend toward subjecting citizens to a *metron*, a quantified limit or threshold, a trend toward measuring them. Some cities required certain officials to meet a *timema*, a monetized wealth requirement, certainly as early as the mid-fifth century in Erythrai.[148] But at Athens, the one city where you can see such practices at work, required no generalized assessment of citizens; rather, a potential officeholder made a unilateral declaration at the moment his qualifications became relevant, apparently as part of his review of office (*dokimasia*). Moreover, until the end of the fourth century, qualifications for citizenship were not quantified. Instead, they reflected the significant or proper activities of citizens (farming, serving in the military, acting with virtue). The evidence suggests that the first quantified thresholds applied not to individual citizens but to the whole citizen body, attempts to define it at a certain number (3,000 or 5,000). Such attempts, however, foundered on their contradictory logic: As Theramenes noted, the number 3,000 was arbitrary if the real criterion was virtue. Similarly, the attempt to limit the number of citizens to 5,000, defined by service to the polis, ended up including nearly twice that number. Both cases reflect the problem of defining the heap—or, rather, they created that problem by separating the unit (military service) from the limit (5,000). But in the late fourth century, under the sway of Hellenistic monarchies, both Athens and Cyrene began to subject individual citizens to a *metron*: a precise, quantified threshold that determined their status, a *timema* of 2,000 drachmas.

Such quantification significantly depersonalized the relationships among citizens and between each citizen and the polis. To some degree, this depersonalization derived from money: citizens were defined no longer by their proper activities but by a monetized threshold. But if money was necessary for this depersonalization, it was hardly sufficient. Cities had long used monetary values to set thresholds for holding office, but they used them in practices that depended on and intensified personal relationships, both the unilateral declaration and the challenge to it. Thus, even more important than monetary values were the ways money was used. The techniques of valuing developed in the Hellenistic period—comprehensive, enduring valuations made by disinterested parties—abstracted citizens from each other and from the polis. If the procedures outlined at Cyrene were typical, censuses relied on disinterested assessors and on previously determined debts, credits, and dowries—values which, from the perspective of the procedure for valuing citizens, were fixed and objective.[149] These procedures mark a shift from personal and interpersonal methods of valuing to impersonal ones. While unilateral declarations of value might be said to constitute man as the valuer and *metron* of all things, comprehensive censuses subjected all citizens to the *metron* of money.

CHAPTER 6

Collaborating

In Athens and other cities, in politics, business, and the military, Greeks did things in and through small groups. Most political officials served on boards or committees—of two, five, or ten members—and this was especially true at Athens, where hundreds of citizens each year were randomly assigned to various collegial offices. Unlike the Assembly or the courts, where hundreds or thousands of people who decided together neither knew nor came to know each other, the boards allowed people to work together closely and get to know each other well. The effectiveness of these boards depended on collaborative practices, which nurtured trust among strangers. Boards functioned effectively not because of a hierarchical structure, not because a ruler was in charge, but because they gave scope for the activities of citizens: practices of equality and of leadership. While conflict and competition could threaten a group's ability to work together, especially through the tendency toward fission, such problems were countervailed by rituals of solidarity, the inability (at Athens, at least) to quit a board of officials, and the ways in which people in groups were held accountable for their activities (the subject of chapter 7). Greek collaborative practices did not repress conflict so much as give it constructive scope and shape: in the exchange of opinions (*gnomai*) among the members, in the impulse toward consensus, which prompted members to consider others' opinions in forming their own, and in the right of dissent, even at the expense of unanimity.

In contrast to the ancient and modern preoccupation with rhetorical language—the technique of deliberation in mass meetings—few have attended to the protocols of deliberation in small groups. True, there are scholarly discussions of particular Athenian boards of officials (like the ten generals); some recent scholarship has considered the external relationships of boards, those between officials and private citizens;[1] and Josiah Ober has described the networks of knowledge that Athenian boards generated and drew upon.[2] But in general, modern scholarship offers few points of leverage in writing about boards as a widespread social and political form in Greece. In this it follows the ancient evidence, which is scattered and indirect. You can read speeches delivered in the courts or the Assembly, almost witnessing the spectacle yourself, but there are no minutes of committee meetings. Thus, to write about the collaborative practices of boards requires a creative use of tangential evidence.

At Athens, where most boards were appointed by lot, officials could not count on antecedent relationships of trust to enable cooperation.[3] In antiquity, some criticized random assignment to official boards for putting the unqualified and unskilled in office. Modern scholars have often understood the lot (in conjunction with the limited tenure of just a year) as a democratic mechanism that prevented anyone from accumulating official power. But it also prevented officials from relying on preexisting relationships with their colleagues, most of whom would be strangers drawn diffusely from thousands of citizens. Indeed, you would expect that boards chosen by lot would reflect the general profile of citizens, and there is evidence that they did so, geographically at least.[4] Thus, trust among board members seems to have been the outcome of their usual protocols and institutional arrangements.

Boards of political officials were important because they nurtured citizens by cultivating action in relations to others, especially through equality and leadership. This perspective differs from the scholarly tradition that sees small groups as promoting the common good by repressing individual interests, whether expressed in laziness or in hyperactivity. So some say that the personal relationships fostered in intimate settings help overcome the free-rider problem, the inclination to shirk and benefit from others' work in creating public goods.[5] Other scholars (Weber most famously) argue that executive boards keep great men in check, thus supporting both aristocracy and democracy.[6] I want to argue, however, that groups did more than repress individuals; they also helped create and nourish citizens through collaboration. I understand citizenship not necessarily or fundamentally as a conscious identity but as a set of relationships with other citizens, relationships realized through action.

I begin by arguing that there were no significant internal hierarchies on Athenian boards; a formal equality prevailed. I then turn to what members of these groups did, examining some of the rituals through which they created and enacted their equality, solidarity, and leadership. I consider in detail the ways in which committees engaged in collegial deliberations—exchange of opinions (*gnomai*), the impulse toward consensus, the use of voting, and the right of dissent. I conclude by analyzing the possibilities and limitations of leadership in a particularly well-documented case of a small group making decisions: the generals who lead the army of the Ten Thousand.

Formal Equality

No member of an Athenian board of officials ruled his colleagues; formal equality prevailed. Although historians have generally endorsed this conclusion, dissenters remain.[7] Especially for Athenian financial boards—for which the evidence from inscriptions is more robust—these historians maintain that one member, a chairman, held a legally superior position and that therefore other boards—for which the evidence from official inscriptions is scattered or nonexistent—may also have had an internal hierarchy. The analysis of the internal structure of boards hinges on two main questions: whether they had an eponym, a modern term meaning a member whose name became the official designation of the board for its term (usually in the form, "X [the eponym] and his colleagues"), and whether boards had a *prytanis* (with the subsidiary question of whether *prytanis* means a higher-ranking chairman or simply a part representing the whole for some function).

Kenneth Dover argued that there was no consistent pattern in the ways that boards were named, so that you cannot speak of an officially designated eponym and therefore cannot infer that any member held a superior position.[8] Considering a range of boards, he showed that documents used several designations (by naming one member alone or with a general reference [e.g., "and his colleagues"], by the name of the secretary [*grammateus*] of the board, by naming two members alone or with a general reference, or by naming all members) and that sometimes the same board was designated by different means. "There is ... only one general principle which accounts for all these cases: the eponym, in any reference to the board, is that member who for any reason is uppermost in the writer's mind at the time of writing."[9] Dover thus locates the eponym in the practices of common language—a speaker's or writer's free choice—not in a technical vocabulary or official practice. He admits that some contradictory evidence must be explained away—especially that from postclassical sources, which often represented one of the generals having supreme command—but he argues that once you remove the preconceived idea that someone must always be in charge of a group, the whole pattern of evidence makes better sense.[10]

Subsequently, Wesley Thompson argued that at least the Treasurers of Athena, the board that oversaw the spaces sacred to this goddess on the Acropolis and managed the vast wealth held in her temple, "had a chairman, a man formally chosen to be the leader of the group throughout their year in office, since this seems to me the natural interpretation of the consistency with which a single treasurer is named in the accounts ... and inventories ... of a given year."[11] Thompson acknowledges two exceptions, instances where different inscriptions referred to the same board with different eponyms, but he conceives some special circumstances to explain these.[12]

By itself, not even Thompson's resolution of the eponym question provides evidence for an internal hierarchy on any board. There is no evidence that the eponym—whether informal or official—was anything but a tag, a way of naming a particular board, an external reference. Even Michael Jameson, who argued that there were chairmen, allowed that an eponym was "an organizational convenience" with no special duties or powers greater than their fellow members.[13]

Some scholars have found stronger evidence for internal hierarchies on boards in the phenomenon of the *prytanis*. The best-known *prytaneis* (plural) from Athens constituted the rotating subcommittee of the Boule, which was on duty day and night for a month. Some documents indicate that other groups too had some sort of *prytaneis*. Thus *IG* I³ 4B, one of the oldest Athenian inscriptions (possibly from 485/84), outlined the duties of the board of treasurers in managing the sacred area of the Acropolis. One clause required the treasurers to be present when they opened the temple (the Hekatompedon) three times a month. If any treasurer was able to attend but did not, he was fined 2 drachmas. "And the *prytanis* is to collect the fine; if he does not, he is to be held accountable."[14] Boromir Jordan finds this "clear and positive proof for a chairman with official, legal supremacy over his colleagues."[15] Doubts are possible,[16] and this is probably the strongest evidence you could muster. The other examples of *prytaneis* don't indicate any internal hierarchy on boards:

- Demosthenes reports that the member of the college of arbitrators who was *prytanizing* (τὸν πρυτανεύοντα) put a resolution to a vote to the whole body.[17] The college of arbitrators, however, was not a small group; it would have had a variable membership but probably at least a hundred men per year,[18] so that its practices would have been more like the Boule than a ten-member committee.
- Pollux, a late, laconic, and sometimes unreliable source, says that one of the *poletai*, the board of officials who sold off public property, was *prytanis*.[19] His description of what this person did—"guaranteeing the things bought"—relates only to the external relationships of the board, not its internal practices.
- Herodotus reports that the *prytaneis* of the *naukraroi* once took action to remove suppliants from the statue of Athena.[20] This report, long

after the fact and at odds with what Thucydides says,[21] has perplexed historians, both because the *naukraroi* remain mysterious officials and because what Herodotus says of them—that "at that time they governed"—does not correspond to anything else we know.[22] Leaving these uncertainties aside, however, Herodotus's use of the plural corresponds less to the idea of a chairman, and more to an on-duty subcommittee, like the *prytaneis* of the Boule.[23] As with the *poletai,* here the *prytaneis* are defined by relationships outside the group.

Taking into account the evidence for both the use of eponyms and the existence of *prytaneis,* Robert Develin has sought a moderate position, arguing that there was no permanent chair or eponym, but a system of rotating *prytaneis,* in which members in turn represented the whole.[24] Develin recognizes the precariousness of the evidence and concludes circumspectly that it is "more consonant with a system of rotating *prytaneis* on financial boards than with the supposition of a permanent annual chairman or a mere eponym."[25] But if you put aside the question whether there was a chairman or eponym and ask instead whether small groups had formal internal organizations, only *IG* I³ 4B might support a positive conclusion. And even here, the *prytanis*'s relationship to other members of the group (assuming he was a member) was a consequence of the ways that Athenians imposed liability on committees, the subject I take up in chapter 7, not an indication of a superior position.

Despite the paucity of evidence for internal hierarchy on most boards, there is one exception. Delegations to religious festivals (*theoria,* a different word from a diplomatic embassy to a state, *presbeia*) were led by a chief envoy, the *architheoron* (the Greek spelling varies). He was the member of the team who spoke and transacted business (as Polybius implies);[26] simultaneously, he was expected to subsidize the delegation's expenses, which included the cost of travel and that of sacrifices and offerings as well. The office of *architheoron* was considered a liturgy,[27] which probably explains why we know more about it and why its holder was superior to his fellow delegates.

Equality and Solidarity

Members of boards did certain things that enacted their formal equality and encouraged group solidarity.[28] In the first place, when they took council, they removed themselves from others: as one litigant noted, a lattice barrier separated the Boule from the crowd, a rope segregated the Areopagus, and all the other officials had their attendants order others to withdraw so that they could meet apart.[29] Officeholders also engaged in

powerful rituals. The strongest evidence for these comes from Demosthenes' prosecution speech against Aeschines, where he anticipated that
Aeschines would attempt to turn the jurors against the prosecution by arguing that Demosthenes was betraying those he had eaten with, his fellow envoys, one of whom was Aeschines. Indeed, Aeschines did make this
claim (though not with the emphasis Demosthenes' anticipatory response
might suggest): "Demosthenes is incapable of speaking for the polis, but
quite practiced in speaking against those with whom he shared food and
drink."[30] Eating and drinking and their linked religious rituals, sacrifice
and libation, can create and strengthen personal relationships, and even
Demosthenes' counterargument recognized the importance of the social bonds formed through such rituals: The *prytaneis* sacrifice, eat, and
pour libations together, the Boule sacrifices and dines together, the generals share sacred rituals, as do almost all the other officials—but none of
that, Demosthenes said, should prevent anyone from denouncing his colleagues when they act illegally.[31] Demosthenes' argument demonstrates
both the ways that rituals created social bonds among members of boards
and, by the resistance which he expected to his attacking a fellow envoy,
the common acceptance of the strength of those bonds.

Collegial Deliberations

For Greeks, official boards operated with their own unique protocols.
Although explicit rules rarely governed their proceedings, members of
such groups nevertheless shared a broad understanding of how to conduct
themselves, as evidenced by a consistency of practice and a lack of evidence of controversy over procedure. Most fundamentally, the majority
determined actions.[32] Yet to leave it at that—as though boards functioned
as miniature assemblies—fails to fully describe how they functioned, and,
indeed, misconstrues the role of voting.

For understanding how boards operated, Herodotus's *History* gives
particularly revealing evidence, though it presents challenges. The text
traces the ways that the large events of history hinged on decisions made
in small, deliberative groups—decisions the value of which usually corresponded to how well the process of deliberation worked.[33] Although the
small groups in the *History* were often informal, ad hoc, or fluid, they can
still provide evidence for Athenian committees since these, too, depended
on similar shared understandings, not formal and specifically Athenian
rules. And although in the *History* many of the group members were not
Greek—particularly in the councils advising the Persian kings—the way
Herodotus has depicted their operation has less to do with the actual politics of the Persian court than with representing that politics as an (often

defective) form of Greek practice. The more serious challenge, on first glance, is that many of the committees in Herodotus were advisory rather than decision-making bodies. (This is true of the councils to the Persian kings and of the Greek generals at Salamis.) Yet in suggesting that presence of an independent and potentially arbitrary ruler deformed collegial deliberations, Herodotus relied on common understandings of how such processes should have worked, understandings that can be inferred from his text.

I would point to five features of the ways that boards conducted themselves. Not every committee discussion showed these features, and such discussions often included other elements as well, but they constitute an ideal description of how boards deliberated. Indeed, the absence of these elements often marked the breakdown of the committee.

1. Boards engaged in collaborative discussion more than adversarial debate. Unhappy with the slow progress of their second embassy to Philip, Demosthenes sought to get the board of envoys to move faster:

> I was constantly telling them, at first as someone giving his opinion (*gnome*) for common consideration, then as someone instructing the ignorant, and in the end outspokenly as to profane men who had sold themselves.[34]

Demosthenes characterized his growing suspicion of and dissatisfaction with his fellow envoys by a progression through three ways of speaking to them: first by attempting to find a common ground (by offering a *gnome* for the group), then by trying to get them to support his position (persuading, which he alternatively characterizes here with a touch of condescension as instruction),[35] and finally, now adversarial, by simply berating them (which indicates he had abandoned the attempt at cooperation).

In the setting of a small group, the art of offering *gnomai* differed from the art of rhetoric (the subject of chapter 8). While a speaker in a large assembly could be said to offer a *gnome*, the speaker was making a motion that the body would either accept or reject.[36] But in a small group, the person who offered his *gnome* was generally committed less to the content of his own ideas (which provided a beginning of discussion instead of an end of debate) and more to a cooperative practical endeavor. You might call it brainstorming.

2. Unlike debate in large bodies, which proceeded by dichotomized choices of formal propositions (approve/disapprove, innocent/guilty), discussion on boards proceeded through multiple ideas, *gnomai*. Thus Thucydides relates that the three generals in charge of the Athenian invasion of Sicily discussed what to do after they arrived and found things were not as they had expected: Nikias offered one *gnome*, Alcibiades and Lamachos

each had their own ideas, but eventually Lamachos gave his support to Alcibiades' *gnome*.[37] Multiple choices could make decisions complex and difficult; indeed, it would be possible for none to have the support of even
a majority. So those offering their ideas frequently built on previous *gnomai*, incorporating what they saw as best in them. Consider the scene in
Herodotus where the seven conspirators who had overthrown the Medes
discuss what kind of government to institute in Persia. Scholars have analyzed in great detail the content of this famous passage. For my present
purposes, notice the form of the discussion as Herodotus describes it:
Otanes begins by criticizing monarchy and recommending democracy.
"Otanes contributed this *gnome*," Herodotus writes after Otanes' speech,
"but Megabyzus urged that they hand over affairs to an oligarchy, saying
this: 'The things Otanes said about ending one-man rule I agree with, but
when he urges us to give power to the people, then he has failed to hit
the best *gnome*.'"[38] After Megabyzus lists his arguments for the rule of the
few, Herodotus writes: "Megabyzus contributed this *gnome*; then, third,
Darius produced his *gnome*, saying: 'To me Megabyzus's arguments concerning the people seemed correctly spoken, but what he said about oligarchy was not right.'"[39] The discussion proceeds by various parties offering their ideas—"These three *gnomai* were laid out"[40]—the last two of
which both respond to and build on the previous ones.

    3. Far from resulting in a paralyzing plurality of choices, the movement
of discussion through *gnomai* in fact aimed at more than simple majority
support; it built consensus. Where initially people thought differently,
the presentation of *gnomai* allowed members to try to articulate a position
that many or most could support. You can see this process in Aeschines'
story about the second embassy to Philip during which he and Demosthenes disagreed about whether to push Philip to renounce his alliance
with Thebes: when all ten envoys voted on what to do, they unanimously
endorsed a compromise.[41] Similarly, the Athenian generals at Arginusai, initially split by the choice between pursuing the defeated enemy or
rescuing their own shipwrecked and dead sailors, subsequently decided
unanimously to try to do both.[42] But the process of offering *gnomai* could
also reveal that substantial agreement already existed, as among the Greek
generals about where to fight after the Persians had sacked Athens in 480:
to the commander Eurybiades' *gnome* that people should suggest the place
to take their stand, most of the *gnomai* of those who spoke (Herodotus reports) favored the isthmus.[43] These and other instances of unanimous or
nearly unanimous decisions, even when opinions seemed initially divided,
point to the ways the exchange of *gnomai* built consensus.[44]

    4. Although groups aimed at consensus, individual members retained
a right of dissent. Because groups did not normally need unanimous con-

sent to make decisions,[45] members could not veto group decisions. But they could resist decisions and compel the group to reconsider. Herodotus exploited this feature of small groups with his figure of the "tragic warner," a lone dissenter whose *gnome* is right (as subsequent events show or Herodotus himself comments)[46] but usually ignored.[47] Hecataeus argues against the Ionian revolt, Artabanus against Xerxes' invasion of Greece, Artemisia against the naval battle at Salamis, and so forth—all presciently but ineffectively.[48] In the Herodotus's narrative these figures function in ways closely related to their counterparts in tragedy—foreshadowing, highlighting rulers' blindness, aphoristically stating universal truths[49]— but they are not just literary devices; they reflect (and implicitly offer advice about) the dynamics of deliberating and deciding in small groups, especially the importance of allowing and considering dissent.

It is difficult to gauge how easily a lone dissenter could have held out in actual practice. The stories of Socrates and of Demosthenes—each of whom, as a member of the committee chairing the Athenian Assembly, objected to allowing a particular vote, despite the approval not only of their colleagues but that of the assembled demos as well, thus exhibiting (depending on your perspective) either great courage or extreme incorrigibility—could be taken to show that it took extraordinary will and self-confidence to resist unanimity.[50] Since the circumstances in these two cases were unusual—thousands of people watched and influenced both boards' deliberations—it may not be safe to generalize.

In informal groups, dissenters could do more than object: they could quit. Indeed, keeping the group intact may have been a prime reason to seek out a broad consensus. Herodotus presents several episodes where the inability to find a common course of action prompted a group to split.[51] Early in the Greek deliberations before the battle of Salamis, Themistokles persuaded the commanding general, Eurybiades, and the other generals in the council to stay and fight by threatening to remove the Athenian fleet, the largest part of the Greek navy.[52]

Athenian officials, however, could not get their way by withdrawing from a board—nor, indeed, could they withdraw without some valid excuse like illness.[53] A board member could occasionally force his position on the others simply by refusing to cooperate, as the Athenian general Nikias did at least twice in Sicily.[54] But such tactics may not have been available to most officials, however, or only at great risk to themselves.

5. Simple majority rule through voting played a limited role. Committees usually made decisions by consensus through *gnomai*; if they took a vote, this seems to have confirmed and ratified the consensus which the members had already reached. For example, in Herodotus's account of the deliberations of Ionian generals—Darius and the Persian army had

crossed over into Europe to invade Scythia, and the Ionians who were guarding Darius's bridge were thinking of destroying it—at first the generals all favored Miltaides' *gnome* (wreck it), but then they all went over to Histiaeus's *gnome* (save it); after that, they voted.[55] In many cases, a vote would have been a formality. This may explain why ancient texts so often describe the decision of a small group with language that does not seem to indicate the careful counting of votes. Take Herodotus's description of the council of Lacedaemonian allies, convened to decide whether to put the former Athenian tyrant, Hippias, back in power. After the Spartans argued for using military force to install Hippias, Herodotus tells us, "most of the allies did not accept their arguments. The rest remained silent, but Socles the Corinthian said the following."[56] At the end of Socles' long speech against taking action, Hippias offered a brief retort (more of a threat than a logical argument). "The remaining allies had held themselves in silence until now, but when they heard Socles speaking freely, every one of them spoke out and chose the Corinthian's *gnome*."[57] Or notice how Aeschines described how the envoys decided to address Philip: they "arranged it among themselves."[58]

Nevertheless, formal voting served at least two purposes. First, voting ratified a consensus, especially in the face of strong dissent. So Demosthenes claimed that when he presented to his fellow envoys a draft of a letter back to the Athenians, they voted to not send it, preferring another version.[59] Second, boards sometimes used voting to make a decision in the absence of a consensus: The ten Athenian generals at Marathon, evenly divided about whether to fight the Persians, offer a rare instance where a close vote (the polemarch, an eleventh member, broke the tie) determined an outcome.[60] Groups used majority decision as a last option, when no consensus had emerged and necessity compelled a decision (so that withdrawal was precluded). The text of a loan on a ship's cargo suggests that when the ship was sinking, the passengers voted to determine what cargo to jettison—at least only such losses could be deducted.[61]

A scene in Aristophanes' *Birds* (lines 1565–1685) shows how voting could function in the context of a board aiming at consensus.[62] A committee of three divine envoys, Poseidon, Heracles, and a Triballian god, arrive to negotiate a peace treaty with Peisetairos, the leader of the new republic of the birds. (The birds have effectively declared war on the gods by using their control of the lower air to intercept and embargo all offerings from humans to divinities.) Peisetairos demands that the gods give over the scepter of rule, and Heracles, perhaps taken in by the delicious food Peisetairos is preparing, immediately "votes yes" (1603). Poseidon, initially hostile to the demand, is open to persuasion and asks the Triballian god what he thinks; he seems to assent. (This god speaks a gibberish that may or may not have meaning.) After more persuasion by Peisetairos, the gods huddle: Heracles "votes yes again" (1627), the Triballian god seems to agree (or so Heracles interprets his barbarian babbling), and Poseidon says, "If these things seem best to both of you, they seem best to me, too" (1630). Voting here—and as Heracles uses the word it doesn't mean *cast a ballot* so much as *declare a preference*[63]—operates not in the context of majority rule, but of the building of a consensus. But then Peisetairos makes another demand: he wants the goddess Basileia ("princess") as his wife. At this point Poseidon changes his mind—one more demand is simply too much: "Let's go back home" (1636). If it were merely a matter of majority rule, Poseidon's defection wouldn't matter, but in fact Heracles remains eager for Poseidon to agree. Poseidon, however, declares that he "votes against" settlement (1676). By now, voting has revealed a deep schism within the group, and Peisetairos notes that "the whole affair rests with the Triballian" (1677). Only when the consensus has broken down does majority rule come into play here. When the Triballian seems to assent again to the agreement, Poseidon says to his colleagues: "You two reconcile and make the agreement. Since it seems best to you, I'll remain silent" (1683–84). Poseidon's silence indicates that he will not attempt to impede his colleagues (as Nikias did in Sicily) or undermine the agreement—that is, after losing the vote he allows a tacit consensus to reemerge—and now Heracles announces that they've resolved to agree to all of Peisetairos's requests. Voting here functions as a means to consensus.[64]

Leadership and Equality on Boards

The absence of hierarchy and the pervasiveness of equality created ample opportunities for exercising leadership. Indeed, you should not understand leadership as the opposite of equality (as ruling necessarily opposes being ruled) but as the effect of practicing equality. One of the advantages of such a system is that the amount of leadership is not fixed: the greater the equality and the more people who exercise their equality, the more opportunities emerge for leadership.

Xenophon's *Anabasis* makes visible the interrelations between equality and leadership on boards. The memoirs of one of the ten thousand or so Greek mercenary soldiers hired by Cyrus, the Persian king's younger brother, to overthrow the king, the *Anabasis* tells the tale of the months-long march almost to Babylon, their victory in battle, and the disaster that followed. Cyrus, their employer and their reason for being there, was killed in the fighting, and a bit later the Persians, having invited the Greek generals to a conference, killed them too. Leaderless, surrounded, and far from home, the Greek soldiers chose a board of new generals (Xenophon was one) and slowly fought their way back to the edges of the Greek world, the shores of the Black Sea. Even here their problems persisted, since Greek cities treated them (circumspectly enough) not as returning heroes but as a huge, dangerous mob of bandits.

If you want to understand how small groups made decisions, Xenophon's adventure story promises to have great value. The author himself witnessed most of what he wrote about, and as a member of the committee of seven generals leading the army, he had unparalleled insight into its deliberations. No Greek historical text gives such sustained and detailed attention to the functioning of a single board.

Nevertheless, it presents significant challenges.[65] Not only did Xenophon probably write it decades after the relevant events, but he wrote a highly personal narrative, one which attempted to justify his decisions and role in the army. He is almost never wrong, and when he is, he corrects himself.[66] He presents himself as the de facto leader of the army, and seems to suppress indications of conflict with his fellow generals. The book is also literarily and philosophically complex; for example, Xenophon the author used Xenophon the character to represent his notions of ideal leadership. He abridged his accounts of the meetings of the generals but included lengthy transcripts of what he claims that he said himself. In the *Anabasis*, Xenophon's speeches often lead to action in unmediated and unproblematic ways.

In the period after the election of new generals and before they got back to the Greek world, a committee of generals ran the army. Unfortunately, the language Xenophon uses to describe their decisions does not clarify how these were reached. The generals did everything, Xenophon says at one point, ἐκ τῆς νικώσης, "in accordance with the prevailing [something]."[67] This phrase raises two related issues. First, as is frequent in Greek, it omits the commonly understood noun, the "[something]." Though "decree" (*psephisma*) is grammatically possible, "opinion" (*gnome*) seems more likely.[68] Second, what would "in accordance with the prevailing opinion" mean? Most have understood this to mean "by majority vote,"[69] but, as Andrew Dalby has noted, there's no explicit statement in books 3–4 that the generals decided anything by majority vote.[70] In describing particular decisions, Xenophon hardly ever uses the word *gnome*[71] but, rather, *edokei*, "it seemed [best]." This was the official language of Athenian government for a proposal passed by the Boule and the Assembly, but since Xenophon uses it variously of the assembly of soldiers, of the council of generals, and of individuals, it cannot consistently mean that something was formally approved by majority vote. How a particular policy or plan came to *seem best* to the generals remains unclear.

So it may be worth looking at the ways that Xenophon narrates the generals' deliberations. Take one of the more detailed examples, from book 4, where the Greeks were approaching a mountain pass in Armenia but found it held by hostile soldiers.[72] Cheirisophos, the general in command of the leading troops, stopped the army and called the generals and captains together. He then said that they should take council, and that it seemed best to him to eat first and then make the attempt on the pass either that day or the next. Kleanor, another of the generals, responded that it seemed best to him to attack as soon as possible. Then Xenophon spoke (and Xenophon the author gives Xenophon the character a speech several times longer than either of the other generals). He said that those ideas were fine if they wanted to attack, but that it seemed best to him to try to "steal" the mountain by secretly outflanking the soldiers on the pass, hoping to scare them off without a battle. (Xenophon then joked that he had nothing to teach Cheirisophos about stealing, since Spartans train their boys to steal; Cheirisophos responded that Athenians like Xenophon were reputed best at stealing—from the public treasury.) Xenophon offered to undertake the outflanking move, but Cheirisophos recommended he stay in command of the troops in the rear. Three officers volunteered to go forward, agreeing to set fires as signals when they had taken the heights. Xenophon's description of the process conforms to what I outlined above: members presented suggestions that responded to and built on previous ideas, culminating in a consensus, which made a vote unnecessary. No one was in charge of this process, though at particular points different people—Cheirisophos, Kleanor, Xenophon, and the three officers—exercised leadership functions: initiating discussion, making suggestions, reframing the question, volunteering to take action.

Scholars have found it difficult to pin down who was in charge of the army as it marched from Babylon to the Black Sea. Among recent historians (who concentrate on the relationship between leaders and the mass of soldiers), Dalby argues that the generals had the power and engineered the soldiers' approval in mass meetings, or that they rarely called such meetings, but Hornblower argues that the soldiers exerted considerable influence on their generals.[73] The same uncertainty pertains to the board of generals. Should you conclude, from Xenophon's representation of his own importance, that "Xenophon and to some extent Cheirisophus" were "actually though not formally the real leading spirit in the community,"[74] or even that "authority for the time being rested with Xenophon and those with whom he wished to consult"?[75]

Some of the reasons that Xenophon's story does not clarify the decision-making process pertain to the text itself: the way it emphasizes and justifies Xenophon's own role in events, and the way it develops models of leadership. But other reasons inhere in the institutional structure he describes, which was always, to varying degrees, being pressured in different ways. The collegial structure of command operated effectively, allowing room for individual excellence and even preeminence. The question of who was in charge, however, cannot be answered definitively because it wrongly supposes that some one person was in charge. There was no ruler, though at various moments leaders emerged.

Weakness of Collegial Organization

Whatever its strengths, such collegial commands would seem to have certain weaknesses, especially for an army. And, in fact, Xenophon reports that after the army reached the Black Sea they, too, had misgivings:

> Since they seemed to be near to Greece, it now came to them how they could come home with something. Therefore they believed that if they chose one ruler, he would be able to use the army (by both night and day) better than several rulers: if stealth were necessary, matters would better be kept secret, and if anticipation were needed, he could act in a more timely manner. There would no need of conversations (*logoi*) with one another, but what seemed best to the one man would be done. Before this, the generals had done everything in accordance with the prevailing opinion [ἐκ τῆς νικώσης].[76]

Single commanders are more effective than boards, everyone knows that.[77] (The fact that in this passage the army was not at war but intending to plunder Greeks and others—Xenophon's "something" is a tiny veil of modesty covering this brutal theft—probably does not affect the analysis.) But Xenophon's text, at least, offers little evidence for this nugget of common sense. At no point does he suggest that collegial command made the army slower, less decisive, or ineffective. You might take this as a whitewash, except that he does show extensive evidence for a different problem, which events subsequent to the adoption of a single command revealed.

The experiment with a single commander lasted only a week before the army split into three parts.[78] (The largest part of this force, the Arcadians and Achaeans, chose ten generals of their own and voted that "they do whatever seemed [best] ἐκ τῆς νικώσης.")[79] But this arrangement, too, did not last long: the Arcadians and Achaeans had been badly beaten by the Thracians after they split up to plunder their villages,[80] and when the whole army got together the assembled soldiers passed a formal resolution to reunite as before, under the command of the board of generals.[81]

The problem was apparently not that a board of generals could not effectively coordinate plundering raids. It was that different generals were competing, for pay for their soldiers and for gifts for themselves. Indeed, Xenophon (the character) says that the soldiers thought "that there would be less stasis with one ruler than with many."[82] Once the army reached the Hellenic world, the circumstances they faced changed, and not only because hostile armies no longer resisted them. More importantly, the primary concerns of mercenaries—pay and plunder—reappeared. They no longer needed to shed their possessions to cross rough country and elude hostile fighters; they could now think about acquiring new possessions. Just as importantly, they now reentered a world of potential employers. For both of these reasons, the previously unified army now manifested conflict, faction, and divisions.[83] Competition for external patrons who could pay the army and enrich the generals (patrons' "gifts" to generals could be extraordinarily valuable)[84] had divided the generals earlier and would do so again.[85]

Thus, the problem was dual: first, external incentives provoked competition among the leaders (and competition for leadership, a potentially lucrative position); second, this competition provoked a tendency for the board to break up. When quitting became possible and external rewards were offered, there seems to have been constant pressure for the board to fragment. (The appointment of Cheirisophos as a single ruler was an attempt, ultimately unsuccessful, to counteract fragmentation.) I would cite two examples of this tendency, one early, one late. Early: when the army withdrew to debate whether to follow Cyrus to Babylon against the king, one of the generals, Menon, urged his men to rush over to Cyrus even before the army had reached a decision, so that they might win extra rewards for being the first to support him.[86] Late: Xenophon picked three hundred of his favorites to set out on a small plundering party to enrich themselves. It was a secret—more men would mean diluting the profits— but word got out, and six hundred others joined them, even though they tried to beat them away so that they wouldn't have to share the profits.[87] The committee of generals operated effectively during the long march back, because during this time there were no incentives or opportunities for individual generals to quit, or for soldiers to follow them.

Conclusion

If Greeks were able to collaborate in small groups, especially through equality and leadership—understood as complementary actions, not structures—the case of the generals leading the ten thousand demonstrates a critical problem: the ways in which external rewards might impel the group to fragment. The next chapter takes up this question in detail, examining how regimes of liability, in distributing both punishments and rewards to groups, affected the ability of members to trust and collaborate with one another.

Apportioning Liability

Just as the previous chapter showed that two external factors—random assignment and irrevocable membership—affected the internal dynamics of boards of officials in classical Greece, so this chapter takes up a decisive third: the regime of liability. Although scholars have written extensively about the accountability of officials in ancient Greece,[1] they have rarely considered how the typically collegial nature of their offices complicated officials' liability for rewards and punishments. Greeks often held members of groups liable for success or failure with equal shares of rewards or punishments. While in some senses rewards and punishments can be seen as linked inversions (so that the denial of a reward is a punishment),[2] when applied collectively to groups their effects might differ. If equal shares of rewards promoted shirking (as the Greeks recognized), the threat of collective sanctions encouraged group participation, solidarity, and trust.

Collective liability avoids two challenges in determining individual liability in groups: calibrating the formula for proportionalizing the penalty with the responsibility and acquiring enough information to apply this formula accurately. For the Greeks, the problem of proportionalizing focused especially on the individual's role in the group's deciding and on the distinction between deciding and executing. Athenian litigation involving groups or their members shows both of these problems. In this chapter I investigate three cases: the trial of a member of a murderous junta who sought to disassociate himself from the acts of his colleagues; the trial of several generals whose joint command had ended disastrously; and the trial of a guardian charged with defrauding his ward in league with his two co-guardians. While these cases raise questions about the ethics of particular regimes of liability (about which Greeks could disagree), my analyses focus more intently on what they reveal about ways in which the practice of collective liability affected the normal relationships of members of a group, even before any sanction was applied. A regime of collective liability—the possibility that all members of the group might be held liable for the actions of any member—prompted colleagues to cultivate and intensify personal relationships of trust (or distrust) with one another. I conclude the chapter with a sustained examination of Xenophon's detailed critical analysis of equally shared liability. Unlike many Greek writers, whose sense of status was affronted by such equality, Xenophon carefully considered how shared liability affected the behavior of associates in groups.

The Challenges of Liability in Groups: Lysias against Eratosthenes

Lysias's prosecution speech against Eratosthenes highlights the two fundamental, interrelated issues regarding liability that conglomerate political bodies gave rise to: first, the challenge of proportionalizing liability to individual members of a group when the whole group made a decision; and second, the practical difficulty of getting information to apply any formula for individual liability.

The defendant Eratosthenes had been one of the Thirty, the antidemocratic governing board that Sparta had imposed on Athens after defeating it in the Peloponnesian War. The Thirty had initiated a bloody purge of Athenians—a reign of terror initially justified as upholding standards of virtue, but quickly devolving into an attack on anyone (especially if wealthy) who supported democracy. The Thirty tasked some of themselves to seize Lysias and his brother Polemarchus, both rich metics (foreigners) who had spent most of their lives in Athens. Eratosthenes apprehended Polemarchus, who was later killed; across town, meanwhile, Lysias escaped through a back door. Jump forward several months. The Athenian democrats have, improbably, retaken Athens by force, and the Spartans, still the dictating military power, have, more surprisingly still, allowed them to stay. Then, to restore civic life, the Athenians agreed to pretend that none of the violence—the arrests, the executions, the confiscations of property—has happened; they instituted an amnesty for everyone but the Thirty and the Eleven, the supervisors of the prison who had carried out the many death sentences. All of these they banished. But look, even here they allowed an out: if any of these submitted to the normal audit for the period during which they held power, and if they passed, they could remain in Athens with full rights. Almost none of the Thirty accepted the gamble, but when Eratosthenes did, Lysias prosecuted him, so as to hold him accountable for Polemarchus's death.

Lysias blamed Eratosthenes not only for his individual act (the seizure, which did not immediately kill but enabled the death of Polemarchus) but also, emphatically and repeatedly, for the collective acts of the Thirty.

His use of names in this speech shows how: he repeatedly used plural nouns, pronouns, and verbs to refer to "the defendants"; he mentioned Eratosthenes by name fifteen times, but the Thirty half again more often; and, by naming "Eratosthenes and his colleagues" (§§52, 79, 87, the language of the Athenian government to describe a board, as I noted in chapter 6), he used Eratosthenes' name to designate the Thirty. Although he described Eratosthenes' individual actions, Lysias spent much more time condemning the Thirty as a group.

Because he spoke first, Lysias had to anticipate Eratosthenes' arguments. Lysias guessed that Eratosthenes would defend himself in three ways. First, he would insist that not all the Thirty were criminals, but only the radical faction led by Critias. Eratosthenes would associate himself with the moderates, led by Theramenes, whom Critias had killed for opposing him.[3] Lysias's ridicule of the idea that Eratosthenes "did the least evil of the Thirty" (§89) points to his claim of being a moderate. Second, Eratosthenes would say that in the Thirty's discussions he had argued against arresting and executing metics (§25). Finally, he would claim that he arrested Polemarchus unwillingly, only because he had been ordered to and because he feared for his own life if he didn't (§§25, 50).[4] In fact, others drawn into the Thirty's acts claimed that fear for their lives had compelled them to act unwillingly.[5] The general amnesty after the expulsion of the Thirty seems premised on the idea that during this dire period many people acted out of a kind of necessity. Some people later believed that the Thirty had ordered so many others to carry out arrests precisely to implicate as many as possible in their crimes.[6] Overall, then, Lysias anticipated that Eratosthenes would treat the Thirty not as a single group but as a collection of individuals (or of factions), with varying degrees of responsibility, and that he would separate the decision from its execution, offering a different plea for his participation in each. Distinguishing himself from the Thirty, Eratosthenes would insist on purely individual liability.

Lysias attempted to forestall each of these arguments. First, he emphatically linked Eratosthenes with antidemocratic extremists, especially Critias (§§41–47), but he also denounced Theramenes' crimes (§§62–78). He claimed that Critias and Theramenes had disagreed not over the justice of executing the innocent but merely over who would hold power (§§51–52). Second, because the Thirty's deliberations had been secret and were known only from Eratosthenes' self-serving report, Lysias urged the jurors to judge Eratosthenes on the basis of what he had done, not what he claimed to have said (§33). Third, he alleged that Eratosthenes had acted willfully—indeed, he killed because it gave him pleasure (§32, cf. §23)— and he could not claim that fear compelled him to act since he had, by his own argument, boldly opposed Critias in the deliberations (§50). Overall, Lysias argued, a good person should not merely have opposed the Thirty in intention or even speech, but should have actively worked to save their victims.[7]

Lysias's indictment of Eratosthenes depended on treating the Thirty as a unitary group. All members of the board were liable for what it did. Instead of separating decision from actions, Lysias sought to knit them more tightly, insisting that Eratosthenes was himself liable for creating the conditions of necessity through which he sought excuse:

> Beyond that, it seems to me that the other Athenians have a sufficient excuse for transferring to the Thirty the blame for what was done. But for the Thirty themselves, if they transfer it to themselves, how can you reasonably accept that? If there had been a stronger authority in the city, which ordered him to kill people unjustly, maybe in fairness you could have lenience for him. But how will you get satisfaction from anyone at all if the Thirty can contend that they did what was ordered by the Thirty?[8]

Despite the extremity of Eratosthenes' predicament, the case against him emphasizes two mundane problems with individual liability in groups. Lysias and Eratosthenes disagreed over what constituted sufficient grounds for dissociating yourself from the decisions and actions of a group. Eratosthenes seems to have claimed that his dissent absolved him, while Lysias demanded more: a refusal to execute a decision, certainly, but beyond that, appreciable actions resisting it. As Lysias also indicated, it was difficult to know what individual members of a group had said or done in its private meetings; therefore, Lysias said, invoking the conventional priority of actions over words,[9] you should give more credence to the evidence of what he admits he did than to what he says he said.

Collective and Individual Liability

In arguing that all public officials at Athens were subject to audit, Aeschines noted that "the law directs that priests and priestesses be accountable, both all jointly and each one of them separately ... and not only individually but also collectively by clan, the Eumolpidai, the Kerykes, and all the others."[10] This unusually explicit statement enjoins two different forms of collective liability: both with whole boards of priests and priestesses, and with the clans from which some of them came.

Although the laws of Greek cities varied in their wording, they would seem to allow that when an official (even a member of a board) acted alone, he would be liable individually. But when it came time to account for the group's actions, any and all members could be held to account.

So far as we know, neither Athens nor any other city had a general law addressing this question, but particular laws, decrees, and rules—about specific boards and specific actions—directed a formally constituted group to act and imposed a penalty if its members did not. These laws usually took the form of a conditional sentence: "If someone (or some group) does (or fails to do) something, then he (or they) will be punished"; or a set of coordinated imperatives: "Someone (or some group) will do something or he (or they) will be punished." (Infinitives, which do not indicate whether subject is singular or plural, were sometimes used in place of imperatives.) Based on their wording, you can identify three classes of rules:

1. One group of laws names the offender in the *if* clause in the singular with the indefinite pronoun, followed by a third-person singular imperative in the consequent clause: "If any one of the officials . . . , let him be . . ."[11]

Most laws, however, name the offender in the first clause with the plural (e.g., as "the officials"). The consequent clause then qualifies this in one of two ways:

2. Many laws qualify the officials (plural in the initial clause) in consequent clause with the singular noun "each" (*hekastos*): "And the Guards of the Hellespont will neither prevent [the Methoniaians] from exporting [grain] nor allow another to prevent them, or they will be penalized 10,000 drachmas each."[12] The consequent clause with *hekastos* can use either a singular or a plural verb.[13]

3. Even more laws keep the plural from the initial clause in the consequent clause (usually with the plural pronoun, *autoi*, "they"): "The *Neopoiai* will exact [the fine] or they will owe double."[14]

The patterns of language in these inscriptions seem to point to two inferences about practices of accountability with boards.

First, the use of the plural in so many inscriptions implies that members of groups could be held liable collectively. While it was possible to single out an individual official (group 1), regulations much more frequently treated the officials as one body, using a plural verb to describe both the prohibited conduct and the punishment of it (group 3 and some of group 2). This would suggest that all members of boards, whatever their individual actions, could be held accountable for what the board as a whole had done, perhaps even that members of boards could be held accountable collectively in a single judgment.

Second the distinction between penalizing the group as a whole and penalizing *each* of the members (group 2 versus group 3) points to different practices of accountability. The distributive force of *hekastos* here does not seem to specify individual liability (that is, it is not equivalent to "they will be judged individually"); rather, it distributes the *penalty* in equal

shares among all members of the group.[15] Laws specifying the penalties
against "each" official invariably set the fine as an exact amount of money
(which is, therefore, equal for "each" official), whereas laws which penal-
ize the whole group often set the fine as a multiple (1, 1½, or 2 times) of an
amount the officials were themselves supposed to collect. In cases where
the penalty was assigned to the whole group, it seems to have been left
up to the group to decide how to apportion it internally. In both cases,
however, the polis established a strict collective liability: if the group violated the rules, all members, regardless of their individual actions, were
punished.

Laws that explicitly refer to the accountability of boards, therefore,
offer three modes of liability, one individual and two strict and collective
(one with equal shares, the other to be allocated by the group itself).

In practice, committees were routinely held accountable collectively
in receiving rewards: formal votes of crowns often recognized the whole
board as an entity.[16] With the Boule, for example, although it was possible to recognize individual members for their specific work,[17] usually the
whole Boule got the crown. As with rewards, so with sanctions. Aeschines
suggested that one year the Boule did not receive their usual gift, a crown,
because they had failed to discipline one of their members.[18] Withholding
a usual reward could be seen as a form of collective punishment.[19]

The principle of equal shares was a common way of allocating liability across members of a group. It seems to have applied as well when the
liability could be divided, as in the case of money. For those who served
as co-trierarchs of an Athenian warship, Gabrielsen notes, "the principle
of equal distribution of any subsequent financial liabilities (for example,
replacement or repair of the hulls and equipment) is ... consistently encountered in the naval records."[20] It is possible, too, that behind the many
inscribed accounts in which the board as a whole is said to do something
(collect or disburse money, hand over objects, etc.), lay a system of strict
collective liability based on equal shares. From the island of Delos in 219
comes an anomalous inscription, which Vial has argued shows that the
two *hieropes* for the year were each liable for exactly half of the value of
their collective monetary transactions.[21] In this document, one of the *hieropes*, Hierombrotos, itemized what he did during his tenure in office:
the list consists of the various revenues collected during the year and the
amounts that certain debtors failed to pay. With two exceptions, each of
the entries consists of exactly half of what was due to the two *hieropes* for
the year. Vial argues that this cannot be because Hierombrotos himself
collected half in installment payments, leaving the others to his colleague
(the calendar won't allow it, and some payments were made only once
during the year). Instead, Vial infers, the *hieropes* divided the sums of each

of their transactions in two, and each submitted at his review a list of exactly half, for which he was liable. It remains unclear, as Vial admits, why only in this one case the official's list was inscribed, and a degree of tentativeness is required for any generalization based on this unique case. (Vial concludes that this practice was normal among *hieropes* at Delos.) Nevertheless, Vial's hypothesis seems better than the alternative (that Hierombrotos collected just half the payments). Thus, at Delos at least, although individuals could act on behalf of the whole committee, they were held liable not for what they did but for an equal portion of what all members had done. Liability was strict (fault did not matter), collective (shared by all members of the board), and equal.

Greeks used forms of collective liability in a variety of business arrangements. A common form of extending liability voluntarily was the practice of giving security. As an alternative to pledging land as security, in leases and other contracts, guarantors (*egguetai*) sometimes promised to make a payment if the principal contracting party failed to. Guarantors could sometimes offer bail in trials, too. In a more complex variation on extending liability, one party to a contract was a group, each member of which guaranteed the fulfillment of the contract by the whole group. Two contracts from the Hellenistic period in which individuals lent cities money established such a collective liability for the borrowers and their guarantors (in one case, for everyone in the city).[22] The Athenian grain tax law of 374/73 allowed groups (*symmories*) to buy the right to collect grain taxes on certain islands, but allowed that the payments could be demanded from the whole group or from any single individual.[23] Finally, investors in maritime loans often insisted on two borrowers, one of whom stayed behind and could be sued for the fulfillment of the contract if the traveling party defaulted.[24] In all of these cases, each party became liable for the full amount of the obligation.[25]

Delegation and Liability: The Athenian Generals at Arginusai

For boards, both the internal rituals and the external constraints, including the persistent possibility of collective liability, helped foster trust in situations where labor was divided or tasks were delegated. The virtues of distributing tasks inside the group contrasts with the risks of delegating them outside, risks that become apparent in one of the most famous instances in Athenian history.

Over by Arginusai, on the coast of Asia Minor just opposite Lesbos, late in the Peloponnesian War, a scrambled armada of Athenian ships defeated the Spartan fleet. Back home, despite this significant victory, many Athenians felt that the generals had failed either to take adequate steps to rescue the Athenian rowers on disabled ships and in the water, many of whom apparently drowned, or to recover the bodies of the dead.[26] The eight generals present at the battle were indicted by *eisangelia*, a procedure in which the Boule and the Assembly first considered the charges and then issued an indictment, which prescribed a trial. In their defense, the generals said that while they were pursuing the remaining Spartan ships, they left Theramenes and other trierarchs (ship captains) behind with forty-seven boats to search for survivors, but a sudden storm prevented the rescue. In this case, the six generals who had returned to Athens were tried together, condemned collectively with a single vote, and executed.

This case has long been a *cause célèbre*, because the Athenians convicted the generals together in unusual, tumultuous proceedings. Modern scholars commonly characterize the whole process as "illegal,"[27] a description found repeatedly in Xenophon.[28] Some care is required here, however, not the least because distress over the procedures may lead to overreaction, as when both Plato and Aristotle refer to the execution of the *entire board of ten generals!*[29] While Xenophon's narrative certainly reveals irregularities and unfairnesses in the proceedings,[30] events were dominated by an attention to process as much as by passion.[31] Condemning these events, however justified, does not really help in understanding them.

The evidence makes it difficult to determine both what happened and why the generals were convicted. The two main accounts, by Xenophon (a contemporary Athenian) and by Diodoros (a writer of the late first century BCE), disagree so strongly about some of the facts and their significance that historians hold no consensus about what actually happened—and may never.[32] In what follows, I will focus on Xenophon's account because it reflects the ideas and assumptions of the classical period. The challenge of Xenophon's history, however, lies not merely in its discontinuities but also in its partisan defense of the generals. Thus, his narrative largely follows the facts in the generals' defense as he reports it, and he devotes far more attention to their defenders than to their accusers.[33] It requires some ingenuity to work against the major source and understand the logic of both the procedures of the trial and the substance of the accusation.

Procedurally, the implicit logic of the single vote seems to respond to the unified actions of the board. On the one hand, the generals involved in the events acted consistently with unanimity. Although some had initially favored rescue over pursuit,[34] none appear to have opposed the final plan to divide the fleet.[35] They all sailed off together in pursuit of the Spartans. In their letter to the Athenians and in their subsequent personal reports to the Assembly, all the participating generals seem to have spoken as one. (Konon, I should note, a general not present at the battle or its aftermath, was not indicted.) On the other hand, multiple trials or votes could create potential unfairness if some were convicted and others excused for collective decisions and actions. This was a perennial problem in the Athenian legal system insofar as it depended on private initiative for prosecutions. Thus, Aeschines complained that it was unfair that he was the only member of the board of envoys who was called to account.[36] Apollodoros, in contrast, prosecuting one of three witnesses from a previous trial for false testimony, reassured the jurors that he would charge the other two witnesses later.[37]

In normal practice, it's true, there was only one defendant in an Athenian trial,[38] but it's not clear that this should be elevated to a "principle."[39] We know of no law establishing the single defendant as a universal norm: MacDowell notes that other than the decree of Kannonos, under which Euryptolemos proposed that the Athenians should try the generals in this instance,[40] there's no evidence of a relevant written law.[41] But the Kannonos decree was not a universal law governing trial procedure, merely a possible (and rejected) legal basis of a trial. If it was the custom to try defendants individually, in this case it ran up against the principle that the demos could "do whatever it wanted."[42] Athenians themselves did not hold consistent views on the wisdom or legality of the process. A while later, they voted to indict five men for deceiving the people in this case.[43] On the other hand, not long afterwards, Lysias cited the punishment of the generals as an excellent precedent for inflicting "the severest penalty" (i.e., death) on the Thirty—and their children.[44]

The substantive controversy turned in part on how to assign liability in situations where tasks had been delegated. The charge against the generals was that they had not picked up the sailors.[45] The generals' defense that the storm had thwarted the rescue seems reasonable; indeed, the Athenians allowed this claim in exonerating Theramenes and the other trierarchs who had been sent to do the rescuing. But many Athenians didn't accept the generals' plea. How to explain this subtle discrimination? A close analysis of the two defenses Xenophon reports, when compared to similar legal cases, shows that Athenians were concerned about the *decision* of what to do, especially the *delegation* of authority.

Xenophon's account consistently evades addressing the liability of those who command. Note the craftiness of Euryptolemos's defense of the generals on this question:

> It is just, therefore, that those who were ordered to go after the enemy
> should have to account for their failures with regard to this, and that

those ordered to go and recover [the shipwrecked and the dead], if they
failed to do what the generals ordered, should be tried for not recover-
ing them.[46]

In Euryptolemos's sentence, the orders to the generals (to pursue the enemy) appear out of nowhere. By urging that the generals be held accountable for what they *did*, it attempts to veil the prior question of their culpability for what they had *ordered*.[47]

Yet what they had ordered might well seem dubious. They left a large
portion of their fleet without an authorized commander. There were times
when men who were not generals were put in charge of troops—for example, Demosthenes and later Kleon at Pylos—but the Assembly authorized both of these.[48] The generals in charge at Arginusai, however, might
have been aware that the Athenian people expected care from commanders
when entrusting tasks to underlings. After all, the people had elected these
very generals after cashiering Alcibiades (in command as a single general)
because he had left his helmsman, Antiochos, in charge of the fleet while
he went off to a conference. In Alcibiades' absence, and despite his orders
to the contrary, Antiochos had attacked the Spartan fleet, losing both the
battle and fifteen triremes. "The Athenians . . . were angry with Alcibiades,
thinking that he had lost the ships because of negligence and abandon."[49]

The delicacy of the generals' situation—a superior attempting to evade
liability for his underlings' actions—finds a close comparison in the defense speech of the producer of a boys' chorus for a competition in a religious festival.[50] This man argued that he shouldn't be held accountable
in any way for the death of one of the boys, because he had put others in
charge of overseeing the training, and he hadn't personally or specifically
ordered the boy to drink the potion that was meant to improve his voice
but that killed him. In his defense, the chorus producer took pains to outline how he had chosen four trusted and experienced men to oversee the
training in his absence,[51] which suggests that he anticipated that the degree of his culpability might have hinged on the care he took in delegating. He also explicitly refused to incriminate his agents, claiming instead
that *aitia* (cause or blame) rested with no one but fortune.[52] Blaming fortune may have been a way out of a bind: had he blamed his assistants, it
might have called into question his own judgment in appointing them and
provoked them to act as witnesses against him to protect themselves. The
arguments offered by the generals paralleled those of the chorus producer.
They absolved their subordinates, insisting that the people they had put
in charge "were competent and had been generals before."[53] Refusing to
blame their agents for the failure, they insisted that the magnitude of the
storm was the real cause of the failure.[54]

Blaming the storm, however, constitutes the ultimate evasion. A military operation is halted not by storm but by someone's orders. Since the generals were gone, the captains left behind must have made this decision. If the storm arose unexpectedly, the captains' mandate—to rescue the sailors—may not have covered this situation, in which case their decision to abort the operation without explicit orders parallels quite closely the events for which Alcibiades had been sacked not long before.

The events at Arginusai demonstrate the dynamics and the dangers of delegating outside the group. Deputizing others created asymmetric culpability: a subordinate could more readily implicate a superior than a superior could blame a subordinate. Thus, in their initial report back home, the generals reported that the trierarchs failed in their assigned task,[55] but when the trierarchs defended themselves, the generals emended their story and, like the chorus producer, exonerated their delegates, ratified their qualifications, and blamed an extraneous cause. But this disparity did not hold within boards, since all members were equally liable, so that all accusations might backfire.

Liability and the Problem of Information: Demosthenes against Aphobos

The allocation of responsibility in equal shares was not just the consequence of democratic ideologies or a cause of group solidarity; it also constituted a simple algorithm for distributing liability in the face of a real and even daunting practical difficulty: the problem of information. Even if you could develop a finely calibrated, objective formula for proportionalizing liability in groups (weighing what a person may have said or done or intended), in order to use this formula you would still face the practical challenge of getting the relevant information. In a world with little writing, it would not have been easy to know who did and said what. It would not have been impossible, of course, but deciding between two competing claims (the norm in Athenian litigation) is probably several orders of magnitude easier than deciding among ten; as I will show in chapter 8, with regard to litigation, dichotomizing makes choice possible, especially by a large group. The allocation of equal shares, then, constituted a kind of "no-fault" system for allocating liability. (Modern "no-fault" systems of insurance provide an apt parallel since their point is to avoid the substantial costs of determining—which is to say, arguing about—liability.)

Demosthenes' prosecution speeches against his guardian Aphobos about his inheritance show the dynamics of equal shares and these problems of information in action. When Demosthenes' father died (in 376), he left behind a seven-year-old son, a younger daughter, a widow, Kleobule,

and a considerable estate.[56] Demosthenes' father, however, had taken care
to appoint three male guardians, two of Demosthenes' cousins and a close
friend, to manage the estate and raise the children; one of these, Aphobos,
was to marry the widow Kleobule. Ten years later, when the guardians
ended their control, Demosthenes claimed that they had embezzled most
of the property, and he began a series of lawsuits to recover it.[57] What had
happened during this decade to so estrange these people is difficult to determine because you can read only Demosthenes' story, which is short on
explanations.[58] According to him, from the beginning the three guardians
disregarded his father's final instructions, began to plunder and abscond
with the estate, and by the end of the decade had reduced it to a fraction
of its original value, now hardly more than a talent. Demosthenes began
by suing Aphobos, his would-be stepfather. Aphobos's defense—as far as
I can deduce it from Demosthenes' speeches—seems to have been that
Demosthenes' father had many more debts than he had admitted when
he died and that these, along with an uncollectible loan and various expenses incurred over the ten years, had seriously diminished the estate's
supposed original value.[59]

   Although Demosthenes charged only Aphobos in this case, his arguments rested on the idea of equal shares of liability for the three guardians.
As he began his speech, it's true, Demosthenes seemed to assign individual
blame to Aphobos, and he claimed near the beginning of his first speech
that "what things of mine Demophon and Therippides [the other two
guardians] have, it will suffice to speak about these when we bring charges
against them. But what this man has—both what the other two convict
him of having and what I know he has taken—I will make my speech to
you about this."[60] However, after arguing in detail that Aphobos took
the dowry but never married Kleobule, and that he never turned over the
profits from a workshop of slaves that he managed for two years (§§13–23),
Demosthenes changed his focus. "On the other hand, the things he plun-
dered in common with the other guardians, and the amounts he argues
that were not left at all, I will now show you one by one."[61] Demosthenes
now spoke only of "the guardians," arguing that "of the things carried
away cooperatively (koine), it's only right that I should recover a third
from him."[62] Indeed, the bulk of Demosthenes' claims rested not on Aphobos's individual liability, but on the collective, equally shared liability of
the guardians. In the end, despite Aphobos's particular actions, Demosthenes claimed from him exactly as much as he sought from the other two
guardians, one third of the total.

   This case highlights the costs of getting the information needed to assign individual responsibility.[63] The situation was admittedly complex:
three guardians, ten years, multiple investments. But before it came to

trial, Demosthenes had had several opportunities to thoroughly investigate the facts: at the time of the guardians' initial report when they turned over what property they had, at the attempt at mediation by a group of friends,[64] and at the public arbitration that preceded the trial.[65] If Demosthenes had himself been too young to understand or remember the guardians' actions, he could get detailed information from his mother and other relatives. His extensive use of witnesses demonstrates his diligence in attempting to ferret out the facts.[66] Nevertheless, he attributed to Aphobos individually only two transgressions, and rested the bulk of his case on Aphobos's equal share in the collective liability of the guardians. Gathering the information to assign individual liability within groups may simply have been too costly and difficult, especially when group members presented a united front.[67]

A fourth-century decree from an Attic deme, Dekelea, underlines the problem of information. What makes this decree unusual is that it states explicitly a formula for excusing some members from the liability of a group. The decree outlines the procedures for admission to a phratry. (By descent, all citizens in Athens belonged to a phratry, a group that had religious functions but was also a recognized part of the polis. Admission to a phratry was an important step in coming into full citizen rights.) At the adjudication where all phratry members voted on admitting those who were coming of age (a vote that hinged on whether they were legitimate sons of citizens), the members of the *thiasos* (a subgroup of the phratry) first voted by secret ballot on the young man's qualifications. "If the members of the *thiasos* vote him to be a member of their phratry, but the other phratry members subsequently vote him out, the members of the *thiasos* will owe 100 drachmas dedicated to Zeus Phratrios, except those who are accusers or who openly oppose him during [in] the adjudication."[68] The rules seem designed to encourage skepticism about candidates' eligibility: both the secret ballot[69] and the immunity of dissenters would operate to neutralize personal relationships of surveillance and trust within the *thiasos*. The exceptional statement of a formula of immunity from liability, however, seems directly tied to its easy application. Because the *thiasos* deliberated and voted in the presence of the whole phratry (the group that would fine the *thiasos* if it wrongly admitted anyone to membership), the other phratry members would already have all the information they needed to excuse anyone from liability.

Collective Accountability and Group Dynamics

Collective liability may intensify the personal relationships of those in groups. Comparative and theoretical literature suggests that when a group suffers a collective sanction, it tends to become a (secondary) enforcement agent itself and to pass on the liability to the member or members at fault. But even before anyone has broken a rule—and this is the secret of the social dynamics of collective liability—group members will work to prevent others' misconduct. To the extent that group members can know each other's blunders or crimes better than outsiders, can inflict a larger range of sanctions (from reprimands to expulsion to informing the state), and can apply sanctions more readily and cheaply, collective liability may produce a level of deterrence that individual liability alone could not. An important corollary, as Levinson has argued, is that collective sanctions not only rely on group solidarity but also provide incentives to build and strengthen it.[70]

Indeed, the Athenians imagined collective liability as a way of ensuring that every member of a group would assume some oversight over the actions of all. In 355, Diodoros and Euktemon charged Androtion with making an illegal proposal, specifically proposing the reward of a crown to the Boule despite its failure to build the legally required number of triremes during the year. Diodoros argued:

> If you acquit Androtion, the hall of the Boule will belong to the orators, but if you convict, it will belong to ordinary citizens. When the majority sees that the Boule has lost its crown through the baseness of the orators, they won't turn over the business to them; instead, they will themselves offer the best advice.[71]

Aeschines recounted a parallel incident: in the Assembly, Pamphilos accused Timarchos, a member of the Boule, of embezzling money, and he urged the Athenians to deny the Boule its usual crown if it didn't punish its own member—which, Aeschines said, is exactly what happened.[72]

In principle, of course, Greek officials were subject to extensive scrutiny, both during and at the end of their tenure.[73] But with few dedicated resources and no power of subpoena, potential outside investigators usually faced significant impediments to gathering evidence. Even Demosthenes faced considerable difficulties in scavenging information to charge his guardians—and these were people and events he knew intimately. And the mutual trust of members, fostered in part by regimes of collective liability, might work against turning one associate against another. Recall here the sense of betrayal Aeschines evinced when one of his fellow envoys, Demosthenes, prosecuted him for malfeasance.

To overcome the problem of getting information, Greeks occasionally commissioned those with knowledge as potential enforcers. In Korope, for example, a body of officials (the *exetastai*) was made explicitly accountable both to volunteer prosecutors and to their successors in office.[74] More directly, Greeks sometimes assigned one member of a group as the enforcer, holding him responsible if he failed to do this. Recollect the inscription from Athens (*IG* I³ 4B, discussed in chapter 6), which says that "the *prytanis* is to collect the fine [from members of the board of treasurers who do not show up when required]; if he does not, he is to be held accountable."[75] Although not formally concerned with distributing penalties, the Athenian institution of the *proeisphora* worked essentially the same: the three richest members of each syndicate (*symmory*) of (a dozen to fifteen) taxpayers had to prepay the tax and subsequently negotiate its distribution within the group on the basis of wealth assessments. The evidence seems to indicate that the prepayment procedures were added after the *symmory* system was already in place, perhaps, Matthew Christ suggests, to facilitate their functioning.[76] Interested and knowledgeable members of the groups were sometimes charged with being internal enforcers of liabilities.

Xenophon's Analysis of Liability and Equal Shares

Contemporary Greeks were not unaware of the way regimes of liability affected boards. Isocrates, for example, thought that making several people responsible for the same areas of competence would cause many to loaf, hoping that others would work. He listed this likelihood as one of the reasons to prefer monarchy to democracy or oligarchy: "Officials in these kinds of governments neglect many things because everyone looks to others, but monarchs neglect nothing because they know that everything happens because of them."[77] The second book of Xenophon's *Kyropaideia* offers the most detailed insight into contemporary debates about the effects of different mechanisms of allocating liability in groups. You may not think of this work as an obvious or even promising source of evidence for such a question: it is an account (largely fictional) of the youth of the Persian king Cyrus the Great, a bildungsroman almost, which purports to discuss Persian institutions. Yet despite its novelistic form, the *Kyropaideia* begins with a general political problem, the instability of states, to which it offers as a solution the practices of Cyrus's kingship. The story of Cyrus's reform of the army, therefore, constitutes part of an attempt to analyze the conditions for a prosperous and enduring state.[78] Formally quite different from Plato's *Republic*, Xenophon's work engages with similar issues. Xenophon also analyzes government in ways that evoke contemporary Athenian democracy. Though he spent much of his life exiled from Athens, his many works frequently show an on-going and by no means hostile concern for his native city.[79]

Book 2 of the *Kyropaideia* concerns Cyrus's reform of the Persian army, but it addresses a specific political problem: how to apportion rewards within a group. In the face of a more numerous enemy, Cyrus decides to arm the commoners like the nobles. Taking away the light weapons they use at a distance, he gives them heavier armor and swords so as to fight at close quarters. In addition to this tactical change, however, Cyrus alters the reward structure for common soldiers. After Cyrus has incorporated common soldiers into the army, one of the nobles, Chrysantas, objects: "If something good happens, everyone [the better and those worthy of less] thinks himself worthy to share equally. But if you ask me, I don't think that anything is less equal among men than the bad and the good being thought worthy of equal shares."[80] Cyrus then proposes a debate: Should everyone continue to receive an equal share, or should each be rewarded in proportion to his deeds and his worth (2.2.18)? To give away the ending: the later proposal will prevail.

In the two speeches against the practice of equal shares, Xenophon presents one of the fundamental practices of equality of the democratic polis (equal shares) as an unproductive and inefficient form of liability. Xenophon's critique hinges on the free-rider problem—collective rewards create incentives to shirk—a problem solved, he argues, by his system of individual accountability. Cyrus begins by arguing that when men who are partners in war all believe that nothing essential will get done unless everyone exerts himself, they quickly accomplish many great things because they will do everything that needs to be done. But when each man thinks that someone else will be the doer and the fighter, even while he holds back, then everyone suffers (2.3.3). Chrysantas continues this argument: "If the powerful strongly take a share in things, I will have a share in some good, such a portion as is just. But if the bad do nothing, and the good and the powerful lose heart, then I fear that I will have a greater share than I would like of something other than good" (2.3.6).

Xenophon's objection to the idea of equal shares focused on a particular contemporary practice: pay for service (*misthos*). Greek cities and armies commonly gave equal shares of pay. Regardless of status, ability, or performance, everyone in Athens doing the same state job—service in office, jury duty, rowing in a trireme, or building a temple—got the same *misthos*.[81] Xenophon marks the transformation of the reward structure of the Persian army as going from pay for hire (*misthophoros*)[82] to prizes (*athla*) based on performance.

Nevertheless, Xenophon defends the system of rewards according to merit as based on equality—indeed, as democratic. Many writers of the fourth century, suspicious of the claims of equality advanced by advocates of democracy but at the same time unable to disavow the idea altogether (that, it seems, would have been unpersuasive), struggled to re-imagine equality. One famous outcome of this intellectual problem was the doctrine of geometric equality, which provided a mathematical justification for bestowing greater privileges on "greater" men.[83] Xenophon's notion of equality, however, bears little resemblance to this. When Pheraulas, a commoner, speaks (2.3.8–15), he claims that Cyrus's system offers a true equality of opportunity, so that commoners can expect to compete equally against nobles. "I believe that we all now start from a position of equality (*ek tou isou*) in the contest of excellence" (2.3.8). They all get the same training, rations, and prizes, and the method of fighting (with a sword) is natural and instinctive (so, by implication, the long training of the nobles gives no advantage). Moreover, the nobles' training in toil is voluntary, but nothing teaches toil better than necessity—that is, the conditions of the life of common people. Pheraulas concludes his recommendation tellingly: He urges his fellow commoners to enter the contest, "since these men have been ensnared in a popular contest [ἐν δημοτικῇ ἀγωνίᾳ]" (2.3.15.)

Xenophon's analyses of the problem of democratic equality were strikingly original in at least four ways. First, while others tended to locate the sources of political instability in inequality (of wealth or office),[84] Xenophon offered a more psychological explanation: the refusal to be ruled by others. At the beginning of the *Kyropaideia*, he claimed that the main problem underlying the instability of states was the fact that "in light of human nature, it is easier to rule any other creatures than people."[85] With Cyrus, however, people obeyed willingly;[86] he not only inspired fear but "was able to implant such a desire to gratify him that they consented to be steered by his opinion."[87] He did this, in part, by creating a system that recognized and realized men's interests better than they could on their own.[88] Hence the force of Chrysantas's endorsement of Cyrus's reform: he will more likely get a share of good things under the system of prizes for merit precisely because the group as a whole is more likely to succeed. Xenophon indirectly linked political stability to the practice of reward for merit (unequal shares) because this practice allows people to get more.

Second, while other writers tended to critique democratic equality on ethical grounds (it was unfair), Xenophon's analysis was largely functional. As he presented it, a system of differential rewards will cause individuals to exert themselves more and the whole group to succeed to a greater extent. Chrysantas phrases his initial objection to Cyrus's plan in the traditional language of status (the good and the bad do not deserve the same, as quoted above), but the subsequent discussion of the system of rewards focuses largely on its effectiveness as a system.

Third, Xenophon's system of differentiated prizes rewards achievement more than status. The traditional language of reward "for merit," *kat' axian*, is perhaps ambiguous, but across authors the contexts tend to show that this *axia* denoted something like "intrinsic worth" or "character" rather than "specific achievements." Isocrates, Plato, and even Aristotle describe rewarding *kinds of people*.[89] For this reason democrats (Aristotle says)[90] rejected justice *kat' axian*. However, while Xenophon retained the aristocratic language, he transformed it: Although his system bestowed rewards *kat' axian*,[91] it rewarded not people of a certain kind but deeds, people's *erga*.[92] Xenophon's system may not, it's true, entirely purge the privileges of status: Cyrus says that reward will be relative to toil, *to ponein*,[93] a term Xenophon generally used to denote the stylized labor of the elite lifestyle.[94] Yet Xenophon's elevation of toil, labor that was supposed to be both real and useful to the city, represented an analogous attempt to rethink and innovate traditional aristocratic claims and practices. By rewarding toil, Cyrus intends to make even the nobles better and to spur them to greater military training. Indeed, Xenophon seems to imagine not abolishing aristocratic status but making this status an achievement. So, he says, Cyrus instituted games and prizes so as to inspire rivalry for "beautiful and good deeds."[95] Moreover, as his language makes clear, rewards for training were always linked to those for achievement in battle.[96] The action, more than the person, determined the reward.[97]

Fourth, Xenophon focused not on the allocation of offices, but on that of rewards. His use of the elevated term *athla*, prizes in games, constituted a significant break with the aristocratic tradition, which understood the problem of equality in terms of *time*, honor or office. Xenophon elsewhere understood *athla* as incentives: to get soldiers to build a wall more quickly[98] or to train more zealously,[99] to get officials to settle disputes with speed;[100] or he conceived them as a general principle to encourage the pursuit of knowledge, commerce, and even agriculture.[101] "When people think that the person who excels won't be acclaimed or receive prizes, then they won't try to better each other. But when the superior person gets a bigger share, then everyone competes most eagerly."[102] Thus, unlike other critiques of democracy, Xenophon's analysis focused not on the democratic practice of using the lot to assign offices[103] but on the common democratic practices of equal shares and *misthos* (pay for service). Aristotle said that payment for service (*to misthophorein*) was characteristic of democracies.[104] *Misthophora*, receipt of wages, could be predicated of Athenian jurors[105] and of other officials.[106]

Points 2, 3, and 4 are closely related, and I would summarize them like this: in place of a moral analysis of the relations between the quality of a person and that person's honor, Xenophon offers a systemic analysis of the relation between a person's achievement and the person's reward. Xenophon offers a profound critique of the common Greek—and especially democratic—idea that all members of a group deserved equal shares, a critique showing an appreciation far deeper than that of others of the ways in which regimes of liability can affect the relationships of people within groups.

Then Xenophon seriously complicates his analysis. The *Kyropaideia* is a notoriously complex work: It is generally difficult to settle whether Xenophon intended Cyrus as a positive model or not, and whether, therefore, he endorsed the analyses of the characters or even of the narrator. I incline toward the position that the *Kyropaideia* is fundamentally ironic or ambivalent in presenting both positive knowledge and a skeptical critique of it.[107] Certainly, by the final book the text offers a judicious reappraisal of its own analysis, particularly on two related problems of implementation, of which the first is resentment. If competition for differential rewards could stir individuals to greater achievement, it could also undermine cooperation. Indeed, the problem of *eris*—competition that could be socially beneficial or destructive, or both—was central to both the Homeric poems and Hesiod's *Works and Days*.[108] Xenophon, too, was aware of the ethical complexities of competition,[109] but also understood its political implications. He devotes a significant chunk of book 8 of the *Kyropaideia*, a book that focuses on how Cyrus constructed his government hierarchically and the role of obedience within this system, to analyzing the mechanisms Cyrus used to make people love him.[110] Cyrus, he says, won praise for setting up contests, which encouraged the practice of excellence. "Among the best men, however, these contests with each other injected rivalries and contentiousness."[111] Although "rivalries and contentiousness" are both things that could have positive or negative connotations, the contrast with the practice of excellence suggests that Xenophon sees them as more counterproductive here.[112] He then describes the way Cyrus set up rules about arbitrating disputes, whether legal cases or quarrels arising from contests, and says that disputants sought out judges who were powerful and friendly toward them. Xenophon remarks, however, that Cyrus's system undercut these social relationships: "The loser was jealous of the victors, and he hated those who decided against him. The victor would at least say that he had won because of justice, and as a result he believed he owed nobody any gratitude." On the other hand, Cyrus's need to enhance his own position promoted these rivalries: "Those who wanted to be first in Cyrus's love were especially liable to jealousy of each other (as others are in cities), so that most people wished to get another out of the way rather than cooperate for some common benefit."[113] Xenophon concludes that Cyrus "caused the most powerful to love him more than each other."[114] Differential rewards come with a cost.

The second, related problem is that of proportionalizing. For the system to work there had to be a mechanism to commensurate the prize with merit. Greeks would have been familiar with this problem since disputes about commensurating Achilles' reward with his merit set the plot of the *Iliad* in motion. Xenophon solved it by having the always fair Cyrus act as judge of the entire army.[115] As Pheraulas says: "I am impelled to the contest with these men especially by this fact: Cyrus will be the judge. He does not judge from the basis of envy, but (I say this with a holy oath) Cyrus truly seems to me to love those whom he sees as no less good than himself."[116] But step back a moment. The problem with this solution was that it was irreproducible, not only after Cyrus's death but even during his reign, because of the size of the army and the empire: the solution wasn't scalable. Thus, by the end of the whole work, Xenophon describes a system for the distribution of rewards—each commander distributes the rewards differentially to those he oversees, and so on down the chain of command[117]—a system that did not depend on the excellence of Cyrus and therefore implicitly reintroduced the problem of measuring merit. It is difficult to imagine that every commander would be a fair or competent judge of achievement, especially since the adoption of the system in the first place seems to have been premised on Cyrus's unique impartiality.

Compared to other contemporary analyses of reward systems, Xenophon's was startling, even radical. Consider his engagement with the problem of *misthos* (considered in chapter 2), which was usually conceived as a static (if difficult) epistemological challenge: How do you determine what something, in this case labor, is really worth? Xenophon's formulation of the challenge of *misthos* was altogether different; his proposed alternative was systemic and dynamic. Downplaying how the reward, the *misthos*, was determined (whether by the seller or buyer of labor), Xenophon emphasized instead the effect of equal *misthos*: a disincentive to achievement. Xenophon's program was not epistemological (the question was not how to determine the true value of a thing, a question that possessed Plato, Aristotle, and Protagoras) but sociological, I might even say managerial. Prizes, *athla*, could create more *axia*, which Xenophon understood not as static or subjective but as dynamic and manipulable. In this case, each person is more likely to come out ahead because all are more likely to contribute to the group's goal, victory in battle. Both givers and receivers of *athla* invest trust not in persons but in a function: the fair commensuration of *athla* with *axia*. The implementation of this system must remain hypothetical, since Xenophon relies on a Cyrus who represents a function, complete fairness; in other words, he can't imagine himself in any system that doesn't rely on personal trust. The virtue of Xenophon's irony is that it allowed him to confront the limitations of his own analysis.

Conclusion: Accountability and Trust

Collective liability complemented the typically collegial nature of Greek offices. Holding all members liable for the actions of the group not only conformed to the common ideology of citizen equality, but also overcame two serious problems of individual liability in group situations: proportionalizing the sanction or reward to particular actions or words, and gathering enough information to do so. These difficulties, as well as a sense that people bear some responsibility for what the organizations they belong to decide and do, show up even in prosecutions of individuals. Both Lysias and Demosthenes argued that their opponents (Eratosthenes and Aphobos) should bear liability for the actions of the groups in which they participated, actions they were alleged to have planned and approved, even if they didn't execute them. Whereas Greeks normally held individual trials, many laws sanctioned each member for the actions of the whole, a response to the typically collegial nature of Greek offices.

Collective sanctions affected the internal dynamics of groups, particularly by repersonalizing relationships. Usually appointed by lot, officials entered office with no antecedent personal relationships to draw on; instead, they had to forge and intensify new relationships—under the susceptibility to collective rewards and punishments—with others on a committee. The dynamics of accountability affected even elected boards, where members were more likely to have already established relationships: When the Athenians sent ten envoys to the Macedonian king Philip, one of them, Aeschines, had proposed to another, Demosthenes (so he later claimed), that they both keep watch on a suspect third member, Philokrates, and subsequently Derkylos had allegedly used Demosthenes' servant to spy on Aeschines.[118] On the other hand, Aeschines related that before the group had addressed Philip and, later, before they reported back to the Athenians, they had met to make sure that they all had something to say, including praise of each other.[119] Whatever the factual validity of these particular claims, they represent collateral strategies of surveillance: in one, members of a group watch their fellows to detect and deter wrongdoing; in the other, they take care to help each other succeed. Whether board members treated each other with trust (delegating tasks or offering constructive counsel) or distrust (watching each other to detect wrongdoing or incompetence), or perhaps both, the possibility of collective liability created a reciprocity of interests that intensified their surveillance of each other.

CHAPTER 8

Deciding

Of all the systems that Greeks relied on, perhaps the most powerful, if the most abstract, was rhetoric. Rhetoric allowed hundreds or even thousands of Athenians to debate and decide matters in the two largest democratic institutions, the Assembly and the courts, and, in doing so, it established relationships of action among citizens—not just between a speaker and a listener, but between competing speakers and among the body of listeners as well—relationships that were, essentially, mediated and impersonal.

I am here going to treat rhetoric as a system for simplifying matters by means of institutional arrangements and conventional language so that large groups could decide things. The inclusion of the institutional context in the definition of rhetoric makes my meaning both broader and narrower than the customary idea of rhetoric as persuasive language. It is narrower because I am concerned only with situations where large groups decided things, not the myriad situations where one person attempted to persuade another. It is broader because I will insist that any analysis of persuasive language in Greek courts or assemblies must consider both the presence of an opposing speaker and the activities of the large, judging audience. I am not claiming that this somewhat idiosyncratic definition of rhetoric is the right one in an absolute sense, merely that it is historically important and analytically fecund.

The chapter begins by considering how the active, judging role of the audience in Athenian courts and assemblies has been obscured by the reduction of rhetoric to persuasion, the action of a speaker on a listener. I am seeking to recover the listeners' essential role, a project inspired by earlier scholars, particularly Finley and Ober,[1] who approached rhetoric historically and systematically. Ober, in his *Mass and Elite in Democratic Athens*, forcefully insisted on the reciprocity between speaker and audience. But in analyzing the ways that elite and ordinary Athenians negotiated their class interests through ideology in rhetorical contexts, he did not study rhetoric itself so much as one of the things that rhetoric happened to do.[2] Here I attempt to give a broad and representative account of the range of rhetorical resources, the conventional ways of representing things that allowed speakers to address large audiences and these audiences to process and decide matters. Finally, I examine the risks posed by rhetoric and the ways these were limited by rhetoric itself.

While this chapter offers a general analysis of ancient Greek rhetoric, it illustrates this analysis mostly with the Athenian courts. The Athenian courts of the classical period were famously unprofessionalized: there were no police, public prosecutors, lawyers, or judges—just two litigants (and their supporting speakers and witnesses) wrangling before several hundred jurors. (I sometimes refer to the audience members in the courts and the Assembly as "judges" to highlight their free use of their reasoning in deciding.) But some litigants did hire speechwriters, and the hundred or so of their speeches that have been preserved allow for a fineness of analysis not possible in other institutions or at other times.[3] Indeed, you cannot conduct analyses of the same subtlety and certainty even for the Athenian Assembly, the core institution of the democracy, since only a handful of speeches have been preserved, aside from the literary versions in authors like Thucydides. Nevertheless, although some of the specifics may have differed (as in the types of rhetorical arguments),[4] the general configuration of rhetoric in the Athenian courts and the Assembly was similar.[5] Although in its quantity and detail the evidence for Athens exceeds that for other Greek poleis, several factors suggest that my conclusions would be broadly applicable elsewhere: the pervasive use of assemblies of citizens and large courts to decide things, the sophists' wide travels, and a pan-Hellenic distribution of rhetorical skill.[6]

Against Persuasion

The usual idea of persuasion as a power a speaker wields on a listener obscures the critical, active exercise of rhetorical skill by listeners. Theories of rhetoric centered on persuasion tend to treat listeners as the passive objects of a speaker's words. Such abject manipulation may have obtained somewhere, sometime, but not typically in the proceedings of the Athenian courts or those of the Assembly, where every speaker could expect that someone else would challenge and disenchant his words and where speeches would be received by listeners wise to all the tricks of language. I don't intend to banish the notion of persuasion but merely to suggest that a speaker's instrumental use of rhetorical resources must always be set against the rhetorical performance of the judging audience.

Ancient teachers of rhetorical language and those who wrote about it elaborated an art of the speaker: persuasion theory. The sophists collected and invented arguments, providing in their verbal instruction and written handbooks (*technai*) treasuries of pleas that speakers might use. Subsequently, Plato made significant theoretical innovations: Thomas Cole argues that Plato first made a theory of rhetoric fully reflexive, discussing the parts and means of persuasion, while Edward Schiappa claims that Plato first clearly defined and differentiated the discipline of philosophy as distinct from its competition, rhetoric.[7] Aristotle continued to articulate and innovate the theory of persuasion, categorizing the types of rhetorical contexts, for example, as a way of understanding what kind of arguments to present,[8] or amplifying the ways that speakers might persuade with argument, character, and emotion.

Despite these meticulous accounts of speakers' powers, persuasion theory offers only an impoverished analysis of judges as rhetorical subjects—in a form I call the theory of the persuadable soul. Most Greek authors expounded some version of this theory. Gorgias provides an early and outlandish description of persuasion's effects when he says it acts like magic, drugs, or force—so irresistible that those persuaded cannot be held accountable for their assent.[9] As Segal interprets Gorgias's psychological theory, persuasion works in a quasi-physical way through a two-stage process: first aesthetic and passive, then motivational and active.[10] Although the listener in some way enables this process,[11] the contingency and power in the process remain with the speaker.[12]

Plato names the theory of the persuadable soul most concisely when his character Socrates defines rhetoric as *psychagogia*, "a kind of soul wrangling."[13] Although fourth-century writers used this term to indicate the effects of poetic language, it had long referred to procedures for conjuring back the souls of the dead.[14] As such, it indicates the powerlessness of the object of rhetoric, the souls of the auditors. And while Socrates' subsequent elaboration of rhetoric contains an account of souls' activities,[15] these are no more than signs that the orator must know how to interpret so as to apply the most effective rhetoric. In regard to rhetoric itself, the soul of the listener remains a passive object.

Nor does Aristotle get much beyond the theory of the persuadable soul. For him, the *techne* of rhetoric was about producing, not listening to, speeches. Thus, although evaluating arguments requires judgment, *phronesis*, Aristotle predicates this only of speakers.[16] He gives no sustained account of how listeners decided; instead, he treats speakers as sovereign agents, as the sole creators and crafters of rhetoric. While Aristotle acknowledges that character and emotion affect the ways that audiences decide, the speaker alone calculates how to project these elements himself and how to adjust his language to take account of them in the listeners.[17]

Because Aristotle gives no sustained attention to the activities of listeners, perhaps the best that can be said is that "there *appears* to be an *implicit* commitment in Aristotle's views to the idea that probable knowledge of the realm of action is acquired through the process of assessing and choosing among competing rhetorical arguments."[18]

These thinkers described the listeners' souls largely to catalogue their defects. Thus Gorgias wrote that persuasion succeeds through constructing false arguments because people have poor memories and cannot predict the future.[19] More concretely, and in line with treating listeners as a final (but passive) cause, Aristotle tended to attribute to them the problems he imagined in contemporary rhetoric: Because listeners are corrupt, style has become important;[20] because of their uncultivated minds, maxims are effective;[21] because listeners are common (*phaulos*), speakers say things outside the subject;[22] because jurors don't have a personal stake in the outcome of trials but listen merely for their own pleasure, litigants stray from the subject;[23] because listeners have weak and simple intellects, speakers don't use long and properly logical chains of inference.[24] Whether Aristotle directly observed or investigated these characteristics of ordinary audience members or simply inferred them from the kinds of things speakers said, his analysis of the practical reason exercised by listeners offers little detail. Instead, his analysis of listeners' character serves a theory of rhetoric founded on persuasion.

You might explain this concentration on the speaker's powers by the demand for instruction. Speakers, vying with other speakers, would pay for an edge, as Aristophanes' character Strepsiades says he'd pay anything to learn how to wrangle out of debts.[25] And while there might even have been a market for the education of slaves in their daily duties[26] (paid for, presumably, by their wealthier masters), there was no incentive for any juror to study to do his job better. This market demand may have spurred the fantastic claims made by teachers of rhetoric about the effects they could produce on auditors.

Common as the persuasion theory was, however, it fails to sufficiently analyze the rhetorical context in four ways: It does not account for symmetry, competition, coordination, or irreducibility. Consider in turn each of these features of rhetoric.

What the audience did, listening, evaluating, and deciding, should get as much attention as what speakers did, attempting to persuade. The persuasion model examines the relationship of speaker and audience from the speaker's point of view, treating the speaker as active, the audience as passive. This model tacitly assumes an absolute disproportion of agency and power. It's better, however, to begin from what John Law calls a *principle of symmetry*, assuming as little as possible, equally investigating all aspects of a situation.[27] Much of what follows attempts to account for the rhetorical competence and activity of the listeners.

Second, the simple pair of speaker and audience fails to adequately account for another fundamental feature of the rhetorical setting: competing speakers. Because the system ensured that there were almost always opposing speeches, no speaker ever had an audience to himself. From a speaker's perspective, the presence of an opposing speech adds another contingency at each point, the opponent's responses, and persuasion theory may describe the ways a speaker might counter these. But for listeners, multiple conflicting speeches exponentially increase the complexity of evaluating and deciding, not only because they must take account of each point of contention, but also because they have to consider the points where one speaker does not respond to his opponent, how to weigh the importance of each point, and, finally, how to turn all of these factors into a verdict. Persuasion theory offers little insight into this process.

Third, in addition to the relationships between speaker and audience, rhetoric created relationships *among the listeners*. Listeners did not simply respond to speeches as a unitary group, nor on the other hand as chaotic, isolated individuals; rather, they coordinated their individual actions into a collective action, a decision. The coordination of these (what might be called) lateral relationships among listeners did not happen so much through conscious articulation and negotiation as through a common competence in rhetoric. The relationships constituted by rhetoric greatly exceeded the simple pair of speaker and audience.

Finally, no decision by listeners can be reduced to or equated with a speech. In the most obvious sense, a decision can't be explained solely by a speech because invariably half of all speeches would fail to persuade. (To say that one speech was persuasive but the other was not does not explain a decision; it merely redescribes it.) Beyond this, the complexity of the rhetorical situation—multiple speeches each making multiple points, sometimes in direct contradiction to each other, sometimes not, and an audience of judges who were themselves seasoned critics of rhetorical language—all this means that even afterwards it can be difficult to explain a decision, and that predicting it beforehand (whether based on the knowledge of one speech, or a general sense of the competing positions) could be futile. You can see this in the scenes in Aristophanes' comedies that depict rhetorical situations.[28] Though often exaggerated—in *The Knights*, for example, Aristophanes takes literally the idea that rhetoric is a form of seduction by having two rival politicians compete as lovers for the attention of Demos ("The People"), offering flattery and trifling gifts[29]—such scenes make an important analytical point: in situations with competing speeches and autonomous listeners, the decision between speeches was far from automatic; it could even defy initial prejudices and expectations.[30]

The Active Audience

In the Assembly and the courts, audiences participated actively. Sometimes they intervened vocally—shouting, heckling, or otherwise making a noise, whether in encouragement or challenge.[31] Scholars emphasize these means by which audiences communicated with speakers, creating reciprocity.[32] However important such communication was, audiences did more than shout their opinions: they decided.[33] Although the available evidence won't support a description of their decision-making as a subjective mental process, it is possible to specify the objective, external features of rhetorical settings that made possible and gave shape to listeners' decisions.

You may begin to appreciate the fundamentally active role of a rhetorical audience by noting the significant differences between the practices of deciding in classical Athens and those found in the earliest Greek sources, Hesiod and Homer. In their poems, where the assembled people witness decisions and in some sense legitimate them (though they do not formally vote),[34] speakers address each other as much as they do the crowd.[35] Michael Gagarin's analysis of dispute procedures clarifies this dynamic.[36] He argues that the lords (*basileis*) in Hesiod's poems act as judges of disputes, but, because they do not merely listen but actively mediate, they—even more than the disputants—need skill in speaking. Meanwhile, as they argue, the disputants might invite such mediation or, abandoning it, engage directly with each other. Nor is there a fixed mediator: different lords might offer different proposed settlements (*dikai*) in an attempt to please both parties. While a crowd of people might watch, they play a minimal role beyond shouting.[37] Insofar as speakers address and attempt to persuade each other, but not the audience, and the audience does not actually decide, there is fine oratory in epic, but no rhetoric in the precise sense I am using the term.[38]

In the political institutions of the classical period, however, auditors were not (or not merely) the objects of a speaker's rhetorical action; they were themselves rhetorical subjects. The conventional nature of much rhetorical language meant that listeners as well as speakers had to acquire rhetorical competence, even if they exercised it differently. While speakers used their rhetorical facility to construct arguments and speeches, listeners used theirs to understand, evaluate, and decide between competing speeches.

Ancient writers occasionally reveal glimpses of the listeners' activities.

Greek writers sometimes attributed a special activity, *krisis,* to the members of the jury or the Assembly. Interestingly, they often define *krisis*—which is usually translated as "deciding" but at its root means separating or distinguishing—in contrast to other activities. Thucydides' characters offer at least two pertinent observations: Pericles distinguishes those who think through a matter from those who decide,[39] and Athenagoras says that the rich are the best guardians of property, the intelligent are the best at planning, and the masses are best at listening and deciding.[40] In these instances, Thucydides differentiates speakers, who act by planning or formulating, from listeners, who act by judging or deciding. Aristotle, on the other hand, distinguishes deciding from another activity a listener could potentially undertake: "The listener must be either a spectator or a decider."[41] Here Aristotle makes his influential distinction between speeches for display (*epideictic* oratory) and speeches for the courts or the Assembly. Whatever problems this taxonomy may generate,[42] it nevertheless rests on two essential differences: listeners in the courts and the Assembly heard opposing speeches and voted for one of the opposing parties; the spectators did not.[43]

Despite the scarcity and brevity of these writers' statements about the activities of a rhetorical audience, several scholars have labored to explicate a fuller analysis. In Thucydides, they often turn to his famous representation of the debate over the fate of the Mytileneans, where Kleon says that the Athenians in the Assembly act more like those who sit and watch sophists than those who take counsel for the city.[44] In this contrast, he proposes two models for the activity of an audience—the proper one, serious and active, and the other, frivolous and passive—and attempts to provoke the Assembly members into the former model. Amplifying these compact remarks, Victoria Wohl finds in Kleon's speech a theory of an active audience: more than spectators, vigorous judges exercise a critical self-mastery in relation to speakers and the pleasures of language.[45] James Andrews, on the other hand, finds an endorsement of *doxa*, ordinary folks' opinions formed on the basis of their experience of actions (*erga*), not of words (*logoi*).[46] Although these scholars are responding to an important hint in Thucydides' history, the few statements he puts into the mouths of his characters are, by themselves, a precarious basis for a historical analysis of the actual functioning of rhetoric in Athens.

Scholars reading ancient rhetorical manuals face similar problems. By reading Aristotle's *Rhetoric*, a manual for speakers, "in reverse,"[47] Susan Bickford offers a sustained account of the activity of *listening*.[48] She argues that Aristotle's theory of the mixed constitution recognizes the inherent conflict in politics, and that just as (so Aristotle says) rulers should not wrong either the ambitious in regard to honor or the masses in regard to money, so citizens must attend to others' needs and interests. Bickford interprets Aristotle's *Rhetoric* as an analysis of this art of paying attention, focusing on the ways that speakers, according to Aristotle, should attend to the characteristics of the audience in order to persuade them. She thus infers from Aristotle's advice to persuade with character, emotion, and argument that listeners must have weighed these same factors. Similarly, Antoine Braet locates the audience's active judgment in the *stasis* theory elaborated by the rhetorical writer Hermagoras (mid-second century BCE).[49] *Stasis* theory attempted to classify all possible types of arguments in a legal case. Although, as Braet acknowledges, *stasis* theory provided explicit guidance only for the speakers, not the judges, he understands it as containing "implicit instructions ... for the judging audience ... to reach an unbiased judgment as rationally as possible."[50]

But you can rely on these ancient authors only so far, since they focus mainly on the actions of speakers, treating listeners, to the degree that they treat them at all, as reactive. Whatever his characters may say (and it's not much beyond the remarks quoted above), Thucydides attributes little rational agency to the listeners in his debates. Virginia Hunter shows that when Thucydides represents crowds acting, they are acting largely irrationally. Pericles, however (at least in Thucydides' view), understands crowd psychology and can use rhetoric to control the mob.[51] Indeed, the distinction Thucydides draws between Pericles and other orators forms the basis of Harvey Yunis's analysis of the possibilities of "mature" democratic decision-making: whereas demagogues *persuade* (that is, use rhetoric to manipulate the audience), Pericles *instructs* (that is, provides full and accurate information on the basis of which the people can decide rightly).[52] Even this Periclean practice, however, does little to modify the persuasion model, since the rational agency of the audience depends entirely on a speaker bestowing it on them. As for Aristotle, as I noted above, whether you understand his treatise as a practical manual of rhetoric or as a theoretical analysis directed for the benefit of his pupils, it consistently takes up the position of the speaker.[53]

Still, these scholars' attempts to scavenge observations about the audience rest on an important insight: the system of rhetoric both enabled and circumscribed (but did not dictate) the activities of judges as well as those of speakers. Recognizing that the system of rhetoric created possibilities of speaking and of judging alike—even if in different ways—infuses a proper symmetry into the analysis.[54] Congruent with this insight, I offer two additional points from a systemic perspective about deciding. First, listeners faced a dichotomized choice—*x* or not *x*—the form of which had been determined outside rhetoric. Nevertheless, as I note later in this chapter, the formation of the choice could be subject to rhetorical critique and therefore the audience's *krisis*. Second, once the rhetorical process had been set in motion, the systemic outcome, a vote, was inevitable.[55] Members of the audience, then, did not need to decide *whether* to vote, but only which way.[56] The decision hung over the proceedings.

The most important element to enable and to shape deciding was what I call rhetorical resources, the kinds of things that typically were said in court. I will describe the major substantive aspects of rhetoric, the particular ways it simplified things, in the next section. Here I would like to concentrate on the three ways these rhetorical resources impinged upon the process of deciding, and on the consequences of this triangulation. First, from any particular speaker's perspective, rhetorical resources were what he could use to construct his speech and to try to persuade the listeners. Despite its limitations as an analysis of the system of rhetoric, persuasion theory accounts for this perspective.

Rhetorical resources affected deciding in a second way, through the opposing speech. Everything one speaker said, the other could potentially answer, critique, or rebut. Of course, few speakers rebutted every single claim their opponents made, but the competitive nature of the setting meant that there was an ineluctable and explicit critical dimension to rhetoric. A critical analysis of rhetorical discourse was an essential rhetorical resource.

Rhetorical resources entered into deciding in a third and decisive way: through the listeners' mastery of rhetoric. Jurors came to court with extensive background knowledge—of general facts, of common sense, and so forth, but especially of rhetoric itself. Audience members were not rhetorically naïve, gullible, or uninformed. For rhetorical language to persuade, it must first be recognized—that is, listeners must be proficient in rhetoric.[57] Further, Athenian audiences, repeatedly confronted with opposing speeches, which often explicitly and critically engaged with the other speech and with the rhetorical setting, must have become, as Thomas Schmitz argues, as shrewd and skeptical as any modern critic.[58] Thus, any speech was potentially judged not just against the opposing speech but against the background of many other speeches in the past. While speakers might attempt to activate the listeners' rhetorical knowledge for their own ends, I would not assume that listeners required such cues in order to call up their own critical rhetorical faculties.

This complexifying triangulation of rhetorical materials—from a speaker, his opponent, and the listeners' past experiences—means that auditors did not simply believe or accept what speakers said—not even the one they eventually voted for. Speeches (even the winning ones) constituted not descriptions of, or even templates for, decisions but only some of the materials for deciding. Thus, to take a trivial but telling example,

Aristotle misapprehends the way deciding worked when he writes that "hearers are affected to a degree also by that topic which speechwriters use all the time: 'Who does not know?' and 'Everybody knows.' The hearer agrees out of embarrassment so as to seem like everybody else."[59] But this can't be right, not only because the opposing speaker could expose this trope,[60] but also because it rests on the assumption that jurors have remembered nothing from their previous decision-making experiences.[61]

Ordinary Athenians acquired their rhetorical expertise in various ways. Although some Athenians may have sought out professional instruction in rhetoric—the scenario played out in Aristophanes' *Clouds* with disastrous results—most seem to have achieved competence through observation and practice.[62] Athenians lived in a world suffused with rhetorical language. Thousands of citizens heard speeches in the Assembly every few days, and the audience for trials included not only the hundreds of jurors but bystanders as well.[63] Like Aristophanes' character Praxagora, they may have mastered rhetoric simply by listening.[64] After their meetings adjourned, Athenians might critique speakers' rhetoric as they gathered in the agora, and they may have practiced their rhetorical skills at home.[65] They also made and heard speeches in their deme assemblies.[66]

To appreciate Athenians' rhetorical competence, return for a while to the shops and stalls of the agora, where many people passed time. Although ancient authors sometimes characterized the conversations in these spaces as joking, chatter, or gossip,[67] people spoke of serious matters, too.[68] At times, conversation may have turned to rumors about people's personal lives (e.g., about a man's sudden wealth)[69] or to boasts of sexual conquests,[70] but lots of the evidence suggests different subjects. In several passages, Aristophanes characterizes men in shops as discussing horse racing, tragedy, "weird and prickly stuff" (a dig at philosophy), and oratory—all topics that modern historians are willing to construe as important politically as well as culturally.[71] It's true that Aristophanes' representations are comic, but the jokes inhere in the language used rather than in the situation itself. Examine, for example, how Aristophanes lampooned the plans of his character Demos ("the People") to reform the polis by banning young men from hanging out in the agora: "I mean these teenagers in the perfume shops, who sit around chattering like this: 'Oh, Phaex is a sharp one, and how resourceful in beating that capital charge! He's intimidative, penetrative, aphoristically originative, clear and aggressive, and superlatively terminative of the obstreperative.'"[72] Aristophanes represents these young men not as gossiping about Phaex, a political figure of the day, not, that is, as spreading rumors about his personal life, but as practicing their ability to critique judicial rhetoric—even if doing so badly. Xenophon shows Socrates sometimes conducting his intellectual inquiries in shops,

even with the craftsmen themselves.[73] I do not intend to perpetuate a ste-
reotype of Athenians as exclusively high-minded intellectuals, but I want
to point out that the evidence suggests a range of conversations, from the
scurrilous to the serious, and that some of these conversations served as
rhetorical education.

People hanging out in the agora did more than talk; at times they acted
collectively, especially as mediators or judges of disputes. A story told by
Eleusinios, a character in one of Menander's comedies, illustrates both the
links between such informal situations and the institutions of the polis as
well as the active role of the people.[74] Eleusinios says he had been outside
the gates to the sacred precinct in Eleusis where people were coming for
a festival (*panegyris* [line 58]), a public space that may have held a temporary market or fair.[75] He came across a crowd (*oxlos*) hovering around a
young woman and two men who were disputing over the woman's status. Then, he says, "those standing around at once formed an assembly
(*demos*)."[76] The crowd, that is, constituted itself as a body to judge the dispute. While the disputants did most of the talking, the crowd (through
unattributed interjections) controlled the debate by cajoling, question-
ing, and challenging the parties and by shouting its judgment as the process went forward. This scene constitutes one of the "forensic scenarios"
analyzed by Adele Scafuro, a set of conventional behaviors shared among
litigation, daily life, and comedy.[77] The scene-setting here is more complex still because it also repeatedly references an earlier trial scene in Euripides' *Orestes*,[78] but the differences between the scenes are as significant
as their shared language. Euripides' character recounts a formal meeting
of the Assembly on the hill marked out for this purpose, not a crowd in an
undifferentiated and possibly commercial public space, which intervenes
on its own initiative. Euripides' formal meeting proceeds by set speeches
of specific individuals, in which the only activity in the audience's role is
to decide at the end, a contrast to a contemporary Athenian trial, where
the jurors frequently and actively intervened in the proceedings. Thus,
through their transformation, Menander's literary borrowings emphasize
how his scene uses the same conventional behaviors found in contemporary trials and daily life. The story Epicrates told the jurors of his conflict
with Athenogenes follows a similar scenario. In his dispute with Athenogenes over a contract, he tracked him down near the perfume shops
and confronted him. There they argued, and then "many people gathered around, and they listened in on the business (since the speeches were
happening in the agora), and they blamed him, and urged us to arrest him
as a kidnapper."[79] Epicrates may have shaped his story for his own ends
in saying that the crowd supported him, but this too shows the actions a
crowd could take in a public place, and it conforms to other stories where

a crowd intervenes in a dispute or fight and attempts to put a stop to it with words, sometimes successfully, sometimes not.[80] Indeed, someone who felt he had been wronged might mingle with the crowd and sit in the shops telling his story,[81] so that shoppers could consider themselves competent judges not only of rhetoric but also of justice.

Rhetorical Resources

Large groups could decide things because rhetorical language provided a simplifying code. Rhetorical resources not only provided the materials for speakers to construct their speeches; they also constituted the framework for large groups of listeners to make decisions. Although I believe the following account represents Athenian legal rhetoric accurately and substantially, it is neither an exhaustive nor a methodical taxonomy. While ancient writing about rhetoric increasingly tended toward such systematization, culminating in the elaborate minutiae of *stasis* theory in the Roman period, the practice of rhetoric in the classical period, at least, did not conform to rigid schemes. My account, while based significantly on my previous book, draws heavily from the many fine scholarly works in the last decade or two on the content of Athenian legal rhetoric. I will describe five broad patterns in Athenian legal rhetoric: narrative form, use of law, construction of character, invocation of emotion, and reliance on probabilities, and then in the next section a sixth, the critical reflection on rhetoric itself. Each of these patterns provided a circumscribed set of possible things to say, which made matters decidable by a large group.

Athenian litigants told stories.[82] The most salient feature of these stories was that they converged on a single, definite act that could be said to contravene a law, in other words a "crime."[83] Although people might articulate grievances that are diffuse and unfocused or complicated and ongoing, prosecutors in court emphasized just one act. Take the case of Ariston, a young man who felt he had been harassed by the sons of a man called Konon. They had tormented Ariston's slaves and hurled insults at him and at his brother as well. This antagonism between groups of young men, however, constitutes background to the decisive incident in Ariston's story: Konon himself struck Ariston and made an insulting gesture.[84] Ariston's narrative embodies an important feature of Athenian legal stories: they dichotomized conflict. Many disputes (like Ariston's) involve multiple parties, each potentially with their own version of the conflict. In court, however, there was a prosecutor and a defendant, and jurors had only to choose between them.[85] Moreover, because only men could address the court, disputes involving others had to be transformed into legal stories about conflicts between men in order to be litigated.[86] In another

instance, a wife,[87] jealous that her husband, Euphiletos, had been coerc-
ing sex from their slave, took a lover, Eratosthenes. The lover's former
mistress, angered that she had now been superseded, informed Euphiletos, who then kept a more careful watch on his wife. One night, when the
lover had sneaked into the house, the husband surprised him and killed
him. One of the dead man's relatives charged Euphiletos with murder.[88]
(Although the law allowed a husband to kill an adulterer caught in the act
with his wife, Eratosthenes' relatives claimed that Euphiletos had lured
him into the house and killed him with callous forethought.) The rhetorical story simplified the situation: The jurors had only to decide between
the two men; the grievances of the three women (the slave, the wife, and
the lover's former mistress) were not—and could not be—at issue.

So far I have described the archetype of a prosecutor's story; defendants had alternatives. Defendants could take up the crime narrative—
and twist it by making the prosecutor the person responsible. One defendant in an assault case freely retold the story of the fight, but made
the prosecutor the initiator of the violence.[89] Defendants might also tell a
story that focused on the prosecutor's decision to litigate, representing the
prosecutor in the stock type of the *sykophant*, an abuser of the judicial system who brought groundless cases for profit, political motives, or petty
personal revenge.[90] In this way the decision to litigate, to initiate the rhetorical process, a decision that was itself extra-rhetorical, could be subject
to rhetorical review and critique. Such stories could represent as trivial
and unworthy of litigation an incident the prosecutor qualified as a crime.
Ariston anticipated that Konon would say just this, dismissing the fight as
tipsy young men scuffling over girls and claiming that the decision to sue
was unreasonable and vindictive.[91] Finally, defendants sometimes simply
denied the logic and coherence of the prosecutor's tale, but offered no alternative story. Few defendants presented their case without a competing
story, however, suggesting that jurors expected and responded positively
to the narrative form.

Athenian litigants invoked the law.[92] When describing an incident as
a crime, Athenian litigants infused their stories with law. They also represented laws as both actual and proper motives and standards for human action, thus using them to delineate their own and their opponent's
characters.[93] Speakers in the Athenian courts frequently paraphrased laws
or had the court clerk read them out verbatim. In making arguments
about the meaning of laws (which frequently named crimes without defining them), litigants appealed to the intentions of "the lawgiver"—the
putative single author of a consistent set of laws—often relying on the
method of "glossing" used to interpret Homer's poems.[94] "The lawgiver,"
however, was a fiction; Athenian laws had been drafted over the course

of a couple of centuries, with hundreds if not thousands of people in-volved each time.[95] No record was kept of the Assembly's meetings. But the fiction of the lawgiver allowed them to see the body of laws as a con-sistent outcome of a uniform intention. That way, an interpretation of one law could be based on others. Take the case of Epicrates, who wished to invalidate a contract he'd made with Athenogenes. (You may recall Epicrates from earlier in this chapter and from chapter 4.) Epicrates had purchased a perfume-making business from Athenogenes and agreed in a written contract to assume miscellaneous, unspecified debts. As it turned out later, these various debts added up to more than five times the pur-chase price. (Epicrates had become infatuated with one of the slaves who worked in the shop and in his eagerness to consummate the sale had failed to inquire about the details.) On his side, Athenogenes could cite a law that held all private agreements to be binding. Epicrates sought to limit the scope of that law to only *fair* agreements (though the law did not in-clude that wording) by invoking other laws, which, he argued, explic-itly made such an exception: for example, the law that invalidated wills made under the influence of compulsion, senility, insanity, sickness, or a woman.[96] Epicrates, then, argued for the real meaning of a particular law by setting it next to other laws, which were said to express the lawgiver's uniform intentions.

Athenian litigants made arguments about each other's characters.[97] Here I refer not just to the projection of *ethos* so prominent in ancient rhe-torical manuals, but to the ways in which they made a defendant's life and character an issue, yet not, to the same extent, the prosecutor's. This may seem natural to us, for whom a prosecutor in criminal cases is an impartial state official, not a litigant. But because Athenian prosecutors were private individuals, often the party claiming injury, jurors in an assault trial, for example, might have to decide which of two litigants hit the other one first. Nevertheless, it was mainly defendants who brought up their litur-gies and other services to the state as important considerations for the ju-rors to weigh. Except in certain kinds of cases (for example, determining the disposition of an inheritance), prosecutors rarely mentioned such mat-ters.[98] On the other hand, litigants did discuss the prosecutor's character with respect to his decision to transform the dispute into a legal case, es-pecially through *sykophancy*. The idea of *sykophancy* allowed Athenians to reflect on their own legal system and litigiousness, but it also enabled de-fendants to make arguments about the validity of the cases against them, including the prosecutor's decision to rely on rhetoric (a necessary conse-quence of the decision to litigate).

Athenian litigants used the language of emotion to appeal to jurors. You should not understand these appeals, however, primarily as incite-ments to irrationality; rather, they invoked structured social relationships of action. Litigants appealed to a reductive dichotomy of emotions, usually anger or pity, prosecutors appealing to the former, defendants to the latter.[99] Such appeals confound simple oppositions between emotion and reason.[100] On their side, litigants invoked emotions by making arguments and providing reasons, so that anger or pity were the *effect* of rational discourse, not an alternative to it.[101] One defendant concluded: "If we seem to have spoken plausibly and to have provided sufficient proofs, men of the jury, by every means and manner pity us."[102] Even more importantly, jurors did not react automatically but actively exercised *krisis*. I emphasized earlier that one of the essential aspects of judgment was that it culminated in a vote; this impending action deeply affected the jurors' empathy. Rüdiger Campe has recently argued that the narrative structures of rhetoric create the possibility of empathy; indeed, he takes ancient rhetoric as the model for empathy in general, because rhetoric—an encounter between the subject and the other framed by rhetorical conventions—shows that institutional frames are a universal condition for the social relation implied in empathy.[103] In his reading of Aristotle, Campe sees jurors as open to passions because of gaps in the determinative conditions of judgment: the law could not cover all aspects of all situations (and so left room for emotions), and jurors were judging the affairs of others, which they could not know completely.[104] Both of these explanations, however, seem accidental: Why should the gaps be filled by emotions, as opposed to customs, social influence, or anything else? But it's possible to point to two necessary reasons—structural conditions of rhetoric—why Athenian jurors might experience empathy, both deriving from the impending vote.[105] First, as many have argued, choice is not possible without an essential emotional component, and jurors had to choose. Second, the emotional narratives that litigants offered to jurors would only be complete with the final verdict. Jurors experienced anger or pity only when they voted for one of the litigants. Indeed, the language of litigants, as in the above-quoted defendant's plea to the jurors, frequently conflated the emotion with the vote. To pity was to acquit. Or, as Danielle Allen (2000) has shown, jurors shared the prosecutor's anger when they punished, that is, convicted. Thus Diodoros concluded his prosecution of Timocrates: "Because of everything I've said, it's important to become angry, to punish, and to make an example of him for others."[106] Here, as often with Greek language of emotions, what mattered was a behavior, not a feeling.[107] The end and completion of empathy was an action, the vote.[108]

Athenian litigants relied on arguments based on *eikos*.[109] Although *eikos* is usually translated as "probability," David Hoffman (2008) makes a strong case that it denoted not probability but likeness or similarity—that it was a qualitative assessment, not a quantitative one. Even when witnesses directly supported litigants' claims, they appealed to *eikos* as well. For example, in the case of one defendant charged with attempted murder, the prosecutor, named Simon, claimed that the defendant had come to his house alone and assaulted him with a weapon, a fragment of pottery. The defendant, after presenting witnesses who testified that the brawl had occurred in the marketplace and that Simon had started it, proceeded to argue what seemed likely: "Who would find it credible that with full intent and deliberation I came to Simon's house in the daytime ... when there was such a large number of people gathered there, unless I was so deranged as to wish to fight alone against large numbers?" This idea, he concluded, is "more unintelligible than likely."[110]

Although this list is not exhaustive, it should be enough to show that rhetoric considerably reduced the complexity of disputes in order to make them decidable. It dichotomized cases, prosecutor versus defendant, reducing all other people with interests to witnesses or just bystanders. It kept both women and slaves from speaking, thus dodging the troublesome issue of how to weigh the testimony of people of different statuses.[111] When litigants appealed to an audience's emotions, they did so in a relatively narrow range, especially on an axis of anger versus pity. When making arguments about their own and their opponent's character, they emphasized dedication to the city and to family (especially to fathers), and, for the prosecutor, what his decision to litigate revealed. Rhetorical conventions constrained both litigants and jurors.

Beyond this, the rhetorical setting consistently imposed a reliance on rhetorical language for arguing and deciding. Litigants did not use physical evidence. Witnesses' testimony during most of the fourth century consisted of a statement drafted by a litigant and entirely subordinated to the litigant's speech; the statement was read out by the clerk, and the witness assented to it (or, sometimes, didn't). No external (nonrhetorical) authority instructed the jurors—about the meaning of laws, for example, which was a subject of rhetorical argument rather than of authoritative pronouncement. And, finally, the balloting was secret, which minimized external influences (whether the surveillance of the powerful or merely the knowledge of previous votes of other jurors in the case) and focused each juror's decision on what people said in the court.[112]

Risks of Rhetoric

Speakers in the Athenian courts routinely commented on the limitations, problems, and risks of rhetorical language. Although such critiques were hardly impartial—they were, after all, interested attempts to persuade—

they performed an important function within the system of rhetoric, stabilizing and checking rhetorical language.[113]

You could point to a number of risks of rhetoric. Speakers might corrupt the process with illegitimate motives: a prosecutor might bring a charge against someone simply to extort money or for revenge, or he might try to gain an advantage by using an incorrect procedure. Aristotle, indeed, attempted to distinguish those *rhetors* who simply exercise their power from the ones who do so on the basis of moral choice.[114] Speakers, including witnesses, might use deceptive language, lie, or conceal or misrepresent the truth. They might introduce irrelevancies, compelling the opponent to spend time responding and perhaps winning over some of the audience with points outside the subject. Listeners, for their part, might lose sight of the ends and concentrate on the means, casting their vote on the basis of the pleasure they derived from a speaker's language rather than the substantive content of his speech. Thucydides' Kleon famously condemns the Athenians for such indulgence, likening them (as I noted previously) to those who took pleasure in sophists' displays.[115] A cunning speaker might work an audience into an emotional frenzy.

Nevertheless, rhetoric took account of and adjudicated almost every risk. For any problem you could name—for all the ones described above and many more—you will find speakers bringing it to the attention of listeners. The competitive structure of rhetoric, the fact that there was always an opposing speaker, promoted a sustained critical discourse on rhetoric. There is no reason to think that jurors decided without having considered the possible perils of the language that provided the materials for their decision. Still, it's important to take account of the particular configurations of this rhetorical reflexivity. I draw your attention to four: the absence of hierarchical authority, the clustering of various factors into a single decision, the potential to rhetorically review the invocation of rhetoric, and system-level recursiveness. All of these relate to rhetoric not simply as a linguistic code but as a system as I've defined it.

Rhetoric was regulated almost entirely rhetorically; that is, just as large groups decided cases based on competing speeches, so they weighed the risks of rhetoric, a process Jon Hesk has called the self-policing of rhetoric. Some scholars have made much of a notable absence: the lack of almost any external and independent authority to control what speakers said or what jurors heard and considered, the equivalent of a modern judge. Although a magistrate presided over trials, he never intervened, and it makes little sense to call him a "judge." Yet despite the absence of such an authority, rhetoric managed to regulate itself.[116]

The recursiveness of rhetoric operated through the jurors' *krisis*, which was formally expressed only once, in their vote, so that all matters were clustered in a single decision. Because of the difficulty of mobilizing the conglomerate authority of hundreds of jurors—who could act authoritatively only through a vote—and because there was no other authority in the court, problematic rhetorical practices were remedied only after the fact through the jurors' final *krisis*, not beforehand through interdiction as a judge in an American court would do. The rhetorical process presented all elements, including considerations of rhetorical risks, holistically. For example, while a litigant sometimes claimed that his opponent spoke "outside the subject,"[117] he could recommend that jurors not only reject such irrelevant arguments,[118] but also count his opponent's inapposite remarks against him when they make their decision. As one defendant put it: "Whenever someone makes an accusation regarding something other than the subject of the prosecution, as in the present suit, it is less proper to trust him than to distrust him."[119] While Athenian litigants may have spoken "outside the subject," they still faced potential consequences.

Even to the degree that the Athenian legal system disaggregated important problems for discrete consideration, these were still decided rhetorically. Three procedures allowed for such disaggregation. The procedure of *paragraphe* allowed a defendant to challenge the prosecutor's procedural choices. The *paragraphe* suspended the original suit and began a second, in which, essentially, the litigants switched roles, the original defendant now charging the prosecutor with bringing a case illegally. (This could occur because the prosecutor had waited longer than the law allowed to bring his case, or because the dispute had previously been legally settled.) Only if the original prosecutor won the *paragraphe* did the original suit go to trial. I offer two observations about this procedure. First, although it separated out an issue for specific consideration, that consideration was still entirely rhetorical, decided by an ordinary Athenian jury. Second, as shown by the preserved speeches from this procedure, both litigants argued not only the specific procedural claims but the original case as well. An older procedure, *diamartyria*, in some cases allowed a witness to assert a fact on oath, which automatically settled the case unless the opponent charged him with false witnessing. (In the fourth century, litigants used this procedure mostly in inheritance cases, where it had the effect of transforming a multiparty case, a *diadikasia*, into a dichotomized choice, guilt or innocence of false witnessing.) As for the third procedure, the suit for false witnessing, though it occurred after the fact (after the *diamartyria* or a case in which someone had testified), it too was adjudicated rhetorically, and speakers routinely rehearsed the original case in addition to the specific procedural claim of false testimony. Thus, none of these procedures completely disaggregated—although they did highlight—the specific procedural point from the whole context of the case. They remained fully rhetorical insofar as they generated a new court hearing, though they also transformed the case by redistributing rhetorical resources to the litigants by changing or reversing their roles.

Even the most decisive extra-rhetorical aspect of rhetoric—the decision to take up rhetoric, to litigate, to formulate the charge or proposal—was routinely subject to rhetorical review. When a man decided to initiate a legal case, whether he thought himself the victim of a crime or stood up as a volunteer prosecutor, just as when a man made a proposal to the Assembly, the decision itself was not arrived at through rhetoric.[120] It was a crucial decision, one that allowed the man great power, and it might be subject to abuse. But in the case of litigation, not only did certain prior factors confer gravity on the decision (the cost of litigation, or the penalty for a prosecutor in a public case who failed to win one fifth of the votes), but the decision was subject to review in litigation itself. As noted above, both the allegation of *sykophancy* and the things defendants alleged about prosecutors allowed jurors to review the appropriateness of the decision to litigate. With regard to proposals in the Assembly, not only could a proposer's motives be scrutinized during debate on the measure, but after it was passed he could be held legally accountable through *graphe* procedures.

One significant limitation remained to rhetorical scrutiny of the invocation of rhetoric: only positive choices to take up rhetoric could be so reviewed; someone who decided *not* to initiate a case or to make a proposal could not be held accountable. So if Athenians litigated too much, as some have argued,[121] their litigiousness may have functioned to allow rhetorical review of more decisions to take up rhetoric. (The system "overproduced" litigation in order to sufficiently scrutinize extra-rhetorical decisions.) But the system of rhetoric was incapable of adjudicating what was *not* brought to its attention, hence the Athenians' concern about those who had dropped or settled cases before trial, or about collusion by their politicians.[122]

There remained one potential problem that rhetoric itself may not have been fully able to regulate: the system itself could fail. A danger in any system is that its functioning may generate conditions that lead to its breakdown; in the case of rhetoric, rhetorical language could prevent (rather than enable) deciding. For example, one side might convince the audience to not even listen to the other.[123] Some speakers may have tried such a tactic,[124] attempting to provoke the audience's *thorubos* to drown out their opponents.[125] Yet rhetoric provided resources to argue against such tactics.[126] In the courts, defendants (who spoke second) appealed for the audience's favor (*eunoia*), citing the jurors' oath.[127] There seems, moreover, to have been a general sense that jurors ought to listen to both sides before deciding, an idea that their oath explicitly required.[128] As the chorus leader in Aristophanes' *Wasps* says, apparently paraphrasing a proverb: "The guy was wise who said, 'Don't judge before you've heard the story from both sides.'"[129] For this argument to be heard, of course, the incitement not to listen would already have to have failed. This, then, represented a rhetorical problem that rhetoric itself could not solve.

A full account of the ways in which the system of rhetoric regulated itself must also consider how the listeners used rhetorical materials in coming to a judgment. The recursive rhetorical language of speakers—which explicitly reflected on the operations and limits of rhetoric—always aimed to persuade, so it could never fully objectify and analyze itself. Because speakers deployed such analyses strategically, they did so asymmetrically, arguing that what they said was truth—facts, not words!—whereas their opponent's speech was deceptive.[130] This was equally true both in the courts and in the Assembly, where Demosthenes' speeches show him repeatedly bringing to the listeners' attention the dynamics of rhetorical practice, its potential limitations or dangers, and their own complicity in it—but always in the service of convincing them he was right, his opponents wrong, in both policy and rhetorical methods.[131]

The judgments of jurors, however, differed in profound ways from the arguments of speakers. Like modern scholars, jurors understood a speech in relation to the possible rhetorical resources; unlike modern scholars, they also considered it in relation to the opposing speech. In the process of judging or deciding, listeners folded the speakers' asymmetric claims into a process that cannot be explained by or reduced to the arguments of either speaker. Although this *krisis* was not objectified or articulated for subsequent use (as in a written justification), it remained available for the individual listener to rely on, if later called to sit in judgment,[132] and it could be shared with others orally in informal discussions of legal cases, legislation, and rhetoric.

Conclusion: Rhetoric and Trust

In the analysis of rhetoric, the concept of trust is an important analytical complement to that of authority. Scholars often theorize the role of language in terms of a speaker's authority. There are competing models of how speakers' authority might work: Ruth Amossy contrasts those (like John Austin) who understand language to create effects, conferring power on speakers, with those (like Pierre Bourdieu) who think that language reflects or expresses the social position of speakers.[133] Amossy herself posits a middle way, which recognizes both speakers' reputations and their ability to linguistically manipulate them.

The concept of authority is not without its uses in analyzing ancient Greek rhetoric. Those who spoke in the Assembly and the courts did so by virtue of a qualifying, pre-rhetorical authority: they were free, male, and usually citizens. Neither women nor slaves spoke in rhetorical settings, and noncitizens did so only under limited circumstances. Thus, when Aristophanes comically staged a female coup d'état in the Assembly, he represented the women of Athens as appropriating the trappings of male citizen authority: their clothes and walking sticks, their beards, and their masculine manner of speaking.[134] Only when guised as men do the ladies both address and vote in the Assembly, thus seeming to confirm the idea that social standing determines authority. But Aristophanes' play also demonstrates the multifaceted way in which speakers had to enact this authority through their appearance, their manner, and their speech. Even the indisputable pre-rhetorical authority of speakers was—or might be—created through rhetoric. As I have argued previously, Athenian litigants frequently attempted to invoke extra-rhetorical authority—of character, of public services, of ritual, of facts, of truth—but always significantly through rhetorical language.[135]

However, the same limitation hampers whatever formula you choose for the relation of speech to authority. Rooted in the persuasion model, the notion of authority does not account for multiple, opposing speakers, all of whom, insofar as they met the social requirements to address the audience, had a qualifying authority; nor does that notion allow any discretion or activity for the listeners, who, in rhetorical situations, did not accede to authority (linguistic or social) but judged and decided between speeches.

The judges' active relation to speech in rhetorical settings is better analyzed with the idea of trust—or, rather, distrust. It is tempting to understand the effect of a speech as creating the listeners' trust in the speaker, as I myself argued in *Disputes and Democracy*. But I now think this argument is poorly grounded. In the contexts I have been discussing here, "trust" is otiose because it merely renames—but does not explain—a listener's vote.[136] The term is also misleading because it seems more likely that the effect of competing speeches was to incite the listeners' distrust of both speakers. It is difficult to know, of course, how jurors reacted typically or in any specific case, but three phenomena arouse skepticism of the trust theory. First, the starkly dichotomized choice presented to listeners—x or not x, a choice imposed on the listeners—must sometimes have seemed unfairly artificial. This sentiment seems to have motivated Hippodamus's proposal that jurors not be forced to vote inflexibly for either condemnation or acquittal, but be allowed to offer a range of intermediate verdicts.[137] Second, speakers persistently attacked their opponents. In particular, the critical reflection on rhetoric offered by rhetoric was usually more about denigrating your opponent's language than firmly establishing your own. Third, if modern scholars offer any guide to how ancient jurors reacted to speeches, suspicion must have been the norm. From William Wyse's ferocious commentary on the speeches of Isaeus to Michael Gagarin's measured assessment of Antiphon's *Against Herodes*, scholars often conclude that the opposing (missing) speech must have been the better one.[138] The jurors' decision, then, must have often come down to a pair of disfavored alternatives, the "lesser of two evils," a choice that hinged on comparative distrust.

Although listeners may often have distrusted particular speakers, they seem to have retained trust in the system of rhetoric as a whole. Impersonal trust usefully names people's continued assent to and participation in the system. But there are limited grounds for asserting a relationship between impersonal trust in the system of rhetoric and personal relations of trust beyond it. As I noted in chapter 1, there is little evidence in Greek antiquity for the civil-society theory of democratic trust, the idea that people's trust in the abstract systems of democracy depends on personal relationships of trust fostered in more intimate settings. Nevertheless, the personal relationships of distrust generated by the system—the suspicion of speakers—do not seem to have reinfected jurors' trust in rhetoric itself. Despite the persistent critical impulse in rhetorical language, people continued to decide things rhetorically. The system somehow limited the distrust it generated. I would suggest two explanations. First, speakers usually aimed their critiques not at rhetoric in general but at their opponent's *misuse* of rhetorical language. The fact that critique always remained subordinated to an attempt to persuade a large audience seems to have insulated the system as a whole. Second, the theory of cognitive dissonance and modern experiments suggest that the necessity of choosing (a necessity that does not weigh on modern scholars) probably resulted in significantly increasing the appraisal of the chosen alternative after the fact.[139] This subsequent unconscious reappraisal would confirm people's sense that rhetoric created good choices.

The intense and sometimes vicious recursiveness of Athenian rhetoric may have generated distrust in particular speakers, or specific speeches, or even in rhetorical language generally, but it does not seem to have produced a widespread rejection of the system of rhetoric. Indeed, the pervasive distrust of speakers and speeches actually seems to have allowed the system to regulate itself, stabilizing it and producing a generalized trust. People lodged this trust not in the character of speakers or the truthfulness of speeches, but in each other, in their individual and collective *krisis*, and in the lateral relationships among citizens that were forged through the process of deciding.

COMMON GREEK
WEIGHTS AND MEASURES

WEIGHTS AND CURRENCY VALUES

6 obols	=	1 drachma
60 drachma	=	1 mina
100 minai	=	1 talent

In Athens a mina weighed 431 grams or about a pound.

DRY MEASURES

4 kotylai	=	1 choinix
8 choinikes	=	1 hekteus
6 hekteis	=	1 medimnos

LIQUID MEASURES

12 kotylai	=	1 chous
12 choes	=	1 metretes

For both dry and liquid measures, the kotyle usually fell between 240 and 270 ml. (depending on the city), just a bit more than a cup.

NOTES

PREFACE

1. *The Education of Henry Adams*, ed. Ernest Samuels (Boston: Houghton Mifflin, 1974), 300–301.

CHAPTER ONE: INTRODUCTION

1. Eubulides first proposed the paradox in the fourth century, possibly in critique of Aristotle's idea of the mean (Moline 1969). Except for bibliographic items, all dates are BCE unless noted otherwise.

2. Prier 1976; Jouanna 2008, 40, 48.

3. Strabo (14.1.27) quotes this six-line fragment (Hesiod fr. 278 [MW]):

θαῦμά μ' ἔχει κατὰ θυμόν, ἐρινεὸς ὅσσον ὀλύνθων
οὗτος ἔχει, μικρός περ ἐών· εἴποις ἂν ἀριθμόν;
μυρίοι εἰσιν ἀριθμόν, ἀτὰρ μέτρον γε μέδιμνος·
εἷς δὲ περισσεύει, τὸν ἐπενθέμεν οὔ κε δύναιο.
ὣς φάτο, καί σφιν ἀριθμὸς ἐτήτυμος εἴδετο μέτρου.
καὶ τότε δὴ Κάλχανθ' ὕπνος θανάτοιο κάλυψεν.

All translations are my own unless noted otherwise. Baldriga 1994 discusses this text and other myths involving Mopsos.

4. μυρίοι εἰσιν ἀριθμόν. Editors, however, usually construe (and accent) the text as μύριοί εἰσιν ἀριθμόν, "the number is ten thousand." This seems less likely because it obviates the adversative force of the next word, ἀτὰρ ("but"), because it leaves the next line and a half superfluous, and because *murioi* does not clearly mean exactly 10,000 until the fifth century (West 1978, 220).

5. Hdt. 1.47.

6. Thus, to represent a profusion, authors described objects in heaps: heaps of grain (Hdt.1.21–22), of money (Aristoph. *Wealth* 269), of salted meat (Theopompos fr. 263), or of dead bodies (Xen. *Hell.* 4.4.12). Along these lines, I might mention "a whole heap of trouble." The heap, however, was multiform: Aristotle sometimes used it to represent a collection that lacked organic unity (Bogaard 1979, 12), a meaning (I hope) not relevant here.

7. Giddens 1990, 100–111, for example, draws this line.

8. Luhmann 1979; 1986; Giddens 1990; 1992. Sociologists have concentrated on trust recently, using it as a way of analyzing the particular configurations, problems, and possibilities of modernity. Misztal 1996 gives an overview of this literature.

9. Putnam 1993; 2000.

10. Arist. *Pol.* 1326a5–b25. Equally famously, Athens was much larger than his maximum.

11. Jones 1999 explicitly draws on modern theories of civil society, arguing that a range of public, quasi-public, and voluntary associations existed in relation to democratic politics. (Connor 1996 covers some of the same ground. Cf. Schmitt-Pantel 1990.) Osborne 1994 sees the groups that citizens belonged to—family, phratry, deme, tribe—as creating an ideological homogeneity that allowed the democracy to function. Millett 1991 argues that the reciprocity among citizens was fundamentally established in the lending and borrowing (of everything from small household items to substantial sums of cash) that pervaded Athenian society. (In his chapter 5, Millett draws his theory explicitly from Aristotle. Cf. Schofield 1998.) Finally, Strauss 1996 argues that the poorest Athenians, the Thetes, gained self-confidence and an appreciation of their political power through service in the navy.

12. J. Cohen 1999, 219–21.

13. Delhey and Newton 2003 find little statistical evidence that individuals' participation in voluntary organizations leads to a general feeling of trusting others. Nannestad 2008 surveys many studies, and concludes there's little evidence for the theory that civil society generates social capital.

14. Luhmann 1979, 71. Giddens 1990, 99–100, suggests both trust and mistrust oppose dread, angst, and paralysis.

15. Arist. *Pol.* 1253b3–13.

16. Arist. *Pol.* 1259a40–b18.

17. Chapter 4 takes this up in detail; it may be that it was simply too exhausting to try to be a despot all the time.

18. Bourdieu 1977; 1990.

19. Because the history of Greece and of Athens during the classical period is relatively well known, and because reliable surveys are easily available (on the web and elsewhere), I have not here provided a potted background narrative.

20. Fr. 125, trans. Kahn 1979, 85. In deference to one of my first teachers of Greek, John McDiarmid, I have to acknowledge that the commonly emended Greek in this especially vexed quotation well may not represent what Heraclitus said (McDiarmid 1941). Still, it's a lovely idea, isn't it, that a heap might contain the most beautifully ordered things?

CHAPTER TWO: HAGGLING

1. Eur. *Cyc.* 137: ἐκφέρετε· φῶς γὰρ ἐμπολήμασιν πρέπει. This seems to have been a variation on a common saying: Plato *Laws* 778c and Dem. 19.12 offer variations.

2. Eur. *Cyc.* 150: δίκαιον· ἡ γὰρ γεῦμα τὴν ὠνὴν καλεῖ.

3. I treat this in detail later in this chapter.

4. Fanselow 1990 makes this point in his critique of the model of the bazaar offered by Geertz 1978. Bresson 2008, 35–39, discusses this information asymmetry in Greek markets.

5. Cicero reports (*de Officiis* 3.50–55) that second-century Stoics used this information asymmetry to explore conflicts between advantage and morality: this focused on whether sellers had any obligation to disclose private information about faults of the goods, which would give buyers an advantage in bargaining. Schofield 1999, 160–77, discusses this passage.

6. Some scholars have doubted Plato's authorship of *Hipparchus*, though it's clearly an ancient text. Plax 2005 is an interesting, if not completely successful, attempt to make sense of this enigmatic work.

7. Plato, *Hipparch.* 225a.

8. Fanselow 1990, 251–52. Alexander 1992, 86–88, may be correct that modern shoppers know less about products than ancient buyers (because of the complexities of the division of labor and the vast number of products), but this creates an information asymmetry between manufacturers and consumers, not between sellers and buyers. (Sales people sometimes know less about complex products than well-informed shoppers.) In the contemporary world, posted prices are related not merely to problems of delegation in large organizations, but specifically to the relative ignorance of sales people about what they're selling.

9. Brown 1994.

10. E.g., Geertz 1978; Alexander and Alexander 1991. Cf. Mayhew 1994.

11. North 1984; 1987; 1991.

12. De Marchi and Moran 1994, 3–4.

13. In an experimental setting Cason, Friedman, and Milam 2003, 241, found that bargaining brought greater profits to sellers than fixed prices did.

14. If Greek writers could imagine a "free agora," an agora purged of all economic activities (Xen. *Kyr.* 1.2.3 attributes this to the Persians, and Arist. *Pol.* 1331a31–b14 ascribes this ideal to the Thessalians), they did so by bifurcating the activities and creating two agoras, one "free," the other commercial. Herodotus (1.153) reports not that the Persians had an agora purged of economics, but that they had neither agoras nor buying and selling, a statement that closely links the place and the activities.

15. One of archaeologists' major concerns has been mapping the Athenian agora: Wycherley 1956 (briefly) and Thompson and Wycherley 1972 (in great detail).

16. Cahill 2002, 266–76, infers the presence of shops in a significant number of houses from rooms that opened directly onto the street.

17. E.g., Xen. *Oik.* 8.22.

18. Thompson and Wycherley 1972, 171–72.

19. S. Johnstone 2002, 247. Alexis fr. 9 (=Athen. 10.431e) mentions carts.

20. De Ligt and de Neeve 1988. Menander fr. 481.

21. Antiphanes fr. 68 (=Athen. 8.358d–e), where a fish seller ventured out into the countryside.

22. Aristoph. *Lys.* 404–19; Theophr. *Char.* 24.7.

23. Gallant 1991, 92–94. Moreno 2007, 37–76, argues that many of the farms in one Attic deme, Euonymon, produced substantial amounts of agricultural produce for the market, where they also must have bought much of what they ate.

24. Arist. *Oik.* 1344b31–34. I discuss this in more detail in chapter 4.

25. Xen. *Poroi* 1.6–7; 5.2–4; Thuc. 2.38; Old Oligarch 2.7, 11–12; Isoc. 4.42; Dem. 8.67.

26. E. Harris 2002, esp. 88–97.

27. Critias fr. 70; Nikophon fr. 9 (=Athen.3.126e–f).

28. Hermippos 63 (=Athen. 1.27e–28a).

29. Aristoph. fr. 569 (=Athen. 9.372b–d).

30. Aristoph. *Peace* 999–1009; cf. Aristoph. *Achar.* 874–80.

31. Compton-Engle 1999.

32. Vlassopoulos 2007, 41–46, discusses these in detail.

33. Aristoph. fr. 139 (=Athen. 3.109f), *Wasps* 238, *Frogs* 858, *Lys.* 457–8, *Frogs* 1346–51.

34. Brock 1994 concerns the kinds of labor women did, which sometimes also involved selling. S. Johnstone 2002 examines some legal aspects of free women as merchants. S. Johnstone 2003 analyzes women's control of property.

35. Brock 1994, 338–41. A character in a fragment of a comedy by Pherekrates says that no one has ever seen a female butcher or fish seller (fr. 64 [= Athen. 8.612a–b]).

36. Although a law limited the value of transactions women could effect (S. Johnstone 2003), women simply didn't have as much wealth as men (cf. Forman and Riegelhapt, 1970, 197).

37. Lys. 22 concerns metic grain retailers.

38. Plato, *Rep.* 371c–d.

39. Plato *Rep.* 557d, Bion fr. 13, and Anaxippos fr. 1 use the *pantopolion* as a metaphor for a place with lots of different stuff. Theophr. *On Stones* 53 attests to ocher; Aeneas 30.1 to arms. Some of these must have been quite modest to judge by the slave in Menander, who imagines operating a *pantopolion* as an independent but humble existence (*Pk.* 283–85).

40. Lys. 1.8 and 16 show a female slave sent to shop on her own, though she also might accompany her owner (§18). Theophrastus says a mistrustful man will send two slaves, the first to shop, the second to check up on him (*Char.* 18. 2).

41. Fox 1996, 147.

42. Aristoph. *Wasps* 605–12; Aristoph. *Ekk.* 228; cf. Theophr. *Char.* 28.4.

43. Xen. *Oik.* 3.10–16.

44. Xen. *Oik.* 7.19–32; 8.22. Moreover, the major expenditure of a wealthy oikos like that depicted in this text was not food or supplies, but liturgies—something a wife had no control over. In fact, the cost of such public services was an impetus to the whole discussion (Xen. *Oik.* 2.1–7).

45. Theophr. fr. 486.

46. Eriphos fr. 2, which I quote below, depicts a girl shopping. Machon recorded an anecdote of the aged courtesan Gnathaena shopping (Athen. 580c–d). Arist. *Pol.* 1300a6–7.

47. On this question, the evidence leads scholars as intelligent as Henderson (1991) and Goldhill (1994) to completely opposite conclusions. Revermann 2006, 111 n. 37, offers a bibliography on the question.

48. D. Cohen 1991 and Nevett 1999.

49. Cf. S. Johnstone 1998.

50. Mansouri 2002 and Vlassopoulos 2007 argue that the promiscuous social world of the agora constituted an important supplement to democratic political practices in Athens. They analyze, however, not economic interactions but conversations that could be understood as political which happened in economic spaces (especially shops).

51. Xen. *On Horsemanship* 1.1–17 describes what to look for in an unbroken colt; 3.1–12 how to examine and test a trained horse. These comprise 29 of the 154 sections. Delebecque 1978, 129, notes that the verb (at 1.1 and 3.1) is probably passive, though it could be a middle ("deceive yourself").

52. Aristoph. *Clouds* 245–46; Plato *Meno* 91b ff., *Prot.* 311b, 349a, *Soph.* 223a. Blank 1985 discusses the topos of payment for sophists. Socrates' practice of refusing payment altogether, a point his followers used as a way of distinguishing—and elevating—their teacher from others, obviously intersects with the discourses of valuing sophists' services. The Socratic refusal of payment constituted a moral critique of valuing wisdom with money. Xenophon reports that when the sophist Antiphon told Socrates that his teachings must be worthless if he didn't charge a price, Socrates responded with the distinction between an honorable and a shameful way of giving out beauty and wisdom. Only prostitutes and sophists charge for such things (Xen. *Mem.* 1.6.11–14). Insofar as the Socratic practice constituted a refusal to engage in valuing at all, it's not directly relevant to this chapter. Corey 2002 argues that in this context the distinction between accepting and refusing pay is morally shallow and indefensible.

53. Plato *Prot.* 313a.

54. Plato *Prot.* 313c.

55. Plato *Prot.* 313d.

56. Plato *Prot.* 314a. It's doubtful that many Greeks behaved in this extreme and obsessive way. Nevertheless, Plato seems to be tapping into an authentic impulse of suspicion.

57. Plato *Gorg.* 519c–20b. Diogenes Laertius (9.56) tells a similar anecdote about Protagoras, but here the student who tries to argue his way out of paying must pay either because he loses the argument or because he wins (which shows that Protagoras instructed him well in rhetoric). Corax, the reputed first teacher of rhetoric in the fifth century, was said to have been involved in a lawsuit over his fee—but the sources are much later than those about Protagoras (T. Cole 1991a, 66–67).

58. Xen. *On Horsemanship* 2.2.

59. Isoc. 13.5–6.

60. Arist. *NE* 1164a22–8: τὴν ἀξίαν δὲ ποτέρου τάξαι ἐστί, τοῦ προϊεμένου ἢ τοῦ προλαβόντος; ὁ γὰρ προϊέμενος ἔοικ' ἐπιτρέπειν ἐκείνῳ. ὅπερ φασὶ καὶ Πρωταγόραν ποιεῖν· ὅτε γὰρ διδάξειεν ἁδήποτε, τιμῆσαι τὸν μαθόντα ἐκέλευεν ὅσου δοκεῖ ἄξια ἐπίστασθαι, καὶ ἐλάμβανε τοσοῦτον. ἐν τοῖς τοιούτοις δ' ἐνίοις ἀρέσκει τὸ "μισθὸς δ' ἀνδρί." Cf. *EE* 1242b34. Plato *Prot.* 328b–c presents a variant: if the pupil disputes the *misthos*, he can go to a temple and swear to what he believes to be the worth (*axia*) of the instruction, paying that. Note that this account too contrasts *misthos* with a subjective evaluation after the fact. I remain agnostic about whether Protagoras did such a thing; my concern in this section is with the idea embodied in the story.

61. Hesiod's *Works and Days* (l. 370) contains a fuller version of this saying: "Let the stated *misthos* for a man who's close be secure [*arkios*]." (μισθὸς δ' ἀνδρὶ φίλῳ εἰρημένος ἄρκιος ἔστω· Aristotle (fr. 598 [= Plut. *Thes.* 3]) attributed the line to Pittheos. West 1978, 249–50, discusses the textual tradition of Hesiod.) The linked and subsequent lines in Hesiod's text—"Smile but use a witness, even with a brother, for trustings as much as distrustings have ruined men"—advise making arrangements which rely as little as possible on trust, even with your closest relatives. Homer refers to *arkios misthos* only twice, both of which point to a situation where both parties have clearly defined the payment for service ahead of time. *Il.* 10.304; *Od.* 18.358; cf. *Il.* 21.445.

62. Arist. *EE* 1242b34 uses the saying for just this distinction: where the return is determined by agreement (versus where the party trusts the other).

63. If, as Seaford 2004, 287–88, argues *panta chremata* means not "all things" but "all goods" or even "all commodities," the statement might stand as an epigram of the pricing practice.

64. The Protagorean practice may seem utopian and impractical, but it resembles the unilateral declarations of value Greeks made in civic contexts, except that it could not be challenged. I treat this in chapter 5.

65. Hesk 2006, esp. 135–36, discusses the ways that comedy represents verbal duels, particularly in the agora. Fox 1996 discusses the problems and possibilities of using Theophrastus's *Characters*. Konstan 1985 and Davidson 1997 deftly use comedy as historical evidence.

66. Hippocrates, *Regimen* I 24. Cf. Hdt. 1.153 with Kurke 1999, 73–74.

67. Diphilos fr. 66 (= Athen. 6.225a–b).

68. Wine (Theopompos fr. 65) or figs (Alexis fr. 128 [=Athen. 3.76d–e]).

69. Wood (Theophr. *HP* 3.10.2), wool (Aristoph. *Frogs* 1387–88), hides (Aristoph. *Knights* 316–18), or wine (Theophr. *Char.* 30.5).

70. Grain (Pherekrates fr. 105), barley meal (Aristoph. *Knights* 1009), or wine (Aristoph. *Thes.* 347–48, *Wealth* 435–36). Chapter 3 takes up the history of standardized measures.

71. Alexis fr. 128 (=Athen. 3.76d–e); cf. Theopompos fr. 65.

72. Aristoph. *Achar.* 34–36; cf. Aesop 2; Xen. *Kyr.* 1.2.3 opposes the commotion caused by the market folks' shouting and rudeness to good order (*eukosmia*).

73. Antiphanes fr. 125 (= Athen. 7.287e).

74. Plato *Laws* 916e–17c. A character in one of Alexis's comedies claims that fig sellers show you ripe ones but switch them for lesser wild figs when you make the purchase, swearing to the fruit's quality (Alexis fr. 128 [= Athen. 3.76d–e]).

75. Xen. *Mem.* 1.2.36; Men. *Sik.* 9–10; Diphilos fr. 66; Alexis fr. 16; Amphis fr. 30; Timocles fr. 11; Athen. 13.580c (Machon, 3rd cent.); Teles II. 104–19.

76. Amphis fr. 30 (= Athen. 6.224e).

77. Alexis fr. 126 (= Athen. 6.226b–c), fr. 200 (= Athen. 226a). Although an unmanly posture, sitting was thought to give them some advantage (cf. S. Johnstone 2002, 247); cf. Aristoph. *Achar.* 837–38, where, in comic inversion, the *buyer* profits by sitting.

78. Amphis fr. 30 (= Athen. 6.224e).

79. Alexis fr. 16 (= Athen. 224f).

80. Antiphanes fr. 218 (= Athen. 6.225f).

81. Antiphanes fr. 166 (= Athen. 6.224c).

82. Diphilos fr. 13 (= Athen. 6.226e).

83. Theophr. *Char.* 15.4. A female character, Metro, reacts with hostility to a cobbler who refuses to name a price in Herodas *Mime* 7, lines 77–78 (which I discuss later in this chapter).

84. Antiphanes fr. 218 (= Athen. 6.225f).

85. Herodas *Mime* 7, lines 79–80.

86. Arist. fr. 558R; cf. Alexis fr. 16 (= Athen. 224f–255a).

87. καὶ ὅτε ... δυσωνοῖντό τι τῶν πωλουμένων, ἔθος ἦν τοῖς πωλοῦσι λέγειν ὅτι μᾶλλον ἂν προέλοιντο Τελεσταγόρᾳ δοῦναι ἢ τοσούτου ἀναδόσθαι.

88. The preserved fragments suggest the work was a comic essay.

89. Dalby 2000.

90. Athen. 228c.

91. Athen. 313f–14a. Of Archestratus, these are fragments 53, 36, and 45 in Olson and Sens 2000 who discuss the particular species of fish referenced and whose numbering I use.

92. Athen. 313f–14a.

93. Hesiod *W&D* 640. Olson and Sens 2000, lvii–iii, discuss Archestratus's epic antecedents.

94. Although the lines surrounding Archestratus's disparagement of the mormyre of the shore are lost, they probably eulogized the preferred kind of mormyre. In fragments 21 and 42 proximity to the shore determines excellence.

95. Alexis fr. 16 (= Athen. 224f–55a])

96. Aesop 88. While fables ascribed to Aesop are known as early as the classical period, the earliest extant compilation, the Augustana collection, which this one comes from, dates from the first to third century CE.

97. Athen. 243f–44a.

98. Millett 1990, 187–90.

99. Theopompos fr. 193 (= Athen. 6.231e–32b).

100. Theophr. *Char.* 9.4.

101. Antiphanes fr. 206 (= Athen. 7.309d–e).

102. Aristoph. *Wasps* 496–99 (trans. Henderson 1998b, 285). Henderson 2003, 163–64, notes that the promiscuousness of such accusations makes it absurd here, but so does the injection of hyperbolic political invective into haggling.

103. Hesk 2006.

104. Eriphos fr. 2 (= Athen. 3.84b–c). Athenaeus reports that Eriphos copied from Antiphanes the lines down to the aphorism.

105. Cf. Hdt. 8.59, where Themistokles, attempting to persuade the Greek commanders to fight at Salamis, gets interrupted by a Corinthian: "Themistokles, at the games those who start early are beaten with a stick." And Themistokles retorts: "Yes, but those left behind are not crowned."

106. Cunningham 1964 (yes); Lawall 1976 (no); Levin 1976 (yes); Rist 1993 (yes). The question, however, should not be, Are the characters or subjects the same? but, How does the juxtaposition of mimes open up interpretive possibilities? Stern 1979, 252 n. 22, briefly adumbrates this approach.

107. Rist 1993, 444, contrasts 6 as private and 7 as public, a difference which, she argues, explains the euphemy of the latter. Lawall 1976, 168–69, too.

108. In addition to those I note below, both mimes begin with the berating of a slave, and in both women are likened to dogs (6.14 and 7.63).

109. 6.65–73 and 7.19–27, 113–21.

110. 6.75–80 and 7.4, 108–12, 127–29.

111. Because the manuscript indicates changes in speakers, but not who speaks, scholars dispute whether Metro alone addresses Kerdon, or another (unnamed) companion does as well. I follow Cunningham 1971, 175, in treating Metro as Kerdon's sole interlocutor. I don't believe it substantially alters my analysis if another woman speaks some of these lines.

112. I provide the translation of Rusten and Cunningham 2002, 259–69.

113. 77–8:

τί τονθορύζεις κοὐκ ἐλευθέρηι γλάσσηι
τὸν τῖμον ὅστις ἐστὶν ἐξεδίφησας;

114. 95: εἶς κνῦσα καὶ κακὴ λώβη.

115. Herodas *Mime* 6.75–80 (trans. Rusten and Cunningham 2002, 253).

116. Cunningham 1971, 185–89, repeatedly notes her sarcasm and abuse.

117. It is possible, as Rist 1993, 443, argues, that the woman giggles because she has happened upon a conversation in coded language about dildos, except that none of the women in the mimes to this point had considered a dildo a laughing matter.

118. Lines 95 and 88, where she uses the term τάλης, which the mother used of her son in 3.35.

119. Arist. *Ath. Pol.* 51.1–4.

120. Arist. *Ath. Pol.* 51.1.

121. Dem. 20.9 and Hyp. 3.14 both allude to this law. Theophrastus recommended that *agoranomoi* should look after "the truthfulness not only of the sellers but also of the buyers" (Theophr. fr. 651 [= Sz-M fr. 20]). From this short fragment it is not possible to tell how he thought buyers might lie—unless he thought that the process of haggling itself was inherently untruthful.

122. Arist. *Ath. Pol.* 51.3 If Seager 1966 is correct in his interpretation of the price regulations for grain at Athens alluded to in Lys. 22, grain retailers were supposed to charge only a specified markup from the wholesale price they had paid. Figueira 1986, however, disputes this.

123. *Laws* 921b: μὴ πλέονος τιμᾶν διαπειρώμενον ἀλλ᾽ ὡς ἁπλούστατα τῆς ἀξίας, ταὐτὸν δὴ προστάττει καὶ τῷ ἀναιρουμένῳ—γιγνώσκει γὰρ ὅ γε δημιουργὸς τὴν ἀξίαν.

124. Alexis fr. 125 (=Athen. 6.226a–b).

125. *Syll.*³ 975. I discuss this law further in chapters 3 and 5.

126. I would point similarly to laws prohibiting resale: *IErythrai* 15 (regarding wool);

*Syll.*³ 975 (the Delian law on wood and charcoal, just mentioned). Plato *Laws* 847d presents a law outlawing profit on the resale of military equipment and supplies. The legendary early lawgiver of Locri, Zaleukos, was said to have legislated against reselling. Such prohibitions against middlemen seem motivated by the same idea, that it's unjust to charge a higher price for the same thing.

127. *R&O* 25. Ober 2008, 220–40, offers an illuminating discussion.

128. Nor is it certain how much of Nikophon's law reiterates this previous law. Alessandri 1984 argues that all of lines 3–36, the portion that establishes a *dokimastes* for the city, are quoted directly from an earlier law. Figueira 1998, 540, follows Alessandri; Rhodes and Osborne 2003, 119, are more circumspect.

129. Stroud 1974; Alessandri 1984; Engen 2005; Ober 2008, 220–40.

130. Some scholars have noted this: Stroud 1974, 179; Figueira 1998, 543.

131. Had the law been directed at everyone, it should have specified "anyone" as a potential target. Other Greek laws on coins applied to everyone: *IC* IV 162.6, which demonetized silver coins and enforced the use of bronze in Gortyn, covered "anyone"; a law of Olbia (*Syll.*³ 218) applied to "whoever buys or sells with another [currency]"; and a law of the Delphic league requiring people to equate the Athenian tetradrachm with four local silver drachmas applied to "anyone living in the cities, either foreigner or citizen or slave, either man or woman . . ." (*FD* III.2 139.3–5).

132. Van Alfen 2005 describes the diversity of types of coins in circulation.

133. Figueira 1998, 28–35, discusses these imitations and provides previous bibliography.

134. Buttrey 1981. Buttrey disputes Stroud's claim that the *dokimastes* "tested" coins (meaning, assayed their silver content). Feyel 2003 attacks Buttrey, arguing that the *dokimastes* must have examined the coins—a point which Buttrey doesn't seem to have denied. (I remain agnostic in their dispute about whether the true meaning of *dokimazein* is "examine" or "approve.")

135. This hardly comports with the way W. Thompson 1982 represents them.

136. Mørkholm 1982, 295; Figueira 1998, 541–42.

137. Buttrey 1981, 90. Engen 2005, 374, dismisses this idea as "fanciful speculation." Feyel 2003, 45–46, is incredulous.

138. Sylla 1976.

139. Timberlake 1981.

140. Mullineaux 1987, 886.

141. In 1896, Sumner wrote in his *History of Banking in the United States*: "It is difficult for the modern student to realize that there were hundreds of banks whose notes circulated in any given community. The bank notes were bits of paper recognizable as a specie by shape, color, size and engraved work. Any piece of paper which had these came within the prestige of money; the only thing in the shape of money to which the people were accustomed. The person to whom one of them was offered, if unskilled in trade and banking, had little choice but to take it. A merchant turned to his 'detector.' He scrutinized the worn and dirty scrap for two or three minutes, regarding it as more probably 'good' if it was worn and dirty than if it was clean, because those features were proof of long and successful circulation. He turned it up to the light and looked through it, because it was the custom of the banks to file the notes on slender pins, which made holes through them. If there were many such holes the note had been often in the bank and its genuineness ratified." (Quoted in Gorton 1999, 39.)

142. Mullineaux 1987, 886.

143. Athen. 159c. The value of all money always varies in what it will buy (more wheat

today, less tomorrow), but if you had to negotiate the value of each coin each time, it would seem a bit like rolling a die.

144. E. Cohen 1992, 18–20.

145. Dem. 50.30; Arist. *Oik.* 1346b24–26, where the Byzantine state sells the monopoly to do this.

146. Le Rider 1989, 164.

147. Dem. 35.24. The agreement required repayment in *argurion dokimon*.

148. I doubt that the amount of the demanded discount was large. A shrewd merchant would make the deduction small enough that it was not worth the buyer's time either to go elsewhere or to continue haggling over the discount.

149. Diphilos fr. 66 (= Athen. 225a–b).

150. Hdt. 4.196.

151. de Moraes Farias 1974 argues that most reports of such silent trade are dubious.

152. Redfield 1985, 110–11, notes that Herodotus represents the center of the world, Ionia, as a sphere of the mixing of cultures, whereas the cultures at the extremes of the world tend not to affect each other.

CHAPTER THREE: MEASURING

1. Lys. 22.5, 6.

2. It occurs repeatedly in the Attic Stelai, a set of inscriptions I discuss in chapter 4.

3. Bissa 2009, 181–82, argues that a phormos equals six medimnoi, based solely on Lys. 22.12. But this passage doesn't mention a phormos, its introduction is unnecessary, and the unmentioned unit on which the price was increased is likely to have been a medimnos, the common measure for pricing, as I argue below.

4. In addition to Bissa, only two recent scholars attempt to explain the use of the word *phormos*. Todd 1993 speculates that the speaker of Lys. 22 used *phormos* to conceal something. Figueira 1986, 156 and 161, suggests that a phormos was about the same as a medimnos, but was used in context where exact measurement was unnecessary.

5. I use "standardized" to mean measures whose size has been formally set and is enforced by the polis. In our world, not only governments set standards, but also trade organizations and nongovernmental organizations (e.g., the International Organization for Standardization).

6. I will not directly address the disputed question of whether Greeks fabricated large transport jars (amphoras) in standard capacities. Garlan, 2000, 67–82, lays out the difficulties in arguing for standardized volumes. As M. Lawall 2000, 74, notes, counting jars (instead of measuring capacities) would not have depended on standardized sizes. Amphoras, like phormoi, could have been used as practical units.

7. Grayson 1975 (esp. chap. 7) considers the contexts of weighing, but does not really address systemic practices. Grimaudo 1998 mostly offers a cultural and ideological history of weights and measures. Greene et al. 2008 is an exception.

8. An attempt to standardize women's clothing sizes seems to have failed utterly because retailers believe it would cost too much and undermine the uniqueness of brands achieved through "proprietary sizing" (Barbaro 2006). Jeacle 2003 discusses the history of the standardization of clothing sizes.

9. Pritchett 1991, 469 n. 696.

10. There were no brands in the ancient world. Brands require three things: first, an entity that can benefit from and exercise exclusive ownership rights over the brand; second, a regime of intellectual property, trademarks, or government regulation, all backed

by a robust (legal) apparatus of enforcement; third, the ability to create consistent quality
of the goods (Barzel 1982, 36), something usually possible only with extensive intervention
in the production process. The only commodity branded in the Greek world was silver, in
the form of coins.

11. Take the case of the pig: "The more similar the swine, the more easily they fit into
the mechanized system, increasing efficiency. For instance, as swine carcasses move down
the conveyor belt, at Hormel's Austin, Minnesota, packing plant, they hit a curved knife,
which slices the cylindrical loin from the inside of the body cavity. If the animals aren't
just the right proportions, the knife will hit the wrong spot, wasting meat or cutting into
bone" (N. Johnson 2006, 50).

12. Cronon 1991, 97–147.

13. The history of the use of moisture content in evaluating grain shows the interrelations between quality and quantity. For much of the twentieth century, moisture content
was used to grade the quality of grain, but after 1985 it was used exclusively to adjust quantity (Hill 1990, 125–30).

14. Even in the modern period, however, the reliance on objective rules was a difficult
achievement. Early on, when the Chicago Board of Trade received complaints that different graders evaluated grain differently so that the process was subjective, the initial reform
was not to further articulate the rules governing grading, but to appoint a chief grader who
oversaw the others as deputies—to rely, that is, on personal relationships (Hill 1990, 15).

15. Rosivach 2000 describes the trade in grain.

16. Garnsey 1988, 107–33; Tsetskhladze 1998, 54–57.

17. Garnsey 1988, 89–106. Whitby 1998 argues for more imports. It's possible that even
in the archaic period some Greek cities imported significant amounts of grain: Figueira
1981, 22–46, argues that Aegina, an island polis near Athens, did this. (Though plausible,
his conclusion is based on a series of assumptions and guesses.)

18. Bissa 2009, 153–210, argues for a significant flow of grain from the peripheries of the
Greek world to the cities around the Aegean. The assumptions required for the math here
make the conclusions contestable if plausible.

19. Isager and Hansen 1975, 55–87, offer an overview.

20. Gofas 1993, 87–91. E. Harris 1989 discusses how two importers would work together, one staying in Athens as surety for the money they borrowed, the other sailing with
the ship. Reed 1984, 35, and Wilson 1997/98 offer speculative arguments for simple delegation in trade as early as the archaic period.

21. Kleomenes, governor of Egypt, organized possibly the largest single grain-shipping
operation during the classical period (Dem. 56.7–8). This involved agents who shipped
grain from Egypt, who accompanied the cargoes, or who sold it at its destination. These
last agents sent letters back to Egypt advising them of prices, so that they could ship grain to
where the price was highest—a practice the speaker of Dem. 56, Darius, represents as very
shady. It is unclear how large this enterprise was, although, since it was organized by an au-
tocrat, it hardly stands at the normal practice of free merchants in the classical period.

22. Wilson 1997/98 discusses the use of letters among merchants in the archaic period.
D. Jordan 2000, 91–92, catalogues private lead letters.

23. Bresson 2000, 144. In Apollodoros's case (Dem. 50), because he was acting as trierarch while awaiting his successor, his expenses (on the ship and its crew) were really debts
(of his successor to him). He kept detailed records of these expenses, as he explained to the
jury hearing his suit for reimbursement, so that his successor could test whether he was
reckoning falsely (Dem. 50.30).

24. In the most detailed and sustained attempt to show the economic rationality of an-

cient accounting, Rathbone 1991 examines the records of one unit (*phrontis*) of a large estate in third-century CE Egypt. Rathbone argues that the systematic nature of the accounting emerges only from a consideration of the whole set of documents, and he cautions that the many other cases where only a single document has been preserved may also have been part of a comprehensive system. Nevertheless, insofar as these monthly accounts recorded what the manager (*phrontistes*) was personally responsible for, and not all the transactions relating to the unit (*phrontis*) (Rathbone 1991, 378–79), they do not analyze an abstract economic entity but monitor a person (cf. Macve 1985). Moreover, although Rathbone shows that central managers *could have* analyzed these accounts to determine costs of production, absent the records of the estate's central administration he is merely making an assumption based on what is already in doubt (that ancient people used written records to constitute and analyze abstract entities).

25. Dem. 34.8.

26. The documents that Wilson 1997/98 interprets as contracts all clearly stated the witnesses' names, however laconic they otherwise were.

27. Todd 1993, 336, on Dem. 32.1. Note that this law did not require merchants to use written contracts, but allowed only those who had used them to initiate this kind of suit. Even without a written contract, they could still use other kinds of suits.

28. Bresson 2000, 119–49, esp. 141–48. I can't treat Bresson's arguments in detail here, but I offer an example: the fact that Romans were able to learn from their papers (as well as from their accents and clothes) that some passengers on a captured Macedonian ship were Carthaginian ambassadors (146–47) does not show that Greek merchants carried officially recognized papers in order to prove their citizenship or destination. The Romans' use of documents in this instance was purely ad hoc, not systematic.

29. This is how merchants' identities are determined in Aristophanes: *Achar.* 818, 909–11 (with an oath); *Birds* 1229. At *Birds* 1213, a *sphragis* (seal impression) and a *symbolon* (token) are ·imagined as possible means of identification—but only to show that someone had come into the city through an official entrance.

30. Cf. Lave 1986.

31. Amyx 1958, 274–75. A phormos should be distinguished from a *thulakos*. This bag was usually made of leather (Ephich. fr. 113; Theophr. *Char.* 16.6) and used especially for carrying *alphita*, barley meal (Hdt. 3.46), which had been bought in the agora (Aristoph. *Wealth* 763, *Wasps* 314, *Ekk.* 820). It seems not to have been very big, as one of Aristophanes' characters says it would have held an obol's worth of contents (*Birds* 503).

32. Hesiod *W&D* 482; Alexis fr. 310; Aristoph. *Wasps* 58. Plato, however, refers to a phormos holding dice (*Lysis* 206e).

33. Polyb. 1.19.3; Aineias 2.2.3; 32.8.8; Hdt. 8.71.

34. Aineias 32.2.2. He says that phormoi of sand, bricks, or stones should be used to build high structures in lieu of wooden towers: ἀνταείρεσθαι πύργους ξυλίνους ἢ ἄλλα ὕψη ἐκ φορμῶν πληρουμένων ψάμμου ἢ ἐκ λίθων ἢ ἐκ πλίνθων. Using the word *phormoi* in this way suggests that they were not rigid. Since sand weighs about twice what wheat does per unit of volume, a full phormos of sand could have been a very unwieldy load. But if phormoi were only partially filled with sand and then stacked, stiff baskets would crumple under the accumulated weight of sand, whereas flexible sacks would allow the sand beneath to support that above.

35. *De Pythiae oraculis* 403C.

36. Aesch. 3.166.

37. Aineias 18.10.2.

38. These sacks may well have been woven out of linen, which was both grown in Greece

and imported. (Herodotus [2.105] mentions two named kinds of linen, one from Colchis, the other from Egypt, and Xenophon [*Kyn.* 2.4] says that hunting nets should be made of Carthaginian or Phasian linen.) There were slaves in Athens who were denominated as "sackweavers" (οἱ σακχυφάνται—Dem. 48.12; *IG* II² 2403; cf. Photius sv. Σακυφάνται. I am assuming that a phormos was a kind of *sakkos*). In Egypt coarse linen was used for sacks (Forbes 1964, 43). Because linen, like other textiles, is perishable, no sacks from classical Greece have been found. But five or six have been preserved in a cave in Israel from the Roman period (Yadin 1963, 259–61). The weave of these sacks was considerably coarser than the linen sheets and woolen garments and textiles found in the same cave. The three whole sacks whose size can be measured show considerable variation in shape and capacity: The largest has about twice the capacity of the smallest. While sacks made in the same workshop or on the same loom may have achieved a greater uniformity, I would not assume that all sacks were exactly the same. *P. Mich. Zen.* 120 is a receipt for two lengths of coarse linen cloth, each 100¼ *pecheis* (forearm lengths) long (about 150 feet total). But while one weighed 35 minas, the other weighed 40.5. It is unclear whether this difference was due to variation in thread, weave, or width of cloth. This evidence would caution against assuming a uniform size for phormoi.

39. Hermippos, a contemporary of Aristophanes, wrote a comedy called *The Phormophoroi*, from which a few fragments survive, one of which (fr. 62) implies that porters had dealings with shopkeepers. Aristotle (fr. 63) reports that porters used a special shoulder pad porters when carrying burdens. (You might doubt his attribution of this invention to Protagoras.) A late archaic vase from Etruria shows a man carrying a large sack on his back (*ARV* 2, 364.52), and the famous Archesilaus cup shows two men carrying packages, though of what and where there is no agreement. (Bresson 2000, 85–94, takes a position and provides bibliography.) Olson 1991, 418, discusses Aristophanes' representation of the chorus in his *Acharnians* as former porters of charcoal. Porters (*skeuophoroi*) carried things for Greek hoplites (Hammond 1983, 27). Later in this chapter I discuss the porters in *IG* 2² 1672. 292–93, 299.

40. While scholars have equated the phormos with a medimnos because that latter's weight of grain, about 80 pounds, seems like a reasonable load for a man to heft, in eighteenth-century France (where human labor was likewise essential to moving the bags) a bag of wheat usually weighed 325 pounds (Kaplan 1984, 366).

41. Burford 1960, esp. p. 3, discusses the extent of overland heavy transport in Greece. Raepsaet 2008 describes some of the technology of land transport.

42. Stroud 1998, 104–7, discusses the roads up to the city.

43. Thuc. 7.28.

44. Rickman 1980, 132–33; Turfa and Steinmayer 1999, 105.

45. Parker 1992b. Cf. Gibbins 2001, 277.

46. Swiny and Katzev 1973, 343–44; Greene et al. 2008, 407.

47. Parker 1992a, 94: "Containers of less resilient material, such as baskets or sacks, are infrequently preserved, but the predominantly manual nature of cargo-handling in Roman times implies that they must normally have been used for most kinds of dry goods, including grain." Rickman 1980, 133–34, inclines toward the same probability for the shipment of grain to Rome. Cf. Casson 1986, 200.

48. Parker 1992a, 92.

49. Sigaut 1988, 21. This corresponds closely to the procedures described by Hesiod in *W&D* 497–82, etc. Isager and Skydsgaard 1992, 22–25.

50. Whittaker 1999, 10, notes that archaeologists have neglected threshing floors but that the few from the classical period that have been identified and published are usually found

near habitation. In early twentieth-century Cyprus, threshing floors clustered on the edges of villages "for ease of transporting the chaff and threshed grain to storage" (13).

51. Cavanaugh 1996, 167; Burford 1960, 10. Cf. Hdt. 7.60, where the Persians count the their army by marching soldiers into an area that holds 10,000 men, emptying the area and filling it again until they reach a total of 1.7 million men. The container is the measure.

52. Olson 1991 elucidates the economics of charcoal at Athens. (What follows derives from this wonderful article.) The urban center of Athens, like Delos, had to import most of its fuel. Although making charcoal from wood is incredibly inefficient (a given amount of wood produces only 15 percent as much charcoal by weight), charcoal has a much higher energy content per unit of weight (65–150 percent more) and is thus more valuable by weight. (Because of its burning characteristics, charcoal was also better, or even necessary, for some activities, like smelting.) At Athens, the poor could go out to the margins, cut down some trees, carbonize them, and carry the charcoal on their backs to the city to sell. The container in which they bore the charcoal was a *larkos* (Aristoph. *Achar.* 333; Alexis fr. 208; and, possibly, Eur. fr. 283). A man wealthy enough to own a donkey, by contrast, might prefer just to load it with wood and drive it to market, skipping the several days it takes to carbonize the wood. As Olson shows, the fuel market at Athens was highly complex, but decentralized. On Delos, however, where all fuel had to be imported by ship, no poor man could haul a *larkos* of charcoal to market. Here men with capital had to acquire charcoal, package it for shipment, and pay to import it. The *kalathos* seems to have been the customary container for this trade.

53. *IG* XI.2 161 A 109 [279 BCE]; *IG* XI.2 203 A 59 [269 BCE].

54. Both the Attic Stelai (see chap. 4 below) and informal capacity marks on amphoras (M. Lawall 2000, 12) show that Greeks treated one half, in a sense, as the smallest unit, one that seems to have been estimated (not necessarily measured) on the basis of a half-full container.

55. *Syll.*³ 975.39–40. The law did not name the measure. Since the same law earlier mandated that wood, timber, and charcoal be sold "using the *stathmoi* for wood" (lines 1–2, 33–34), it's possible that the charcoal measure was the same as that for wood. But *stathmoi* would normally refer to weights, not measures, and the *hieropoioi* who in who in 279 bought charcoal by the *kalathos* also bought wood by the talent, a weight (*IG* XI.2.161 A 108). It's possible that *stathmoi* here could be understood generically as "weights (or measures)."

56. Amyx 1958, 271–73, provides most of the evidence about *kophinoi*. She notes, however, that the evidence does not allow the reconstruction of the exact form of a *kophinos*.

57. Migeotte 1993.

58. *SEG* 34.558.

59. *IG* VII. 2712.65.

60. *SEG* 38.380.

61. Feyel 1942, 84–85, discusses the equation; Knoepfler 1988, 290 n. 99, registers the uncertainties about size.

62. The statement that a *kophinos* of *alphita* (barley meal) costs 4 drachmas is just "comic fantasy," whereas the claim that a *kophinos* of wine equals 3 *choes*, as does a *kophinos* of wheat—now that's a fact! No one has explained the humor here—and this equation could be the punchline—which is unsettling for any math. Am I the only one who suspects a joke behind the line: "A basket (*kophinos*) of wine equals 3 *choes*"? Is it possible that the humor here is in systematizing an unstandardized container? I might also note that three would be an unusual number of smaller measures to go into a larger one; such fractions were usually based on 2, 4, or 6.

63. Particularly inscription 2 (*SEG* 34.558.34–36), which fines cities which fail to deliver

on time their contribution for the shipment to Rome 2 staters and 9 obols per *kophinos*. Inscriptions 1 and 3 could as easily refer to customary baskets as standardized measures.

64. Theophr. *Char.* 4.14; *IG* I³ 386.132; 387.45. In the Attic Stelai, *kophinoi* were sold as implements, not as containers of other things. This suggests that at Athens, at least, they were not typical storage containers.

65. Aristoph. fr. 349; Aeneas 38.7. Dung: Xen. *Mem.* 3.8.6 and Aristoph. fr. 662.

66. Arist. *HA* 629a13. In the gospels, the remnants of the loaves and fishes were taken up in *kophinoi*, twelve in number (e.g., Mark 6:43).

67. Rhodes and Osborne 2003 #59.20–25. The translation is by the editors (with modifications).

68. Mahir 1987, 81.

69. I would offer two comparisons. Lawall 2000, 74, suggests with regard to imported shipments of wine that "the concern portside was primarily with the numbers of jars and not the specific quantity of contents of any one jar.... The assumption on the parts of the buyers and sellers must have been that roughly the expected quantity of liquid would be present in any given jar (of a known type ...)." Similarly, Mayerson 1998a argues that in Egypt under Roman rule people could simply count bags of grain because the sack was standardized to 3 artabas. Although he argues that this sack size was standardized, the evidence he cites (p. 191 n. 7) suggests that if 3-artaba sacks were common, they were not universal. Merchants and others could use customary containers as units not so much because the containers were standardized as because of their expertise in sizing them up.

70. *R&O* 45, ii, 1–22.

71. Bousquet 1985, 234.

72. E.g., Heraclides gave the Athenians 3,000 drachmas for grain and sold them 3,000 medimnoi of wheat at reduced prices (*R&O* 95.9–13 [325/4]). Cf. *IG* II² 363 [324/23] and *SEG* I 361 [end of the 4th cent.].

73. Had it been remeasured in local medimnoi, a discrepancy of even a tenth of 1 percent would have shown up as 2 medimnoi different from the conversion formula.

74. The loss is arbitrary because the unit price—if there was one—is unknown, merely chosen to sound plausible.

75. This undermines Casson's conclusion (1956, 235) that the most common size of an ancient grain ship was a capacity of 3,000 medimnoi, which he inferred because this is the most common number mentioned in inscriptions recording gifts of grain to cities (3 out of 10 times—the fourth case he mentions must be disqualified because the number has been restored). However, this requires assuming that the inscriptions records "the exact amount of grain involved" (234) and that in each case the donor sent a precise shipload of grain.

76. Dem. 34.39.

77. Disputes over the accuracy of the Consumer Price Index have often hinged on whether it fails to take account of the qualitative changes of goods (Bureau of Labor Statistics 1997). Some economists believe that it overstates inflation because some goods have become better—that is, though the CPI treats "automobiles" as fungible over time, they really are not.

78. Thus, they may study changes in prices over the long term (inflation or deflation), which may be seen as changes *in the average*, or over the short term (seasonal or even daily swings), which may be seen as deviations *from the average*.

79. Duncan-Jones 1990, 145; Rathbone 1997, 193; Drexhage 1991; Reger 1993, 308.

80. Rathbone 1997, 199, raises the question of the qualitative variability of wheat, but then asserts that it was "pretty uniform."

81. I discuss accountability in more detail in chapter 7.

82. *IG* II² 1672. The precise numbers preserved in this text have, sirenlike, lured scholars against their own better judgment to founder on the shoals of specious math (Stroud 1998, 35−37). I have tried to lash myself to the mast of statistical restraint.

83. Stroud 1998, 60, gives the references.

84. Loomis 1998, 111−14, lists the instances from *IG* II² 1672.

85. If he were using a half-hekteus measure, the largest approved standard measure mentioned in an Athenian inscription in 222/21 (discussed below), with a capacity of about 4 liters, he would have to fill it some 1,200 times to measure out a hundred medimnoi.

86. This does not include the cost of the time of the *Epistatai* who oversaw the measuring.

87. Garnsey 1988, 98, presents the individual contributions in tabular format.

88. Stroud 1998, 59 followed by Rhodes and Osborne 2003, 125.

89. It's hard to imagine how it would work. This hypothesis requires that there be a way to measure the degree of compacting and its deviation from the proper—but what would this be and how would it be quantified? If the grain was supposed to be compacted, why wouldn't they just compact it and then top it off for a full measure?

90. This depends, however, on how you read two of the instances, where it's possible to read (for example, in line 298) not "of barley medimnoi 43, having four half-hekteis as the *epibole*" but "of barley 43 medimnoi four half-hekteis with the *epibole*." The latter seems the less likely alternative, though, since the third instance clearly quantifies the *epibole*: "10 medimnoi and *epibole* five half-hekteis" (line 285). I do not, however, know of any parallels for this meaning.

91. This idea goes against the common claim that the year in question (as well as others around that time) saw a grain shortage. (Isager and Hansen 1975, 200−204.) But as Stroud 1998, 35−36, points out, the evidence for this shortage is not strong. Even if you accept Garnsey's arguments (1988, 98−101) that Athenian harvests were poor that year, Garnsey also shows that at Lemnos they were quite abundant. And even if there were high prices at certain times, that does not mean there were always high prices.

92. This seems to have been the case in a public lease in late third-century Thespiai (*I Thesp* 62.25−26).

93. It's unclear whether this *epimetra* was a one-time premium, or was calculated per year.

94. Gargola 1992, 17; Garnsey 1988, 79−82.

95. *Syll.*³ 976.53−63. Gargola 1992 discusses this inscription in detail.

96. Isocrates refers to perquisites customarily given to magistrates (Isoc. 12.145), a passage you might reasonably suspect of hyperbole, but all officials were audited for theft, culpable neglect, and accepting gifts (Arist. *Ath. Pol.* 54.2, with MacDowell 1983, 58−59). Scholars, following the evidence available, have focused on the most sensational kinds of bribery—of ambassadors, politicians, and groups of jurors—and had little to say about the opportunities for petty gain available to ordinary officials (e.g., MacDowell 1983; Harvey 1985).

97. That officials so openly used such a fiction suggests it was a common practice. It may have been less culpable than not selling the grain at all.

98. I acknowledge that there are gaps in my account that must be filled by hypothesis, but the only alternative account (the theory of compacting) is based entirely on hypothesis.

99. *IG* I³ 78. 27−30 required the *hieropoioi* at Eleusis, the predecessors of the *epistatai*, to measure and record the grain they received as firstfruits offerings. I discuss this inscription in chapter 4.

100. Kurke 1999, 71–80.

101. Lang and Crosby 1964, 49–55. It is true that two small fragments of pottery which they classify as possible measures (nos. 70 and 71, p. 55) can be interpreted as consistent with what may have been a measure as large as a medimnos, but the identification of them as official measures is very uncertain, and their original size more speculative still.

102. Vanderpool 1968 *SEG* 24.157.

103. Inscriptions from two other cities provide evidence for actual measuring devices as large as (but no larger than) a half-medimnos: *Syll.*³ 945, where the measures are listed in descending order by size, and *I. Délos* 1820.

104. In Schilbach's (1999) catalogue of official measuring vessels from Olympia, the two common sizes were around 200 ml. (a half-pint) and around 816–968 ml. (a quart). There may have been a handful of cups twice the size of the latter (Schilbach 1999, 324). We don't know exactly how all these measuring vessels were used, though Schilbach 1999, 336, guesses that the itinerant traders who showed up to supply tourists at the festivals may have use them. At Heraclea, renters of temple lands paid in grain measured out "with the public chous" (*IG* XIV 645 I.103), a chous being a size between a medimnos and a choinix (*IG* XIV 645 II.36), probably around 3.3 liters or a bit less than a gallon (Uguzzoni and Ghinatti 1968, 182–3).

105. *IG* II² 1013. 7–11.

106. Bettalli 1985 discusses these locations.

107. *IG* XII suppl. 347; Arist., *Ath. Pol.* 51.1.

108. Vélissaropoulos 1980, 207–14.

109. The language of Dem. 20.31–2 might suggest that Leukon collected the "thirtieth" on exported grain in kind, but since Demosthenes wanted the jurors to understand the tax exemption that Leukon granted merchants exporting to Athens as a gift to the Athenians, it better served his case to characterize the savings of a "thirtieth" as an amount of grain that came to Athens, not as an amount of money a merchant didn't have to pay.

110. Dem. 32.18 and 34.34 show that the records of tax collectors would usually have indicated at least who paid the tax. Dem. 34.7 shows that the tax collectors would have recorded the declared value of the cargo.

111. *IG* I³ 1453 § 10. I have not translated all of the editors' restorations, some of which seem to me to be questionable, if still plausible.

112. Figueira 1998 takes about 600 pages to interpret this law. His revisionist understanding—that the law did not (as the orthodox interpretation claims) ban the allies of Athens from using their own coins, weights, and measures, but only required that they accept Athens's—has been both embraced (Evans 2001) and derided (Mattingly 1999; Crawford 2001) with a vehemence that the intricacies of epigraphy seem especially to provoke. If Figueira's analyses are not entirely persuasive, he has shown how precarious those of others are. Uncertainties abound because the text has many gaps, including the beginning, a section of unknown length, which would have actually stated what the law's main provisions were. (Historians routinely infer that the addition to the oath of the Boule restated these.) Historians fill the smaller gaps with restorations whose plausibility depends on an overall understanding of the law, the precise issue at stake. There is no direct evidence for the purpose of this law, though scholars speculate that it was meant to symbolically impose Athenian hegemony on its nominal allies, or to facilitate trade by providing a set of public goods (standard weights, measures, and coins), or to streamline the collection of tribute. Moreover, attempts to measure the law's effectiveness by examining coins minted by allies or the sizes of their amphoras (presumed proxies for measures) have been indecisive or contestable. In particular, the analysis of amphora sizes depends on many questionable assumptions (that

they were officially standardized and that amphoras themselves were systematized to abstract measures). The one consequence that seems clear (because the law specifies it) is that the Athenians imposed the cost of this decree on their allies, who apparently had to pay the Athenians a fee for reminting their coins (§5). Reminting, by the way, likely imposed a further cost on the allies: the probable loss of metal during the process (at Delphi, reminting resulted in a loss [*apousia*] of 6–15 percent [CID II 75; Raven 1950]).

113. In chapter 4 I discuss other aspects of this law.

114. *R&O* 26. 21–27. Trans. Rhodes and Osborne 2003, 121.

115. Stroud, the first editor, understood the clause about the *sekoma* to mean "filling up the measuring table (*sekoma*) to the [rim?]," a procedure combining weighing and measuring to verify the density of the grain (Stroud 1998, 54–61). He suggested this with considerable hesitation, as this is the only clause of the law that cannot be read with certainty. While there can be little doubt that the buyer of the tax was supposed to weigh out the grain—in four separate places the law explicitly called for weighing it (lines 16, 21–22, 24–25, and 40)—the possible reference here to measuring seems doubtful, both because the procedure seems largely redundant, needlessly exhaustive, and extraordinarily complex and because the linguistic parallels Stroud cites are weak. There are four problems with these. 1. Stroud (1998, 58) provides two parallels for understanding σηκώσας as "dispose" (Plut. *Moralia* 928d) or "equalize" (First Augustan Edict from Cyrene, *SEG* IX.8). However, both parallels cannot be valid since these are different (and, indeed, incompatible) meanings in their original passages. Moreover, while Nicolet 1991, 497, may be correct that σεικωθεισῶν translates the Latin *aequare*, the equalization was achieved in part, at least, by weighing, so that the Greek names the process and the Latin the effect. It seems unwarranted to insist on a novel meaning when the more basic one still pertains. 2. It's unclear how "disposing or equalizing the table" can mean "leveling the grain." 3. The objects modern scholars call *sekomata* do not provide a valid parallel for τὸ σήκωμα in the inscription. We don't know what Greeks called these blocks of stone with holes of various capacities in them, and in *I. Délos* 1820, the only of these objects that uses the word σήκωμα, it probably does not refer to the table itself, but to the validity of the capacity of its cavity. It does not name itself with the words "*sekoma* of a half-medimnos of grain," but rather certifies its capacity. (Mayerson 1998b argues that, in reference to wine in Roman Egypt, σήκωμα refers to a measuring jar of a definite, but arbitrary, capacity. While all σηκώματα were necessarily jars, only jars of a definite capacity were σηκώματα.) 4. All of the parallels Stroud provides come from 300 to 500 years after the passage in question. This law, then, does not outline a procedure for determining or verifying the density of grain, but determining the volume of grain by weighing it.

116. Grayson 1975.

117. *NH* 18.63–68; Mayerson 1998a.

118. Rathbone 1983, 271.

119. Rhodes and Osborne 2003, 125. As they note, although Theophrastus says that wheat from Lemnos was heavy, the weight of a medimnos in the law's formula, about 33 kg., is significantly less than the lightest weight in Pliny's collection of conversion formulas (39 kg.).

120. Theophr. *HP* 8.4.4–5.

121. Theophr. *HP* 8.4.5.

122. Amouretti 1979, 62.

123. Trans. Grenfell and Hunt 1906, 271. The editors have made a number of small restorations of the Greek, none of which affect the mechanisms analyzed here.

124. Because there were different sized measures, specifying which one could be important. In *P. Hib.* 74 (c. 250 BCE), one official wrote to another: "Measure to Nobonchis the

agent, and Horus son of Semtheus, and Harsemphtheus the subordinate of Teos 2368¾ *artabae* of olyra on the receiving measure, which are on the spending measure 2500, and make two receipts with them, one in the name of Cleomachus for 1600 artabae, equivalent to 1684 on the spending measure, the other in my name for 768¾ artabae, equivalent to 816 on the spending measure." (Trans. Grenfell and Hunt 1906, 228.) In addition to the receptacle, receipts sometimes specified the implement used to level the top, e.g., "a fair smoothing-rod" (*P. Lille* I 21, 23; *P. Sorb.* inv. III) or "a fair and just smoothing-rod" (*P. Tebt.* 3.823).

125. *P. Oxy.* 7.1024 (129 CE): "pure, unadulterated, unmixed with earth and sifted."

126. *P. Hib.* 39 and 98.

127. Gofas 1993, 91–2. *P. Hib.* 54.

128. The author of *P. Hib.* 74 (quoted above) directed an official to issue receipts when disbursing grain.

129. S. Johnstone 1994.

130. Rickman 1998 documents the extensive efforts of the Roman government to undertake, organize, and oversee the grain supply for Rome.

131. *P. Oxy.* 4.708. Editor's trans. with modifications. (=*W. Chrest.* 432). The rest of the papyrus contains a copy of a similar letter about a different shipment.

132. It was not a "weighing" (as the editors translate it). Weighing samples would not reveal impurities.

133. Mayerson 2002.

CHAPTER FOUR: KEEPING TRACK

1. Arist. *Pol.* 1257b14–16. Roller 1983, 310–12, discusses ancient variants of this legend.

2. Mickwitz 1937; de Ste. Croix 1956; Macve 1985. Rathbone 1991, 331, takes up the debate. Scholars have used double-entry accounting as the standard for economic rationality because Max Weber highlighted it as one of the key features in the rationalization of modern capitalism. Carruthers and Espeland 1991 argue, however, that merchants adopted double-entry bookkeeping in the Renaissance more for its symbolic than its technical virtues.

3. P. Miller 1998.

4. Aristoph. *Clouds* 643–45. Cf. Krates fr. 20.

5. Aristoph. *Peace* 1144.

6. Adespota 895, 896 (Edmunds v. 3 p. 353, ## 108, 109). The math (such as it is) in this speech is driven by the need to make a pun on the number seven.

7. Aristoph. *Wasps* 715–18.

8. Plato *Laws* 746d–47c.

9. Plato *Laws* 771a–c.

10. Theocritus 5.58–59.

11. Mayerson 1998b shows that in Hellenistic Egypt estates sometimes had idiosyncratic measures.

12. Given the scattered and anecdotal evidence, it's not surprising that scholars disagree about the abilities of Athenians to read and write. W. Harris 1989 (followed by Whitley 1997, 639, and Morgan 1999, 59) sees few citizens having much facility; Pébarthe 2006, on the other hand, argues that many citizens had these skills. In any case, there were variations: in areas outside Athens fewer still may have been literate (as Whitley 1997 shows for Crete), reading and writing became more common components of education during the fourth century (Morgan 1999), and women had fewer of these skills than men (S. Cole 1981, 219).

13. I argued this in chapter 3. Pébarthe 2006, 79–110, discusses the private use of writing

in daily life. All of Pébarthe's evidence concerns writing as a way of stabilizing relationships external to the household. Theophrastus imagines a tightwad making a written inventory of half-eaten radishes left over from a feast so that the diners' slaves don't take them (*Char.* 30.16), but this is not evidence for households organizing consumption through writing. The humor in the scene seems to come from the absurd inappropriateness of his cataloguing; he records not his supplies but others' potential debts.

14. Dem. 27.40–1, 49 (with the comments of E. Cohen 1992, 124–25); Lys. 32.14, 26. Cf. Aristoph. *Clouds* 18–31; Theophr. *Char.* 24.12; Finley 1951, 21–27; Millett 1991, 137.

15. W. Johnson 2000, who argues for understanding reading not as an isolated act but as a social and cultural system.

16. Hyp. 3.8, 10. The social function of this second act of reading was in part to mobilize his friends and relatives to support him in his dispute with Athenogenes. I discuss Epicrates' case further in chapter 8.

17. Kula 1986 discusses the imposition of the metric system in France; Cronon 1991 the imposition of quality standards for grain by the Chicago Board of Trade. Similarly, Hopkins 1980 argues that the requirement that taxes be paid in coin impelled the use of coinage throughout the Roman empire.

18. Osborne 1988, 323; Burford 1993, 180, notes a few instances where payment was required in produce.

19. The great exception might be the Spartan Helots. It is unclear whether the Helots paid a set rent in kind or a share of the crop. The source for the former, Plutarch (*Lyc.* 8), is late, influenced by propaganda, and refers to the Helots in Lakonia, whereas the source for the later, Tyrtaeus (fr. 6), is writing a poetic simile that refers to the Helots of Messenia. Myron (at Athen. 657d) wrote simply that the Spartans took a share (*moiran*) from the Helots. Hodkinson 1992 argues for a 50 percent sharecropping arrangement.

20. Lewis 1959, 243–44; Gofas 1969, 351–52; Gallo 2000.

21. Thuc. 6.54.4 says Pisistratus's tax was one twentieth, Arist. *Ath. Pol.* 16.4 says one tenth, and D.S. 9.37.3 says "a share." The name suggests (but does not prove) it was paid in kind. A law in Kolophon attempted to discipline tax farmers, including those who stored things for them in their courtyards (lines 14–15) (Étienne and Migeotte 1998).

22. A *hekteus* was literally a "sixth" of a medimnos, a half-hekteus "half-sixth."

23. *IG* I³ 78, lines 4–10, 14, and 27–30. Cavanaugh 1996 offers a detailed study of this document.

24. Meiggs 1972, 302–4.

25. Theoc. 7.32.

26. Theophr. *HP* 8.2.7.

27. For those of us used to thinking in percentages, it would be easy to say the solution is a bit more than 66 percent of a hekteus, a bit less than 75 percent. But Greeks do not seem to have imagined proportions as percentages, but as sums of fractions with numerators of one. Fowler 1999, chap. 7, discusses Greeks' use of fractions and ratios. Thomas 1987 shows how challenging the English found the comparison of proportions in the early modern period.

28. I don't know how those compelled to make a firstfruits offering to Demeter and Kore in Eleusis would have felt about it—the amount was almost trivial, but it would have been enough to have a nice feast at home; it was imposed by the Athenian state, but it fulfilled a religious obligation and carried a blessing (*IG* I³ 73.45)—but the decree was minimally exploitative in transferring wealth from subjects to Athenians. The grain was used first to make a *pelanos*, a cake offering; the rest was sold with the proceeds funding a series of sacrifices of bulls and a permanent votive, which would bear an inscription describing its origins (*IG* I³ 73.36–44). The mechanism the Athenians set up allowed ordinary folks, both

Athenians and their allies, to easily send an offering to the goddesses at Eleusis, a religious opportunity that may have been welcomed.

29. *R&O* 26, lines 5–8.

30. Stroud 1998. The law was first excavated in 1986.

31. Stroud 1998, 44–46, suggests the shifting verb tenses result from using both "technical" and legal language.

32. Most scholars have understood "the twelfth" to be a proportional tax on grain production (Stroud 1998; Rhodes and Osborne 2003). ("The fiftieth" is taken to be the well-known import-export tax.) E. Harris 1999, however, argues that "the twelfth" refers to a tax on grain in transit through the islands. Rhodes and Osborne, unpersuaded, argue that a transit tax would have been counterproductive (diverting grain away from Athens), that the phrase "the grain of the islands" more naturally refers to grain produced there, and that the schedule in the law is linked to the agricultural, not mercantile, calendar (Rhodes and Osborne 2003, 123–24). Although indirect, these arguments seem more persuasive to me.

33. Stroud 1998, the first publication, is the most detailed consideration. Rhodes and Osborne 2003, 118–29, supply the bibliography up to their publication and offer their own interpretation. Moreno 2003 and 2007, 103–15, and Hansen 2009 have appeared since.

34. Scholars have generally followed Stroud 1998, 79–80, who argues that the law converted taxes due in cash to taxes due in kind. The law does not say this, however; and if the law converted the payments by the buyer (the tax farmer) from cash to grain (presumably, the grain he had collected as taxes), it's possible that these taxes had always been collected as grain. Hansen 2009, 145–46, argues that they had always been collected in that form.

35. Moreno 2003. He interprets "the twelfth" as a ratio in relation not to the actual harvest but to the notional taxable capital of the farmer.

36. In chapter 5 I discuss unilateral declarations of value.

37. As I noted earlier, comparisons should consider the possibility of differences as well as similarities. I explicitly denied some similarities between Greece of the classical period and Hellenistic Egypt because of the much greater scale of economic enterprises in the latter (chap. 3). In this case, however, it is precisely because of the absence of the impersonal mechanisms that structure larger organizations (precise measuring) that it seems fair to consider it similar.

38. *P. Rev. Laws* cols. 24–25. They did not measure the agricultural produce, grapes, but the processed result, wine.

39. *P. Rev. Laws* col. 29.

40. Cf. *W. Chrest.* 250, where a farmer estimates (*suntimasthai*) both the amount of his wine production and the monetary value of his fruits and garlands.

41. *P. Rev. Laws* col. 42.

42. *P. Rev. Laws* col. 43 twice refers to measuring in fragmentary contexts.

43. *P. Rev. Laws* col. 42.

44. *P. Rev. Laws* cols. 27–28; *W. Chrest.* 250.

45. *SB* XXII, 15558; *P. Rev. Laws* col. 28.

46. *P. Rev. Laws* col. 29. The *timesis* here seems to refer to an estimate of its money value.

47. *P. Cair. Zen.* 59236; Préaux 1939, 184.

48. Arist. *Ath. Pol.* 7.3–4.

49. I discuss this in detail in chapter 5.

50. E.g., Chrimes 1932.

51. Skydsgaard 1988, 52.

52. Connor 1987, 47–49.

53. Lave 1986.

54. Netz 2002, 329.

55. This resembles the way I account for gasoline. I measure the capacity of the car's tank not by *gallons* but by *quarters of a tank*, and these quarters (especially the last one) I understand not as volumes but as distances (about 100 miles). I think in gallons only when I buy it—and even then this information matters mostly because it's part of the more important statistic, the total cost. I tend to gauge my patterns of usage by how often I fill up, time not volume.

56. *IG* I³ 421–30.

57. Lewis 1966.

58. *IG* I³ 421.20–21, 22–23, 29–30; 422.81–89.

59. 422.94–95 (barley), 130 (an unknown substance). There were two instances of houses sold with *pithoi*, I presume because they couldn't be moved (426.46–47; 430.1–2).

60. Pritchett 1956; Amyx 1958.

61. Osborne 1985, 47–63, argues that various sources show that the rich often owned scattered properties, even if these tended to cluster around their home demes.

62. Euphiletos, the speaker of Lys. 1, spent time in both (§11, 20), though his wife remained in the city. Cox 1998, 136–37, discusses the evidence for the wealthy owning multiple homes.

63. Arist. *HA* 596b26: "People who control many properties summer in cool places and winter in sunny ones."

64. *W&D* 475, 600, 613. In one of these instances, Hesiod advises that you "gather [the grain] well in vessels with measure" (1.600: μέτρῳ δ' εὖ κομίσασθαι ἐν ἄγγεσιν·). This probably does not indicate physically measuring the grain with a measuring device (as lines 349 and 397 do, which I discuss below). Rather, it seems reflect the archaic sense of *metron* used adverbially: "with fullness," that is, filling the containers completely (Prier 1976, 162).

65. Samuel 1966, 428.

66. Lines 815, 819. West 1978, 248–49, notes that Hesiod may have imagined substances other than just wine stored in *pithoi*—e.g., grain.

67. *W&D* 368–69: Ἀρχομένου δὲ πίθου καὶ λήγοντος κορέσασθαι, μεσσόθι φείδεσθαι· δειλὴ δ' ἐν πυθμένι φειδώ.

68. *W&D* 766–67. The monthly portion corresponds to the *pithos* of wine, except that the slaves had to figure out how to make it last.

69. *W&D* 559–60.

70. Prier 1976, 162, however, argues that even if these passages refer to measuring with a physical measure, the more fundamental sense is of "a completion of a process seen in the existence of a specific amount."

71. Xen. *Oik.* 8.10; 9.9. Small 1997, 227–30, notes the similarities and differences between Ischomachus's methods and those of contemporary memory systems.

72. Xen. *Oik.* 9.10.

73. Xen. *Oik.* 9.8: χωρὶς δὲ καὶ τὰ κατὰ μῆνα δαπανώμενα ἀφείλομεν, δίχα δὲ καὶ τὰ εἰς ἐνιαυτὸν ἀπολελογισμένα κατέθεμεν. οὕτω γὰρ ἧττον λανθάνει ὅπως πρὸς τὸ τέλος ἐκβήσεται.

74. Xen. *Oik.* 7.36.

75. Xen. *Oik.* 7.33.

76. 10.10: παραστῆναι δὲ καὶ ἀπομετρούσῃ τῇ ταμίᾳ. Only this once does Ischomachus allude to actual measuring on his farm, and he does not describe it in any detail. (You must, for example, infer the object of the verb of measuring.) Ischomachus may here allude to an otherwise unmentioned system of accounting through measuring, or the housekeeper may

be measuring out rations to other slaves under the supervision of the matriarch (a practice I discuss at the end of this chapter). The latter requires fewer assumptions.

77. Arist. *Oik.* 1345a19–24: ἐν δὲ ταῖς μεγάλαις, διαμερισθέντων καὶ τῶν πρὸς ἐνιαυτὸν καὶ τῶν κατὰ μῆνα δαπανωμένων, ὁμοίως δὲ καὶ περὶ σκευῶν χρήσεως τῶν καθ' ἡμέραν καὶ τῶν ὀλιγάκις, ταῦτα παραδοτέον τοῖς ἐφεστῶσιν. Ἐπὶ τούτοις καὶ τὴν ἐπίσκεψιν αὐτῶν διά τινος χρόνου ποιητέον, ἵνα μὴ λανθάνῃ τὸ σῳζόμενον καὶ τὸ ἐλλεῖπον.

78. The name does not indicate that this was done only in Attica, any more than the "Persian" system the same text mentions (the master organizing and overseeing everything himself) was exclusive to Persia. Cahill 2002, chap. 6, argues that in Olynthos in the fourth century, some households stored food extensively while others bought it as needed. There seems to have been a middle way: buying when the price was low (Xen. *Mem.* 2.10.4) and storing it.

79. Arist. *Oik.* 1344b33–34: ἀποδιδόμενοι γὰρ ὠνοῦνται, καὶ ἡ τοῦ ταμείου θέσις οὐκ ἔστιν ἐν ταῖς μικροτέραις οἰκονομίαις. In conjunction with this source, scholars usually cite Plutarch's story that Pericles sold off all the produce of his estates and used the money to buy things when necessary (*Pericles* 16.3–6). This, however, is a precarious piece of evidence. Stadter 1989, 197–98, notes that we don't know the source of the story: the origin could be history, comedy, or philosophy. It also contradicts the advice in the *Oikonomika* that this system is appropriate for smallholdings.

80. Lys. 32 and Aristoph. *Clouds* show the former. Note that the use of written lists in these circumstances parallels Hesiod's use of measurement.

81. Horden and Purcell 2000, 177–78, argue that buying and selling produce was a primary response to risk, indeed an essential part of self-sufficiency (273).

82. Dem. 42.6–8.

83. Aristoph. *Ekk.* 817–20 recounts a man selling his grapes and going straight away to buy *alphita*. Philocleon imagines spending his jury pay on lunch and wine on the way home, or having his daughter or wife try to finagle the coins (Aristoph. *Wasps* 605–19).

84. Although Hesiod's poem seems to present itself as a straightforward manual describing how to farm, it is a literary piece, which omits much and sometimes places emphases on strangely impractical things (Nelson 1996). Despite these distortions in the overall picture, however, it describes actual farming practices in elaborating its themes (work, timeliness, thrift, etc.). Indeed, Millett 1984 argues that the poem describes a consistent and plausible peasant society. Similarly, Xenophon's treatise is not a transparent description of an Athenian household. The specific household practices it refers to have been selected and organized to support political and ideological arguments (Johnstone 1994). But here, too, the problem of veracity is less about specific details and more about the overall picture.

85. Small 1997, 229, says that the housekeeper uses the list only to memorize the items, but the passage says merely that the husband and wife hand over the items to the housekeeper and make a list. I infer that Ischomachus uses the list to hold the housekeeper accountable. Pomeroy 1994, 283 (followed by Pébarthe 2006, 60), deduces from the plural participle in 9.10, γραψάμενοι, that Ischomachus's wife was literate. Through sections 9.6–9.13, Ischomachus uses the first person plural to describe actions that he plans, directs, and executes but in which his wife assists. His shift to the plural seems to indicate that he imagines she is being assimilated into his scheme of management. Inferring her literacy from the plural participle is a generous—if not impossible—conclusion. The idea that this passage shows that "literacy is regarded as essential to domestic management" (Morgan 1999, 54) exaggerates its implications.

86. Contrary to Pomeroy's claim (1994, 57), Xen. *Oik.* 6.3 refers neither to written accounts nor to a household. After Socrates suggests that he and Kritoboulos reiterate their

discussion, the latter replies: "Yes, just as it's pleasing when partners in a monetary enterprise go over it without dispute, so is it also when we, who are partners in a conversation, recapitulate it in agreement."

87. Arist. *Pol.* 1338a15–17. Cf. Theophr. fr. 662.

88. Arist. *HA* 580b12–13 refers to a container (*aggeion*) of millet that was shut tightly and later opened.

89. Dem. 42.6–9.

90. Money: Dem. 25.61; Theophr. *Char.* 18.4. Women's clothes: Aristoph. *Lys.* 1199; Theocritus 15.32. Note the way a woman's clothes were closely associated with the containers that held them at Menand. *Sik.* 388–9. Xen. *Oik.* 9.3 says that the valuable blankets and equipment should be put in a secure storeroom (*thalamos*).

91. Xen. *On Horsemanship* 4.1–2.

92. Aristoph. *Thes.* 418–28 is a prime piece of evidence for this. I discuss it below.

93. Xen. *On Horsemanship* 4.1–2. At *Oik.* 9.3, in fact, he stresses the dryness, not the security, of the room for storage of food.

94. These two possibilities in part reflect the kinds of evidence available: comedy depended on conflict (often domestic), while Xenophon sought to show Ischomachus as such a good manager of people, including his wife, that conflict never arose. But the ambiguity also reflects the possible differing positions of a free women in a slave-holding patriarchy, positions each type of writing exploited for its own ends.

95. Aristoph. *Thes.* 418–28.

96. In Aristophanes' *Frogs* (971–79), Euripides himself is made to say that he put calculation and examination into his plays so that Athenians have come to understand everything, especially how to run a household. And this consists specifically of questions: How's that? Where's that? Who took that? Here the implementation of distrust consists not in controlling space more closely but in techniques of inquisition.

97. Theophr. *Char.* 18.4.

98. Pritchett 1956, 236 and 248.

99. Nevett 1999 has shown that, despite this vocabulary, Greek houses were not rigorously divided by gender.

100. One Athenian litigant, Euphelitos, described how he had temporarily taken over the "women's room" so that his nursing wife could wash their baby without having to descend the stairs. One night, he said, she slipped out to meet her lover, shutting the door to and barring him, Euphiletos, in the "women's room" (note that it secures from the outside) with a jesting excuse that she didn't want him to get out and seduce the slave woman (Lys. 1.10–13). Euphiletos implies (with a pathetic irony) that the door was meant to prevent, not enable, illicit sex. Ischomachus is more direct: the purpose of the bolt on the door is to prevent slaves from taking things and having sex without his permission (Xen. *Oik.* 9.5).

101. Theophr. *Char.* 30.11; Herodas *Mime* 6.5–8; Xen. *Oik* 10.10 (discussed above). Theophr. *Char.* 4.10 describes the distribution of ground grain as rations, but only a supplemented text (on the model of 30.11) refers to measuring. Aristoph. *Peace* 1246–9 refers to weighing out figs for slaves working in the fields. The humor in this passage derives not from the weighing (which is the mundane assumption behind the joke), but from the material the scale was made of. It's impossible to say how often Greek masters measured slaves' rations.

102. The text here is uncertain, and some scholars have taken it to refer not to miserly measures but Pheidonian measures—a standard smaller than the Attic. Ussher 1960, 260–61, discusses this.

103. Theophr. *Char.* 30.11. This fellow's niggardliness—and the humor in the vi-

gnette—seems not to consist so much in his measuring as in the nitpicking way he follows
the norms of measuring.

104. Herodas *Mime* 6.4–8:

μᾶ, λίθος τις, οὐ δούλη
ἐν τῆι οἰκίηι <κ>εῖσ'· ἀλλὰ τἄλφιτ' ἢν μετρέω
τὰ κρίμν' ἀμιθρεῖς, κῆ<ν> τοσοῦτ' ἀποστάξηι
τὴν ἡμέ[ρ]ην ὅλην σε τονθορύζουσαν
καὶ πρημογῶσαν οὐ φέρουσιν οἱ τοῖχοι.

CHAPTER FIVE: VALUING

1. Netz 2002.

2. Zelizer 1989 and 1994.

3. Descat 2000, 18, briefly notes this.

4. Stroud 1998, 27 n. 42, collects references to the *pentekoste* at Athens; Vélissaropoulos
1980, 208–11, discusses it more generally.

5. Aineias 29.3.

6. *Syll.*³ 975. I discussed this law above in chapters 2 and 3.

7. *Syll.*³ 952.

8. In particular, it's unclear what "the writing" (*syngraphon*) is, although the law invokes
it in relation to penalties for violation.

9. Arnaoutoglou 1998, 41, takes the verb in the last sentence not to mean that the shipper
"values insufficiently" but that an official "imposes a lesser penalty." Since the verb is unique to
this inscription, its context here is all that can decide the question. I think his interpretation less
likely, because if an official failed his duty in this way, I'd expect a clause punishing him, whereas
this law simply makes up the difference between what was required and what was paid.

10. Arist. *Oik.* 1352b33–53a4. The text includes this in a long list of money-raising
schemes governments could use.

11. *Nomina* I, 106 A 11–18. Cf. Arist. *Ath. Pol.* 39.6.

12. *Syll.*³ 976.

13. *IG* IX.1 694. 9 and 44.

14. McCabe, Teos 48.10–11.

15. *Syll.*³ 736.46–47.

16. *Syll.*³ 1047.63–66.

17. It's not clear what 30 staters would have been worth in Erythrai (van Effenterre and
Ruzé 1994, 378).

18. Arist. *Ath. Pol.* 39.6.

19. *Hell. Oxy.* 16.2.

20. *Pol.* 1278a25, where it concerns "sharing in office." At 1321a26–28, he makes this
a requirement for "sharing in the *politeuma*" (i.e., the group of citizens eligible for office:
Mossé 1979, 247–48).

21. 1319a15. Newman 1902, v. 4, 517, remarks that this probably concerns a tax like the
eisphora, not qualification for citizenship, but if Aristotle thought that this would promote
agriculture, there should have been a reward (citizenship or office), not a cost (a tax) associated with land ownership.

22. The "Themistokles Decree," a fourth-century inscription that probably presents a
redaction of an Athenian decree of 480, required trierarchs to own a land and house in Athens (*GHI* 23.20–21).

23. Chapter 4 discusses the origin of these classes.

24. Arist. *Ath. Pol.* 7.3; cf. *Pol.* 1274a15–21.

25. Of these, he records only that they opened the Archons to Zeugetai in 457/6 (*Ath. Pol.* 26.2).

26. *Ath. Pol.* 8.1; 47.1. De Ste. Croix 2004, 9, accepts his silence in the case of other offices as evidence of absence.

27. De Ste. Croix 2004, 11–13, discusses them.

28. De Ste. Croix 2004, 5–72.

29. Arist. *Ath. Pol.* 7.4. Aristotle registers some uncertainty about his inference: "Nevertheless, it's more reasonable [εὐλογώτερον] that [the Hippeis] were defined by measures, just like the Pentakosiomedimnoi."

30. De Ste. Croix 2004, 30–32; Rosivach 2002, 39.

31. De Ste. Croix 2004, 46–49. Historians continue to rely primarily on etymology in arguing for the basis of the classes: de Ste. Croix, for example, tries to imagine the original definition of the classes based on the etymology of each.

32. Yet one that would solve the intractable debates about the original basis of the classes, and when and why these bases were changed. It is consonant with Connor's idea (1987, 47–49) that membership was self-declared, though he does not suggest it. The virtue of Connor's brief treatment of Solon's classes is that it shifts the question away from abstract, objective definitions (the quest of scholars, modern and ancient) to the question of the contexts and processes of using the classes.

33. Rosivach 2002, 43–45, catalogues the references to the classes in the classical period.

34. Rosivach 2005, 597–98, notes this briefly.

35. Arist. *Ath. Pol.* 7.4: διὸ καὶ νῦν ἐπειδὰν ἔρηται τὸν μέλλοντα κληροῦσθαί τιν' ἀρχήν, ποῖον τέλος τελεῖ, οὐδ' ἂν εἷς εἴποι θητικόν. He reports, too (47.1), that in his day although the law required the Treasurers of Athena to be from the Pentakosiomedimnoi even poor men were appointed. If, as I have argued, the Solonian classes were not formally defined, you don't have to deal with the problem of massive lying on the part of poor Athenians— and the tacit collusion of all others. Note, below, Thrasyllos's allegation that Pronapes stood for an office reserved for a Hippeus although he had declared a small *timema* in another context.

36. Dem. 43.54.

37. Isae. 1.39.

38. Similarly, members of the Boule swore an oath in which they promised "not to imprison any Athenian who provides three financial sponsors classed in the same class as himself" (Dem. 24.144). No source directly explains how the Boule verified the status of the sponsors, but I would suggest that this law compelled the wealthy to provide wealthy sponsors, not by appraising their status through records, but by threatening to imprison them if the Boule was not convinced of their self-declared *timema*.

39. In the case of the heiress, she probably did not declare her status herself, but the volunteer prosecutor or the Archon did. (In this case her guardian would not, since he would be the person charged with wronging her.)

40. E.g., *FD* 3.238.18–19 or *ID* 503.

41. *I Beroeae* 1 B76 ff. The same law allowed judges of male beauty contests to avoid service by swearing off (B52). It's unclear what would have constituted an inability here, perhaps an incapacity to avoid partisanship.

42. Dem. 19.124; Aesch. 2.94.

43. Arist. *Ath. Pol.* 49.2, and note the comments of Rhodes 1993, 567.

44. It is possible (as some have claimed) that valuations themselves were guaranteed by

oaths, but the evidence for this is late or indirect. Gofas 1969, 342 and 353–54, cites only the Ptolemaic Revenue Laws and a law of the emperor Hadrian. *IG* 12, Suppl. 349, the subject of Gofas 1969, is too fragmentary to yield any independent confirmation.

45. Dem. 42.18: ἀποφαίνω τὴν οὐσίαν τὴν ἐμαυτοῦ ὀρθῶς καὶ δικαίως. Gabrielson 1987, 20.

46. De Ste. Croix 1953, 34.

47. S. Johnstone 2003.

48. Isae. 7.39. Wyse 1904, 582, comments that Thrasyllos "comes dangerously near the undemocratic sentiment that poverty is a disqualification for office." Thrasyllos provided no witnesses for these allegations.

49. De Ste. Croix 1953, 43–44, discusses the incorrect and correct interpretations.

50. Christ 2007, 65–67.

51. *Syll.*³ 364.

52. *Syll.*³ 364.68–69.

53. The law's limitation on interest rates, line 75 (cf. line 91), suggests that high interest rates were a problem.

54. This constitutes a windfall because people did not lend money intending to foreclose on property, but in order to earn interest and have the principal repaid.

55. *Syll.*³ 364.1–10.

56. *Syll.*³ 364. 52, 78, 87–88, where arbitration is explicitly mandatory.

57. Willetts 1967, 33. Cf. *Iscr. di Cos* ED 129A.9–12 (c. 280) where a group of men reconciles (διέλυον) most of the parties in dispute over contracts, and with the rest "issues a verdict with all justice" (διέκρινομ μετὰ πάσης δικαι[οσύνης]).

58. *IJur* 43.

59. *Syll.*³ 364.6: ἐπὶ τοῦ δικαστηρίου. This functions like the Athenian practice of arbitration on stated terms, where the arbitrator's ruling merely repeated the disputants' compromise, thereby ratifying it (Isoc. 17.19; 18.10, 14).

60. Rubinstein 2003.

61. Arist. *Ath. Pol.* 55.2–4. There is some doubt about the correct reading of the text here and whether it refers to the payment of taxes or the man's Solonian class. Rhodes 1993, 618, shows why it probably refers to taxes. If it does refer to the man's class, this would be clear evidence both that class membership was determined unilaterally and ad hoc and that it could be challenged by a volunteer.

62. Arist. *Ath. Pol.* 55.4.

63. Schaps 2004, 27–28.

64. Xen. *Oik.* 2.3.

65. An estate worth only 500 drachmas would seem to be low for someone who served as a hoplite as Socrates did, an ironic assessment.

66. S. Johnstone 2003.

67. Consider how land values at Ephesos plummeted in response to war in the previous section.

68. Xen. Oik. 20.22–24: Ischomachus says his father increased the *time* of undeveloped land many times over by investing in it. Cf. Isae. 9.28, where the speaker claims that his father doubled the value (*axion*) of an orphan's land that he oversaw by planting and cultivating it.

69. Cahill 2002, 278, argues that houses in Olynthos nearer the agora tended to cost more.

70. Wallace 1989 discusses the *proeisphora*.

71. Gabrielsen 1987 explains the *antidosis* in detail.

72. Gabrielsen 1987, 29, says the speech shows "the subordination of substance to sleight-of-hand employment of argument and rhetoric."

73. Dem. 42.5. A stade is a bit over 600 feet, so the total distance would be 4.6 miles.

74. De Ste. Croix 1966.

75. De Ste. Croix 1966, 112.

76. Hdt. 1.185; 2.149; 2.41. Cf. Theophr. fr. 599.

77. Polyb. 9.26a.1–6.

78. Polyb. 4.39.1; 4.65.3; 4.83.4; 6.32.1; 10.11.4; 10.27.9.

79. Think about estimating the linear distance across a small lake versus estimating its surface area.

80. Dem. 42.5.

81. Finley 1951 studies these *horoi*; his book begins with this incident.

82. There was nothing illegal in Phainippos's decision to contest the *antidosis*.

83. The procedure required both parties to swear to "disclose rightly and justly the property" (Dem. 42.11, 18; cf. Gabrielsen 1987, 20).

84. The speaker embedded these accounts of Phainippos's income within a narrative of his violating the laws by selling off his property after the lawsuit had begun (§19). He reported them, however, less as diminishment of capital than as large income.

85. Arist. *Ath. Pol.* 49.4, though this text specifies the subsidy as 2 obols.

86. Isoc. 15.154.

87. Isoc. 15.155–58.

88. Xen. *Oik.* 1.7–14. The passage I quoted at the beginning of this section, in which Socrates imagines what his and Kritoboulos's estates might sell for, continues this argument by considering the opposite of income, expenses. Socrates says that although Kritoboulos's estate is worth a hundred times more than his, the richer man is poor because he has greater obligatory expenses (sacrifices, benefactions, entertainments, liturgies, the *eisphora*, etc.) and friends who are unlikely to aid him in need (Xen. *Oik.* 2.4–8.). Socrates does not monetize these expenses, but rather treats them as debts so that he can narrate a story of financial ruin.

89. Plato *Laws* 955d–e makes the difference clear.

90. As I argue in chapter 7 regarding Demosthenes' inheritance, what a man says his estate is worth may not correspond to what it might realize. Inheritance valuations were not negotiated, verified, or contested.

91. We make comparable the value of land and houses by describing the price per square foot—a still not fully adequate statistic.

92. Lambert 1997, 263, discusses the hypothesis (for which the evidence is not strong) that sometimes the value of land was inferred from the rent by multiplying by 12.5.

93. I discuss his case and his accounting more fully in chapter 7.

94. Dem. 27.9–11. He marks the transition at the beginning of §10 and again in his summary at the end of §11. Within the latter group (items that do not bring regular income), he distinguished items "at home" (slaves, raw materials for making sofas, money, furniture, etc.—all of which were literally in his house) and those "at sea," invested maritime loans, as E. Cohen 1992, 122–29, shows. Land and sea, however, were not the main—but only subsidiary—categories of his accounting (contra E. Cohen 1992, 121–22).

95. *IG* XII.9. 191.

96. *Syll.*³ 306. Heisserer 1980, 205–29, discusses the inscription in detail.

97. *Syll.*³ 306.16–19. Heisserer 1980, 208–9 (trans. modified).

98. Heisserer 1980, 213–15, and Thür and Taeuber 1994, 60–61, uphold distinct positions.

99. Merker 1975 publishes a fragmentary tariff from a Greek or Hellenized city in Syria or Palestine from the late Hellenistic period.

100. *Syll.*³ 44.

101. Billows 1990, 213–14.

102. *Syll.*³ 344.112, 119–20.

103. *Syll.*³ 1185.14–17.

104. Arist. *Ath. Pol.* 4.2.

105. Arist. *Ath. Pol.* 29.5; Thuc. 8.65.3–66.1 uses almost the same phrase. Rhodes 1972 argues that the Five Thousand denominated those with citizen rights, not just those eligible to hold office.

106. Thuc. 8.65.3 says five thousand was the upper limit; Lys. 20.13 implies the same.

107. Arist. *Ath. Pol.* 29.5 and 32.1–2; Thuc. 8.97.1.

108. Lys. 20.13: καταλογεὺς ὢν ἐνακισχιλίους κατέλεξεν, ἵνα μηδεὶς αὐτῷ διάφορος εἴη τῶν δημοτῶν, ἀλλ' ἵνα τὸν μὲν βουλόμενον γράφοι, εἰ δέ τῳ μὴ οἷόν τ' εἴη, χαρίζοιτο. The speaker had every reason to exaggerate his father's liberality (for which he provided no witnesses), but most of the jurors themselves would have been familiar with the process of registration, which had happened only a couple of years prior to the speech. Gomme et al. 1981, 201–6, discusses the difficulties of this speech.

109. Arist. *Ath. Pol.* 36.2.

110. Xen. *Hell.* 2.3.19.

111. Aristotle says that these men were meant to be "moderates" who were known for virtue (*arete*) (*Ath.Pol.*36.2).

112. Xen. *Hell.* 2.3.51.

113. Lys. 25.16; Isoc. 18.16; 21.2.

114. Dion. Hal., *Lys.* 32: Φορμίσιός τις τῶν συγκατελθόντων μετὰ τοῦ δήμου γνώμην εἰσηγήσατο τοὺς μὲν φεύγοντας κατιέναι, τὴν δὲ πολιτείαν μὴ πᾶσιν, ἀλλὰ τοῖς [τὴν] γῆν ἔχουσι παραδοῦναι, βουλομένων ταῦτα γενέσθαι καὶ Λακεδαιμονίων.

115. D.S. 18.18.4–5. Plutarch (Plut. *Phocion* 27.5) says that "they were governed by the ancestral constitution based on an assessment" (πολιτευομένοις δὲ τὴν πάτριον ἀπὸ τιμήματος πολιτείαν).

116. D.S. 18.74.3.

117. The problem of anachronism—writers interpreting earlier times as similar to their own—would tend to undermine patterns of change.

118. Although the text is undated, the consensus of scholars favors 321 based on circumstantial evidence. (Laronde 1987, 85–89, provides the details of the inference for the date.) As Laronde 1987, 89–91, also argues, this *diagramma* was not a constitution but a royal directive to the city, outlining a set of laws it should formulate.

119. Fraser did not provide a complete text, but only an extensive apparatus on many lines. Where Ferri and Oliverio disagree, Fraser consistently endorses Ferri's readings. Fraser 1956–58, 120–21, discusses the unjustified certainty with which the text has sometimes been treated.

120. I provide the text of Cary 1928:

(7) πολί]τευμα δ' ἔστω οἱ μύριοι· ὑπαρχόντων δὲ οἱ φυγάδες οἱ ἐς Αἴγυπτον φυγόντες

(8) οὓς] ἂν Πτολεμαῖος ἀποδείξηι καὶ οἷς ἂν τὸ τίμημα ᾖ τῶν χρημάτων τῶν ἀ[θα

(9) νάτων σὺν τοῖς τῆς γυναικὸς μνῶν εἴκοσι Ἀλεξανδρείων ὃ ἂν οἱ τιμητῆ[ρ

(10) ε]ς τιμήσωσι ἐλεύθερον, καὶ ὅσοις εἴη ὀφειλόμενον μναῖς εἴκοσι Ἀλεξανδρείοι[ς

(11) σὺν τοῖς τῆς γυναικὸς [ἀθ]ανάτοις τετιμημένοις μὴ ἐλάττονος τοῦ ὀφειλ

(12) ή]ματος καὶ τοῦ τόκου· καὶ ἀνταπομνυόντων οἱ ὀφείλοντες, [ἐ]ὰν οἱ γείτονες [μὴ

(13) τ]ιμὰς ἔχωσι· ἔστωσαν καὶ οὗτοι τῶν μυρίων μὴ νεώτεροι τριάκοντα ἐτῶν. τι[μ
(14) η]τῆρας ἀ[ν]αιρείσθων οἱ γέροντες ἐκ τῶν μυρίων ἄνδρας ἑξήκοντα μὴ νε[ω]
       τέρ[ους
(15) τρι]άκοντα ἐτῶν ὀμόσαντες ὅρκον νόμμον· οἱ δὲ αἱρεθέντες τιμώντωσαν ὅσα [ἂν
(16) ἐν τοῖς νόμοις γραφῇ· τῶι δὲ πρώτωι ἔτει πολιτεύσ[θ]ωσαν ἐκ τῶν πρότερον
       τιμημάτων.

121. Mossé 1979, 247–48 (followed by Poddighe 2001, 47), argued that the term *politeuma* indicated that those excluded from the Ten Thousand were "passive" citizens, that is, formally excluded from all political power.

122. Pagliaro 1956, 103–4.

123. Pagliaro 1956, 104–5, argues that "deathless" means real estate, while Christophilopoulos 1950 argues on the basis of other inscriptions that the term means something permanent, though this may or may not have had a technical meaning. In this inscription, its contrast with credits in the next clause suggests it means material wealth.

124. Fraser 1956–58, 123, draws attention to the anomaly of the wording here, but offers no solution.

125. Pagliaro 1956, 107–8.

126. From Pagliaro's exegesis, I infer he would translate lines 10–12 like this: "Let those who owe make a counterdenial on oath, [and the neighbors too swear], but if the neighbors do not have the *time*, these [those called to swear instead of the neighbors] should be from the Ten Thousand if not younger than thirty." (I have added his inferred supplements in square brackets.) Pagliaro's interpretation also requires another supplement: that the debtors swear about the debts whereas the neighbors swear about something different, the person's movable property.

127. As I noted earlier in this chapter, one Athenian litigant alleged that Phainippos, his opponent, had concocted fake debts so as to seem to be less wealthy.

128. Poddighe 2001.

129. Poddighe 2001, 45 n. 38. She cites (p. 47) Oliverio's version of lines 46–50 but Fraser 1956–58, 124–25, notes that "in most places I can read few of the letters read by Oliverio, and . . . a great many of his readings do not make sense."

130. Poddighe 2001, 47.

131. Cary 1928, 234–35. Fraser offers no guidance on this choice, though he agrees with Ferri that the last half of line 46 is completely unreadable.

132. I have translated Oliverio's text, on which Poddeghi relies. Ferri's differs in some of the particulars.

133. It is possible that at Athens, too, there was a link between the abstract wealth requirement and the census (*exetasmos*) that Demetrius of Phaleron conducted (Ktesikles, *FHG* 4.375; Athen. 272c).

134. Seaford 2004 (e.g., pp. 301–4) has analyzed such incommensurability.

135. Homer, *Il.* 6.235–37.

136. Many scholars have attempted to make sense of this puzzling episode (recently Donlan 1989, Scodel 1992, and Harries 1993). Homer's interjection makes clear that the exchange was inadvisable; the quantification confirms this.

137. *IG* II² 1629. 193–96.

138. My analysis concerns Solon as the figure to whom Greeks attributed quantification. I remain agnostic about whether Solon himself ever quantified anything beyond the ten periods of life, though the maneuvers attributed to Solon—quantifying, valuing, and setting ratios—look a lot like those of early law collections (Whitman 1995).

139. Solon fr. 5 (W).

140. Hdt. 1.32.

141. Seaford 2004, 81 and 194–95.

142. Plut. *Solon* 23.

143. Arist. *Ath. Pol.* 7.4.

144. Arist. *Ath. Pol.* 13.2.

145. Dem. 43.54. This is obviously not exactly 5:3:2.

146. D.L. 1.55. Plut. *Solon* 23.3 gives the first two, right before another ratio of 5:1 (the bounty for a wolf versus a wolf cub).

147. If the modern impulse is often to create incommensurability—first, second, and third construct a hierarchy but not a ratio, much as gold, silver, and bronze do—Greeks as often as not sought to quantify in ratios, rewarding crowns, for example, in explicit ratios of 5:3:2 (*IG* II² 1629. 193–96). Much more beyond Harvey 1965 could be written about the social uses of ratios by Greeks.

148. If the chapters of Aristotle's *Ath. Pol.* concerning Drakon can be trusted, the earliest case would be dated to the seventh century.

149. Interpersonal negotiations may have initially determined these values, but for the purposes of the citizen's *timema* they were fixed. What you pay for your house is negotiable; for your taxes, what you paid for your house is not.

CHAPTER SIX: COLLABORATING

1. Rubinstein 1998; Wallace 2005.

2. Ober 2008, esp. 156–59.

3. Most Athenian officials served cooperatively, as Aristotle's catalogue shows (Arist. *Ath. Pol.* 43.1–62.3). Although three of the most important—the archon, the king archon, and the polemarch—did not serve on a committee, they did collaborate with their assistants (*paredroi*) (Kapparis 1998). Hansen 1991, 225–45, gives a fine overview of Athenian offices.

4. Taylor 2007 shows that the proportion of known Athenian officials selected by lot from the demes in and around the city versus those further away roughly corresponds to the proportions of seats in the Boule (the small differences aren't statistically significant), while the proportion of known elected officials is about 12 percent higher from urban demes than the proportion of seats in the Boule (a difference that is statistically significant).

5. Fine and Harrington 2004, 348. I take up the problem of shirking in more detail in chapter 7.

6. Weber 1978, 217–82. Wallace 1992, 107, argues this for Athens.

7. Kahrstedt 1969, Dover 1960, and Hansen 1991. W. Thompson 1970, Jordan 1979, and, in modified form, Develin 1986 have contested the conclusion.

8. Dover 1960.

9. Dover 1960, 68.

10. Dover 1960, 76.

11. W. Thompson 1970, 58–59.

12. W. Thompson 1970, 60.

13. Jameson 1955, 75.

14. *IG* I³ 4B 22–24. Trans. Jordan 1979, 21.

15. Jordan 1979, 63.

16. Only two letters (PY) of the word *prytanis* are preserved on the fragmentary stone, a restoration that Jordan finds "inescapable" but that Piérart 1971, 543, questions. Nor does the inscription indicate that the *prytanis* was a member of the board, and Aristotle (*Pol.*

1322b26–29) says that *prytanis* was a common name for a religious offic a¹ ;though it's otherwise unattested in Athens).

17. Dem. 21.87.

18. Lewis 1955, 28.

19. Pollux 8.99.

20. Hdt. 5.71.2.

21. Thuc. 1.126.8.

22. Gabrielsen 1994, 20–21.

23. Develin 1986, 68–69.

24. Develin 1986.

25. Develin 1986, 79.

26. Polyb. 28.19.3.

27. Lys. 21.5; Arist. *NE* 1122a25. When the Athenians honored Kallias of Sphettos in 270/69, the citation of his benefactions recognized that when he had been chosen as *architheoron* to the festival for Ptolemy, he turned down the fifty minai of city funding (Shear 1978, 3 [lines 60–61]; *SEG* 28.60).

28. Dow 1976.

29. Dem. 25.23.

30. Aesch. 2.55; cf. 2.41, 126, 163.

31. Dem. 19.188–91.

32. Hansen 1991, 237; Kahrstedt 1969.

33. Thucydides adopted this Herodotean project but extended it to debate in larger groups: hence his concern with paired, opposing, rhetorical speeches before audiences that decided between them, and with factors—like self-deception or the debasement of language—that corrupt debate.

34. Dem. 19.156: πολλὰ λέγοντος ἐμοῦ καὶ θρυλοῦντος ἀεί, τὸ μὲν πρῶτον ὡς ἂν εἰς κοινὸν γνώμην ἀποφαινομένου, μετὰ ταῦτα δ᾽ ὡς ἀγνοοῦντας διδάσκοντος, τελευτῶντος δ᾽ ὡς ἂν πρὸς πεπρακότας αὑτοὺς καὶ ἀνοσιωτάτους ἀνθρώπους οὐδὲν ὑποστελλομένου.

35. Yunis 1991, 198–99, and Mader 2007 argue that Demosthenes often represented himself to the Assembly as one who instructed in the Periclean mode, which as Mader 2007, 158, notes, often shaded off into censure.

36. Karavites 1990.

37. Thuc. 6.47–50.

38. Hdt. 3.81.

39. Hdt. 3.82.

40. Hdt. 3.83.

41. Aesch. 2.107.

42. I discuss this case in detail in chapter 7.

43. Hdt. 8.49.

44. Hdt. 3.73; 3.76; 4.137; 5.36; 5.93.

45. Exceptionally, Drako's law on homicide (*IG* I³ 104) specified that the male relatives of a victim of unpremeditated killing could pardon the killer only if they agreed unanimously.

46. E.g., Hdt. 5.118.

47. Lattimore 1939. Gray 2002, 299–302, traces the permutations this story takes.

48. Hdt. 5.36; 7.10; 8.68.

49. Saïd 2002, 122–23.

50. Plato *Apol.* 32b, Xen. *Hell.* 1.7.14–15, and *Mem.* 1.1.18 and 4.4.2 recount the case of Socrates, and Aesch. 2.82–84 that of Demosthenes. The size and method of choosing the

presiding committee differed between these two incidents, though the Boule supplied the members of both committees (Hansen 1991, 140–41).

51. Hdt. 4.11; 4.119; 7.219.

52. Hdt. 8.56–63. Darius, too, by threatening to betray them, compelled the other six conspirators against the king to carry out their plot immediately rather than wait (Hdt. 3.71–73).

53. I discussed the procedure for declining an office in chapter 5.

54. Thuc. 7.47–49; 7.50. Hamel 1998, 95–99, examines these in detail. Phrynichos similarly forced his position on his colleagues (Thuc. 8.27).

55. Hdt. 4.137–38.

56. Hdt. 5.92.

57. Hdt. 5.93.

58. Aesch. 2.22.

59. Dem. 19.174. He does not clarify how many of the other envoys voted against his letter, though in his narrative of the embassy he presents himself as a lone dissenter.

60. Hdt. 6.109–10. In Herodotus's story, the seven Persians discussing what type of government to impose determine this by majority vote (Hdt. 3.83).

61. Dem. 35.11. The exigent circumstances may have prevented the (possibly protracted) formulation of a consensus, especially on such a contentious issue as whose stuff to ditch.

62. Katz 1976 offers suggestive if inconclusive parallels between the three divine envoys and the three Athenian generals who led the Athenian expedition against Sicily.

63. As at Thuc. 7.47.3.

64. Thus it oversimplifies to claim that in this scene "decisions are made by majority vote" (Katz 1976, 354).

65. Lee 2007, 13–15, discusses these.

66. Xen. *Anab.* 3.3.11–20.

67. Xen. *Anab.* 6.1.18.

68. The word "decree" does not appear in the *Anabasis*; the related word for "vote" (*psephizein*) does, but only in reference to votes by assemblies (1.4.15; 3.2.31; 3.2.33; 5.1.4; 5.1.14; 5.6.11; 6.2.12; 7.3.14; 7.6.14; 7.7.18), not the committee of generals. In Herodotus, a *gnome* was commonly said to "prevail" (1.40; 1.61; 3.82; 5.36; 5.118; 7.175).

69. Nussbaum 1967, 43.

70. Dalby 1992, 22 n. 44.

71. Xen. *Anab.* 1.6.9–10; 5.3.37.

72. Xen. *Anab.* 4.6.6–21.

73. Dalby 1992; Hornblower 2004.

74. Nussbaum 1967, 47.

75. Dalby 1992, 22.

76. Xen. *Anab.* 6.1.17–18.

77. Certainly oligarchically inclined Greeks thought so: Isoc. 3.24; Theophr. *Char.* 26.2.

78. Xen. *Anab.* 6.2.12–16.

79. Xen. *Anab.* 6.2.12.

80. Xen. *Anab.* 6.3.1–9.

81. Xen. *Anab.* 6.4.10–11.

82. Xen. *Anab.* 6.1.29.

83. Many reacted badly to Xenophon's scheme to found a new city on the Black Sea, not so much because it would keep them from getting home, as because it would prevent them from being mercenaries (6.4.7–8 with Roy 2004). Note that these two things had caused divisions in the army before Cyrus was killed.

84. Azoulay 2004.

85. E.g., Xen. *Anab.* 2.5.28; 7.2.2.

86. Xen. *Anab.* 1.4.13–17.

87. Xen. *Anab.* 7.8.11.

CHAPTER SEVEN: APPORTIONING LIABILITY

1. Piérart 1971; Roberts 1982; Fröhlich 2004.

2. Levinson 2003, 376.

3. Lys. 12.62. Xenophon's favorable portrait of Theramenes in the *Hellenika* (2.3.15–19, 22–56) suggests there were some who remembered him as the noble victim of the Thirty's terror rather than as one of the agents behind it.

4. Defendants rarely used this plea of necessity. In twenty-five defense speeches, only one argued for lenience because of acting under necessity, and this was on an issue peripheral to the main case (Lys. 18.2). Indeed, the main evidence for defendants using this argument lies in prosecutors' speeches (Lys. 12, 13, and 22). In two of these cases, the prosecutor trapped the defendant into the argument in cross-examination (Lys. 12 and 22). But in none of the cases can you be sure that the defendant actually made as much of the argument as the prosecutor said he would. Defendants may have been reluctant to employ this plea because it required admitting having done the deed. Paradoxically, the idea that crimes performed unwillingly should be pardoned was most often used by prosecutors—to provoke the jurors' anger against defendants who, the prosecutors alleged, had acted intentionally (e.g., Lys. 31.11).

5. Lys. 13.52; cf. Isoc. 18.17.

6. Plato, *Apol.* 32c–e.

7. Such a man would be *chrestos* (§32) or *agathos* (§48).

8. Lys. 12.28–29.

9. I discuss this in chapter 8.

10. Aesch. 3.18: τοὺς ἱερέας καὶ τὰς ἱερείας ὑπευθύνους εἶναι κελεύει ὁ νόμος, καὶ συλλήβδην ἅπαντας καὶ χωρὶς ἑκάστους κατὰ σῶμα,… καὶ οὐ μόνον ἰδίᾳ, ἀλλὰ καὶ κοινῇ τὰ γένη, Εὐμολπίδας καὶ Κήρυκας καὶ τοὺς ἄλλους ἅπαντας.

11. *IG* II² 1013.12 (Athens, late 2nd cent.); Dem. 24.50 (Athens, before 353); *Syll.*³ 976.71–74 (Samos, after 188); *Syll.*³ 671 A.11–12 (Delphi, 160/59); *Syll.*³ 577.61–62 (Miletus, 200/199). If the restoration is correct, *IG* I³ 4 B.13–16 (Athens, 485/84) would also belong here.

12. *GHI* 65.36–39 (Athens, after 430).

13. Singular: *GHI* 46.35–37 (Athens, third quarter of the 5th century); *GHI* 69.36–38 (Athens, 425/24); *Syll.*³ 226.49–51 (Athens, 344/43); *IG* II² 1631.385–93 (Athens, 324/3); *Syll.*³ 577.24–25 (Miletus, 200/199); *Syll.*³ 1220.8–9 (Nisyros, 3rd cent.); Dem. 24.22 (Athens, before 353). Plural: *GHI* 65.36–39; *GHI* 73.18–21. (If restored correctly, *IG* I³ 133.18 [Athens, late 5th cent.] would be included here.) Indeterminate (an infinitive): *GHI* 43.8–9; *IG* I³ 84.9–11 (Athens, 418/7); Dem. 24.22 (Athens, before 353).

14. *R&O* 59.44–45 (Arkesine, Amorgus, mid 4th cent.). Also *IG* I³ 6C.26–30 (Athens, before 460); *R&O* 100.238–42 (Athens, before 325); *Nomina* I.84.13–15 (Erythrai, 5th cent.?); *IG* XII.8.265.8–10 and 10 (Thasos, 4th cent.); *Nomina* II.95.11–13 and 48–49 (Thasos, 463–60?); Pleket 2.II.4–6 (Thasos, 425–400); *R&O* 25.26–28 (Athens, 375/4); *GHI* 43.12 (Miletus, 470–440); *I Beroeae* B.33–35 (Beroia, early 2nd cent.); *GHI* 43.6–7 (Miletus, mid-5th cent.); Dem. 24.22 (Athens, before 353); Dem. 43.71 (Athens, before the mid-4th cent.); *Syll.*³ 672 (Delphi,160/59); Nomina I 16.7–8 (Gortyn, early 5th cent.?); I Cret. III. 7.16–20 (Itanos, beginning of 3rd cent.); *Syll.*³ 1157 (Korope, 100); *Syll.*³ 577 (Miletus, 200/199); *IG*

XII.8.267.14–15 (Samos, 4th–3rd cent.); Buck no. 4 A.15–18 (Chios, 5th cent.). If restored correctly, *IG* I³ 4 B.16–17 (Athens, 485/84) would also belong here. Cf. *IG* IV.554.6–7 (Argos, 6th–5th cent.), which makes the whole council "liable to Athena" if the members fail to act.

15. The distributive force of *hekastos* refers to something shared among a group (Dem. 21.67), often a *meros*, a part or share (Dem. 3.34; 45.18; Isae. 5.16).

16. Aesch. 2.46.

17. Rhodes 1985, 14 n. 9.

18. Aesch. 1.111–12.

19. Dem. 19.31–32.

20. Gabrielsen 1994, 176.

21. Vial 1984, 167–70; *ID* 353.

22. *IG* VII.3172.29; *Syll.*³ 955.25.

23. *R&O* 26. 33–36. I discussed this law in chapter 3.

24. E. Harris 1989.

25. In American law, this would be joint and several liability.

26. In this massive sea battle, the victorious Athenians lost twenty-five ships, sunk or disabled, with about 200 rowers and others per ship. It's unknown how many of these were saved.

27. E.g., Lang 1990.

28. *Hell.* 1.7.5, 14, 25.

29. Plato, *Apol.* 32b; Arist. *Ath. Pol.* 34.1. Cf. Ps.-Plato *Axioch.* 368d.

30. The decision not to allow the generals a full defense before the Assembly that voted on their fate (Xen. *Hell.* 1.7.9) and the threats to silence those with qualms about the procedures (1.7.13–15) seem unfair.

31. When it became too dark to accurately count hands, the first meeting of the Assembly was suspended and the matter referred back to the Boule (1.7.7). The Boule formulated a proposal (to try the generals collectively), which it submitted to the Assembly (1.7.9–10). In the ensuing debate, the Assembly first voted for an alternative proposal (to try them individually), then reversed itself and endorsed the Boule's proposal (1.7.34). It subsequently voted to condemn the generals (1.7.34). The people of Akragas, on the contrary, when upset with their generals, spontaneously stoned most of them to death (Diod. 13.87.5). Cf. Thuc. 5.60.6.

32. Lang 1990, 25. As Andrewes 1974 shows, Xenophon's account defends the generals, whereas Diodoros's vilifies the Athenian people, while exonerating Theramenes.

33. In Xenophon's narrative of the initial Assembly meeting, the generals' defense (1.7.5–7) runs about twice the length of Theramenes' accusation (1.7.4), and while for a later meeting he quotes the resolution of the Boule stating the charge (1.7.9–10) and summarizes the accusation of one of the surviving sailors (1.7.11), he allows Euryptolemos a lengthy defense speech (1.7.16–33).

34. Xen. *Hell.* 1.7.29; Diod. 13.100.1.

35. Xen. *Hell.* 1.6.35 says simply ἔδοξε δὲ καὶ τοῖς τῶν Ἀθηναίων στρατηγοῖς. In Diodoros, the storm arises before any decision is made (13.100.3).

36. Aesch. 2.178. Cf. Lys. 27.4.

37. Dem. 45.7.

38. Rubinstein 2000, 78–87.

39. Hansen 1975, 67, says that "the principle 'one person, one trial' [was] adopted by the Athenians themselves in their administration of justice as fundamental for the democracy."

40. Xen. *Hell.* 1.7.34.

41. MacDowell 1978, 189. Pownall 2000 and Mehl 1982 argue that the charge of illegality is hard to maintain.

42. Xen. *Hell.* 1.7.12.

43. Xen. *Hell.* 1.7.35; Diod. 13.103.1–2.

44. Lys. 12.36.

45. Xen. *Hell.* 1.7.4, 9, 17.

46. Xen. *Hell.* 1.7.31.

47. This parallels Xenophon's brief summary (1.7.5–6) of the generals' own defense.

48. Thuc. 4.2 and 29.

49. Xen. *Hell.* 1.5.16. In the last phrase δι' ἀμέλειάν τε καὶ ἀκράτειαν, the second term, ἀκράτεια, usually means "lack of power [over yourself with regard to pleasures]." The first term, ἀμέλεια, seems to refer to Alcibiades' irregular and ineffective delegation of authority while gone (which Plutarch [*Alc.* 36.1–2] elaborates).

50. Ant. 6. The date of this speech is uncertain, but falls somewhere in the 410s, several years before the battle.

51. Ant. 6.12–13.

52. Ant. 6.15.

53. Xen. *Hell.* 1.7.5.

54. Xen. *Hell.* 1.7.6.

55. Although Xenophon does not include this report, Andrewes 1974 shows that his narrative implies and requires it. Later in his history, Theramenes refers to it (2.3.35).

56. Athenian law recognized only the father's custody of children; his death made them legal orphans.

57. You can read five of these: Dem. 27–31.

58. S. Johnstone 2003, 265 n. 86. The death of Demosthenes' father's suddenly changed the relationships between some of these people. Aphobos, who was supposed to become Demosthenes' new stepfather, was probably still a young man in his twenties, and Kleobule, unlike many Athenian brides who were teenagers and often ten to fifteen years younger than their betrothed, was nearly his age or even older (Davies 1971, 118 and 121). Demothenes alluded to a conflict between his mother and Aphobos.

59. Scholars' consistent acceptance of Demosthenes' claim of fraud and embezzlement is remarkable, especially since at least some of them recognize that the details of his case are hyperbolic and unreal (as Davies 1971, 132–33, characterizes it). This trust stems in part from Demothenes' liberal use of witnesses and his vindication by the jury (though scholars are fickle in acknowledging the wisdom of other Athenian verdicts, like Socrates' conviction), but probably also from the knowledge that he would go on to become the great defender of Greek freedom as well as the story of his youth, which casts him as rich and well-born yet also self-made. We cannot know what really happened, but we could accord the unfortunate Aphobos the courtesy of attempting to understand what he would have said in his defense. Here's my attempt, based on hints in Demosthenes' speeches: Demosthenes' father left the impression of a considerable fortune when he died, and the guardians acted in accord with this, selling off some assets (27.18, 43) so that they could disperse the funds designated for themselves, and valuing the estate for tax purposes in the highest class. But it gradually became apparent that Demosthenes' father, through inadvertence, incompetence, or bad luck, had failed to account for many debts he owed (27.49, 54), that he had foolishly lent money to someone who subsequently defaulted (27.25), and that it was prudent or necessary to pay off debts to the state incurred by Kleobule's father (28.1). The estate, in other words, had *never* really been worth anything like what Demosthenes said it was when his father died—not 14 talents, but only 5 (27.62). (Aphobos may also have claimed that he had

turned over all he held, though the other guardians had not [27.52].) On top of this, much of what Demosthenes claimed the estate should have been worth when he came of age depended on exuberant assumptions about the rate of return on investments: somewhere between 12 and 20 percent each year, *after* all deductions, expenses, and losses. Demosthenes' speech does not hint at how Aphobos responded to some specific claims (e.g., what happened to the will, or the raw materials used in the workshops?), but it would be dangerous to conclude that no reasonable response was possible.

60. Dem. 27.12.

61. Dem. 27.23.

62. Dem. 27.29; cf. 29.59–60.

63. Lysias, too, had discussed this problem in his prosecution of Eratosthenes (Lys. 12.33).

64. Dem. 27.1; 29.8; 30.2.

65. Dem. 27.49 ff.

66. Mirhady 2000, 186–95, discusses his use of witnesses in the speeches against Aphobus.

67. Demosthenes' attempt to find contradictions in the guardians' claims (27.42–43), shows only one disagreement: Aphobos said that Therippides had received 70 minae, but he denied it.

68. *R&O* 5.88–94.

69. I discuss how the secret ballot operated in rhetorical settings in chapter 8.

70. Levinson 2003, 378.

71. Dem. 22.37.

72. Aesch. 1.110–12.

73. Hansen 1991, 258, describes the oversight of officials by the Athenian Boule; Fröhlich 2004 catalogues the phenomenon throughout the Greek world.

74. *Syll.*³ 1157 (1st cent.).

75. *IG* I³ 4B 22–24. Trans. Jordan 1979, 21.

76. Christ 2007, 67 n. 70.

77. Isoc. 3.18.

78. Indeed, late in the work (8.1.14–15), Cyrus uses his military innovations as the specific model for reforming his political institutions.

79. S. Johnstone 1994. Despite his physical exile, Xenophon remained an Athenian through his writing.

80. Xen. *Kyr.* 2.2.17.

81. The form of differential reward structure sometimes used in construction projects was piece work.

82. 2.1.18. Cf. Xen. *Kyr.* 2.1.2. Our term "mercenary" mistranslates *misthophoros* in these passages since the soldiers were serving for pay in the army of their own country. Cf. Trundle 2004, 16–21.

83. Harvey 1965. This theory contrasted an arithmetic proportion, where the *difference* between numbers is equal (2, 4, 6, 8, etc.), with a geometric proportion where the *ratio* between them is equal (2, 4, 8, 16, etc). The latter, the advocates of this theory argued, was the truer equality.

84. E.g., Arist. *Pol.* 1301b27–1302a8.

85. Xen. *Kyr.* 1.1.2; cf. 8.1.1–7.

86. Xen. *Kyr.* 1.1.3.

87. Xen. *Kyr.* 1.1.5: ἐδυνάσθη δὲ ἐπιθυμίαν ἐμβαλεῖν τοσαύτην τοῦ αὐτῷ χαρίζεσθαι ὥστε ἀεὶ τῇ αὐτοῦ γνώμῃ ἀξιοῦν κυβερνᾶσθαι.

88. Xen. *Kyr.* 1.6.21.

89. Plato *Laws* 757a–c (πρὸς τὴν αὐτῶν φύσιν ἑκατέρῳ). Isoc. 7.21–2. In 3.14–16 he consistently used the language of aristocratic status to describe reward (κατὰ τὴν ἀξίαν), though he did imply that this would consider both men's natures and their actions (καὶ τὰς φύσεις τῶν ἀνθρώπων καὶ τὰς πράξεις). As Harvey 1965, 114–17, notes, Aristotle's theory pushed him away from rewarding people's natures, but he couldn't break with traditional thinking. Schofield 1996, section IV, discusses Aristotle's idea of ἀξία. Ober 1989, 285–89, analyzes tensions in popular discourse between birth and achievement.

90. *Pol.* 1317b4.

91. Xen. *Kyr.* 2.3.15, 16.

92. Xen. *Kyr.* 2.2.18, 20, 21; cf. 8.4.5.

93. Xen. *Kyr.* 2.2.20; 2.3.4.

94. S. Johnstone 1994.

95. Xen. *Kyr.* 8.2.26.

96. Xen. *Kyr.* 2.2.20; 2.3.4.

97. To simply refer to Xenophon's scheme as a case of "geometric" equality (Gera 1993, 163–64, Mueller-Goldingen 1995, 137–39) therefore misrepresents it. Insofar as Xenophon's scheme was proportional, it was analogous to this theory, but the theory of geometric equality always justified rewarding different statuses or characters differently, precisely the key break Xenophon made.

98. Xen. *Hell.* 3.2.10.

99. Xen. *Hell.* 3.4.16; *Agis.* 1.25; *Kyr.* 1.2.12, 6.2.6; *On Horsemanship* 1.26.

100. Xen. *Poroi* 3.2.

101. Xen. *Hiero* 9.3–11.

102. Xen. *Kyr.* 8.4.4.

103. As does Isoc. 7.21–2 or Plato, *Laws* 757b–c. Cf. *Dissoi Logoi* 7.1–6. I discuss the random choice of officials in chapter 6.

104. Arist. *Pol.* 1317b34.

105. Arist. *Ath. Pol.* 27.4.

106. *IG* I^3 82.20.

107. As Nadon 1996 and Whidden 2007 argue.

108. Thalmann 2004.

109. Thalmann 2004, 391–92.

110. Xen. *Kyr.* 8.1.46–8.2.28.

111. Xen. *Kyr.* 8.2.26: τοῖς μέντοι ἀρίστοις οἱ ἀγῶνες οὗτοι πρὸς ἀλλήλους καὶ ἔριδας καὶ φιλονικίας ἐνέβαλλον.

112. Cf. 3.3.10, where Cyrus attempts to mitigate the jealousies among the soldiers his competitive training causes by leading them into battle, where common dangers induce them to strive for the common good.

113. Xen. *Kyr.* 8.2.28.

114. 8.2.28. This comes close to reproducing the language of 8.1.48. The pairing marks the beginning and end of Xenophon's discussion of how Cyrus made the powerful loyal to himself.

115. Cf. Isoc. 3.15: "Monarchies apportion the most to the best man, the second-most to the one after him, and the third- and fourth-most to others according to the same proportion (*logon*). And if this isn't true everywhere, it is at least the purpose of the constitution."

116. Xen. *Kyr.* 2.3.12.

117. Xen. *Kyr.* 7.3.1; 8.4.29–30; cf. 8.3.2.

118. Dem. 19.13, 175.

119. Aesch. 2.21, 43–47; cf. Dem. 19.253.

CHAPTER EIGHT: DECIDING

1. Finley's still-bracing study of Athenian demagogues (1974 [original 1962]) brilliantly analyzed the operation of the Athenian Assembly as a system that produced effective results irrespective of the participants' motives. Although Finley may have underemphasized the risks in the system, his crucial insight was that moralizing about speakers' motives was probably an important part of the system and constituted (to some) a powerful polemic against it, but does not fully explain how the system actually operated.

2. Ober 1989.

3. There are limitations of this body of evidence: Most of the speeches were written by professional speechwriters for wealthy clients; very rarely is the opposing speech or the verdict extant; and the preserved written speeches may not correspond exactly to what the litigants said in court.

4. S. Johnstone 1999, 128–29.

5. Aristotle noted (*Rhet.* 1354b25) that most writers on rhetoric discussed only how to speak in court.

6. Since the historians Thucydides and Xenophon provide much of the evidence for this last point, their own Athenian rhetorical expertise may have contaminated their representations of other Greeks.

7. T. Cole 1991b; Schiappa 1992 and 1999. Since both Plato (e.g., *Gorg.* 465a) and Xenophon (e.g., Xen. *Mem.* 3.10.1–15 with S. Johnstone 1994, 234–35) depict Socrates as insisting on and offering theoretical accounts of practices, this may have been one of his tricks, picked up by both students. O'Sullivan 1993 and Schiappa 1994 disagree on whether Plato invented the term "rhetoric."

8. Arist. *Rhet.* 1358a36 ff.

9. Stunning and elusive as Gorgias's *Helen* is, Porter 1993 has interpreted it as a critical unshrouding of rhetorical language, which demonstrates through its own outrageousness that such language is powerless to deceive except for the self-deception of its auditors. If Porter is right, Gorgias himself stands outside the tradition of the theory of the persuadable soul, though his text testifies to its prevalence.

10. Segal 1962, 124–26.

11. Porter 1993, 296, shows how the speaker's deception depends on the self-deception of the listener.

12. Segal 1962, 121–22, argues that persuaders invoke a power ultimately beyond their understanding and control.

13. Plato *Phdr.* 261a: ἡ ῥητορικὴ ἂν εἴη τέχνη ψυχαγωγία τις. In *Euth.* 298e–90a Plato likens the art of making speeches to enchanting vipers, scorpions, and the like, except that it's directed not at these pests but at jurors and other crowds.

14. de Romilly 1975, 15; Gellrich 1994, 280–81.

15. Murray 1990.

16. Warnick 1989.

17. Abizadeh 2002, 284.

18. C. Johnstone 1980, 13 (emphasis added).

19. Gorgias, *Helen* 11.

20. Arist. *Rhet.* 1404a9. He adds, however, that style doesn't matter as much as people think.

21. Arist. *Rhet.* 1395ʰ −4.

22. Arist. *Rhet.* 141.b. 6.

23. Arist. *Rhet.* 12.4b29−55a1.

24. Arist. *Rhet.* 1. /a11−13; 1357a3; 1419a18−19.

25. Aristoph. *Clouds* 245−46.

26. Arist. *Pol.* 1253. 25.

27. Law 1994, 9−12.

28. He offers several scenes with opposing speakers and a third party as decider: *Wasps* 521−735, 894−991; *Knights* 624−82, 724−1128; *Frogs* 871−1471.

29. *Knights* 724−1128.

30. *Frogs* 1411−13, 1433−36, 1467−68; *Wasps* 725−35.

31. Bers 1985; Tacon 2001.

32. Ober 1989, 104; Hansen 1991, 146−47.

33. Demosthenes (8.77) noted that shouting in the Assembly was different from acting.

34. Hammer 2005, 113−15.

35. Homer *Il.* 1.53−305; 2.84−393; 19.54−237; *Od.* 2.6−259; the trial scene depicted on Achilles' shield may follow a similar pattern (*Il.* 18.497−508).

36. Gagarin 1992. His analysis of how disputants and lords interacted (66−71) draws heavily on the *Iliad.*

37. As Westbrook 1992, 74−75, shows, the disputants in the trial scene (*Il.* 18.497−508) address not the assembled crowd but the nobles, who act as judges.

38. I offer this comparison to make clear the particular features of the situation in classical Greece. I address neither the difficult question of whether or how these poems depict a historical reality nor the vexing problems of how political and legal institutions evolved from the archaic to the classical period.

39. Thuc. 2.40.2.

40. Thuc. 6.39.1

41. Arist. *Rhet.* 1358b2−3. Couloubaritsis 1996 discusses Aristotle's analysis of *krisis.*

42. Schiappa 1999, 185−206, argues that the category of *epideictic* (which Aristotle seems to have invented) obscures the possible political import of such speeches.

43. Aristotle later attempts to keep epideictic speeches within the fold of rhetoric— since rhetoric exists, Aristotle claims, for the sake of deciding, *krisis* (Arist. *Rhet.* 1377b)— by saying it's directed to a spectator *as if* he were a decider (Arist. *Rhet.* 1391b). But, he admits, this is not the usual sense of the word. However, the crucial point remains that only listeners to speeches in the courts and the Assembly engaged in *krisis*, deciding. Walker 1996, 252−56, discusses this important difference.

44. Thuc. 3.38.7.

45. Wohl 2002, 95−96.

46. Andrews 1994, 33−39. While this draws on Thucydides' pervasive use of the *logos/ergon* binary, any speaker's injunction to his listeners to judge based on *egra* (facts), not *logoi*—the former, of course, to be found in his own speech, the latter in his opponent's—was not a deeply original analysis but a common rhetorical argument, as I note below.

47. Bickford 1996, 418.

48. Bickford 1996. Like many political philosophers (including Aristotle himself), Bickford melds the descriptive and the prescriptive in her analysis, such that her reading of Aristotle ultimately serves to ground her theory of political communication.

49. Braet 1987. Hermagoras's writings have not survived, but scholars can reconstruct their contents from descriptions by later authors.

50. Braet 1987, 84−85.

51. Hunter 1988, 25.

52. Yunis 1991; Mader 2007. Hesk 1999, 183, however, rightly cautions against treating Demosthenes as unique: "One suspects that *all* major *rhetores* of the mid-fourth century would have sounded 'Periclean' at certain points in their deliberative addresses to the *demos*." The idea of *instruction*, that is, was primarily a rhetorical resource to be used against your opponents, not a disinterested analysis. Even Aristophanes contrasted his good instruction with the fawning, bribing, and bamboozling of others (*Achar.* 656–58).

53. McAdon 2004. Aristotle's treatise is problematic as well because it includes many prescriptive elements and bears an unreliable relation to actual Athenian rhetorical practice.

54. I should note that neither Bickford nor Braet intend to accurately describe Athenian rhetoric: Bickford attempts to turn Aristotle against those who find in him an endorsement of certain theories of civil society, and Braet argues that Hermagoras anticipates modern legal thinking.

55. In the Assembly, Athenians might put off a decision on a motion, but could do so only by a vote.

56. In the courts, if you did not vote, you were not paid.

57. Cole 1991b, 14. Hesk 2007 shows how various speakers advanced innovative arguments that depended on the audience understanding the conventional ways that such arguments were usually framed.

58. Schmitz 2000, 58–59. The fact that modern critics can read the speeches closely and repeatedly may allow a kind of critical analysis that listening once might not so easily have supported. On the other hand, except in two or perhaps three (probably heavily redacted) cases, we don't have the opposing speech. I sometimes wonder if our critical distance doesn't allow an overly critical appraisal, so that the speech we *don't* have must have had the better case (S. Johnstone 1999, 142 n. 64).

59. Arist. *Rhet.* 1408a33–37.

60. Aeschines famously relied on *pheme* (common knowledge) in one speech (Aesch. 1.125–31; cf. Dem. 19.243–44) and challenged his opponent's use of it in another (Aesch. 2.144–45). Hesk 2000, 227–30, analyzes the litigant Mantitheos's critical discussion of this argument at Dem. 40.53–54.

61. As Trevett 1996 argues, Aristotle's treatises do not demonstrate that the was familiar with much forensic oratory, either in written or oral form. Carey 1996 argues that his prescriptions do not closely match actual legal rhetoric. Mirhady 2000, 185–86, and 2002, 268–71, documents the divergences between the limited strictures about the use of witnesses in rhetorical handbooks and actual rhetorical practice.

62. Similarly, Revermann 2006 argues that audiences in the theater acquired competence to understand plays through performance and repeated exposure. Several scholars have argued that Athenians became competent judges in the Assembly and the courts in part through their experience as spectators in the theater (e.g., Ober 1989, 152–55; Goldhill 1998; Monoson 2000, 88–110). Despite some significant similarities, there were important differences between the theater and the courts (S. Johnstone 1999, 121–22). Theater spectators did not have to decide, nor did poets operate within a linguistic system that simplified matters in order to make them decidable. If anything, drama relentlessly complexified.

63. Lanni 1997 emphasizes how bystanders would have learned about laws, and the same applies to rhetorical language.

64. Aristoph., *Ekk.* 244.

65. Xen. *Oik.* 11.23–24. In this passage Ischomachus describes practice at speaking more than at judging, though the two would have been related.

66. Whitehead 1986, 86–120, discusses deme assemblies. As Dem. 57.9 indicates, these speeches may have gone on all day.

67. Theopompos fr. 283b; Aristoph. *Ekk.* 303; Pherek. Fr. 64 [=Athen. 13.612a].

68. Vlassopoulos 2007, 40–41, emphasizes the extensive political discussions in the agora. Demosthenes describes the agora as the location of political discussions (Dem. 19.122).

69. Aristoph. *Wealth* 337–39.

70. Athen. 13.581d.

71. Aristoph. *Birds* 1439–45; *Clouds* 1003; *Knights* 1375–80.

72. Aristoph. *Knights* 1375–80 (trans. Henderson 1998a, 401–3 with modification). The humor of the passage depends on a series of made-up adjectives ending in ικός, a method of forming words just then becoming popular (Peppler 1910, 432–34). These five words used of Phaex's language all derive from forceful physical actions—restricting, piercing, pressing, striking, and seizing—and could be said to represent a theory of rhetoric that sees persuasion as a form of violence. Dover 1993, 30–31, comments on the passage.

73. Xen. Mem. 4.2.1; 4.2.8; 3.10.1–15; Oik. 6.13. Cf. Teles IVB. 21–23.

74. Men. *Sik.* 176–271.

75. De Ligt and de Neeve 1988. In Menander fr. 481 (Koch) a *panegyris* is associated with an *agora*.

76. Men. *Sik.* 190–91 (trans. Arnott 2000, 251).

77. Scafuro 1997. Scafuro's study focuses on arbitration and the settlement of disputes and does not treat this scene of informal litigation.

78. Eur. *Or.* 866–956; Arnott 2000, 200 and 246–61.

79. Hyp. 3.12. Another litigant, Demo, represents the dockside bystanders in the Piraeus actively intervening in a dispute over a ship's cargo (Dem. 32.15–16).

80. Hdt. 3.137; Lys. 3.16; 13.23.

81. Isoc. 18.9.

82. S. Johnstone 1999, 46–69, and Gagarin 2003.

83. Although the American legal system distinguishes criminal from civil law and litigation, the Athenian system did not. Therefore, it had no "crime" in the precise sense that we would use it. I use the term loosely to describe an act that could be said to violate a law, whether we would term it "criminal" (e.g., assault) or "civil" (e.g., failure to fulfill a contract). Aristotle uses the Greek verb *adikein*, to do wrong, to mean a wrong willfully committed in violation of the law: ἔστω δὴ τὸ ἀδικεῖν τὸ βλάπτειν ἑκόντα παρὰ τὸν νόμον (*Rhet.* 1368b6–7).

84. Dem. 54.

85. Litigants' reliance on supporting speakers (*synegoroi*), especially in *graphai*, may complicate this somewhat, since, as Rubinstein 2000 shows, their speeches were not always subordinated to that of the main litigant. Christ 2002, however, cautions against inferring a cacophony of voices. In any case, the jurors' choice was still dichotomized, even if "the litigant" was a team. Exceptionally, the *diadikasia*, used primarily to adjudicate inheritance disputes, allowed any number of applicants, all of whom were formally equal (i.e., neither prosecutor nor defendant).

86. S. Johnstone 1998 explores the consequences of this transformation for the lives of slaves and women. Free males who were not citizens could appear as defendants or, in some situations, prosecutors (in maritime cases, or in private cases if they were metics). Whether metics could prosecute in public cases is not clear: As Todd 1993, 196, notes, the laws authorizing some such cases granted prosecution to "Athenians" only. In the case brought by Epainetos of Andros (Dem. 59.64–71), which is sometimes taken to show that even free for-

eigners could initiate *graphai*, his status is unclear (he may be a metic) and the procedure (as Apollodoros describes it) so peculiar (a *graphe*, which only the victim could initiate) that it may be unsafe to generalize to other *graphai*.

87. Typically, Athenian litigants did not name women but described them by their relationship to a man, usually their husband (Schaps 1977).

88. Lys. 1.

89. Lys. 3.

90. Christ 1998 discusses this concept in detail.

91. Dem. 54.13–14.

92. Johnstone 1999, 22–33 and 62–66. Yunis 2005 discusses the ways that litigants attempted to get jurors to identify themselves with the speaker's interpretation of the laws.

93. De Brauw 2001.

94. Johnstone 1999: 24–33; Ford 1999. Rhetorical handbooks referenced this argument: Arist. *Rhet.* 1374b12 (cf. *NE* 1137b23–24); *Rhet. ad Alex.* 1422b1–25, 1443a31–35.

95. In a nonrhetorical context, Xenophon suggests that the people or the majority (*plethos*) could be considered the author of a law by their consideration and approval of it (*Mem.* 1.2.42).

96. Hyp. 3.13–22.

97. Lanni 2006, 59–64.

98. S. Johnstone 1999, 93–100.

99. Allen 2000 analyzes the former; S. Johnstone 1999, 109–25, Konstan 2000, and Gärtner 2004 the latter. The prosecutor of Alcibiades the Younger starkly contrasts pity and anger as the jury's two choices (Lys. 15.9).

100. Konstan 2000 emphasizes this.

101. Defendants' appeals to pity were sometimes accompanied, however, by nondiscursive rituals: weeping, supplication, the parading of children (S. Johnstone 1999, 114–20).

102. Lys. 19.53.

103. Campe 2008.

104. Campe 2008, 373.

105. The vote was a necessary structural feature of rhetoric, because even before the speeches began, each individual listener had already chosen to vote, and because from the perspective of the system there would be a verdict even if many jurors chose not to vote.

106. Dem. 24.218.

107. Dover 1974, 195–96.

108. Thus, contrary to Remer's idea (2008, 191) that *pathos* moves listeners to act on their rational knowledge, at Athens, at least, the impending and inevitable action, the verdict, made jurors receptive to emotion.

109. Schmitz 2000.

110. Lys. 3.29, 31. Cf. Arist. *Rhet.* 1402a.

111. It's often said that the procedure of the *proklesis*, challenge or dare, was a way to "introduce" the testimony of slaves or women. This, however, misapprehends that procedure (S. Johnstone 1999, 70–92), which was essentially a tactic in the private negotiation of disputes. Whenever a litigant wanted to let jurors know what a slave or woman had witnessed, he just told them himself.

112. S. Johnstone 1999, 105–6.

113. In what follows I concentrate on the rhetorical setting of the Athenian courts; J. Miller 2002 discusses how the rhetorical language of the Assembly contained its own critique.

114. Arist. *Rhet.* 1355b18–21.

115. Thuc. 3.38. Aristotle, too, said audiences sought pleasure (*Rhet.* 1354b29–55a1).

116. There was possibly one exception to this generalization that rhetoric was policed only by rhetorical means: Before the trial, the official who accepted the charge may have exercised some discretion in determining its formulation and whether to accept it. With limited evidence, it is difficult to come to firm conclusions about what happened at these preliminary procedures, especially the *anakrisis*. (Harrison 1971, 94–105, and Todd 1993, 126–29 [more skeptically], discuss the question.) Such proceedings were not rhetorical in the precise sense I have been using: Arguments were not directed toward a large group, the procedure involved interrogation of litigants (whether by the opposing litigant or the official), and the presiding official could order a litigant to answer a question. But in general the official's discretion does not seem to have significantly affected the process.

117. Lanni 2006 analyzes this phenomenon.

118. As Aeschines did (Aesch. 1.170, 176).

119. Ant. 6.10.

120. The legal procedures of *eisangelia* and *probole* complicate this generalization: in these procedures a preliminary consideration and vote by the Assembly (a rhetorical procedure) preceded and authorized the prosecution. Still, the decision to pursue the initial process in the Assembly was extra-rhetorical.

121. Christ 1998.

122. Din. 1.99–102 and Dem. 58.39–40 both express concern that politicians' public attacks on each other are merely a distraction from their private collusion.

123. This differs from situations where someone used nonrhetorical violence to silence an opponent in a debate: as Odysseus against Thersites (Homer *Il.* 2.265–69), or Critias against Theramenes (Xen. *Hell.* 2.3.50).

124. Aeschines claimed Demosthenes had tried to so incite the jurors (Aesch. 2.1). Apollodoros (Dem. 45.6) claimed that in a previous trial his opponent's lies had caused the jurors to refuse to listen to even a peep of his case; one suspects hyperbole. As for direct evidence, some speakers invited the audience to refuse to listen to their opponents *on certain subjects* (Bers 1985, 9 nn. 32–33).

125. It's worth noting that the audiences sometimes shouted not to silence but to *provoke* speech: Thuc. 4.28.3–4; Aesch. 3.82; Dem. 19.122.

126. Demosthenes sometimes began speeches to the Assembly by requesting that the audience not attempt to silence him (Dem. 5.15; 13.3; Tacon 2001, 179–80, discusses his *Exordia*).

127. S. Johnstone 1999, 61–62.

128. Dem. 24.149–51 provides one version of the oath. Lys 19.4–5 offers the commonplace sentiment.

129. Aristoph. *Wasps* 725–26.

130. S. Johnstone 1999, 87–97.

131. Yunis 1991; Mader 2007.

132. Although speakers could attempt to activate listeners' memories of previous decisions, there is no reason to assume that auditors would remember the past only when reminded.

133. Amossy 2001. In this she follows Bourdieu himself (1991).

134. Aristoph. *Ekk.* 25–30, 507, 149 ff.

135. S. Johnstone 1999.

136. If trust is treated as an action, trusting, then the vote is trusting; if trust is a psychological state that motivates and enables the action, however, it must be inferred entirely from the vote, so that this cause is no more than a hypothesis.

137. Arist. *Pol.* 1268a1–67. Aristotle notes that this proposal would "turn the juror into an arbitrator" but is unworkable because so many jurors cannot deliberate together about the decision (1268b4–22). Aristotle highlights the essential link between the size of the body of deciders and the simplifying, dichotomized choice.

138. Wyse 1904; Gagarin 1989.

139. Shultz, Léveillé, and Lepper 1999, 48, argue that "choosing between relatively unattractive, qualitatively distinct objects is difficult to do, is particularly dissonance arousing, and can yield large increases in the value of the chosen alternative."

BIBLIOGRAPHY

Abizadeh, Arash. 2002. "The Passions of the Wise: *Phronesis*, Rhetoric, and Aristotle's Passionate Practical Deliberation." *Review of Metaphysics* 56: 267–96.

Alessandri, Salvatore. 1984. "Il Significato Storico della Legge di Nicofonte sul *Dokimastes Monetario.*" *Annali della Scuola Normale Superiore de Pisa. Classe di Lettere e Filosofia* 3rd ser. 14: 369–93.

Alexander, Jennifer, and Paul Alexander. 1991. "What's a Fair Price? Price-Setting and Trading Partnerships in Javanese Markets." *Man* 26: 492–512.

Alexander, Paul. 1992. "What's in a Price? Trading Practices in Peasant (and Other) Markets." Pp. 79–96 in Roy Dilley, ed., *Contesting Markets: Analyses of Ideology, Discourse and Practice.* Edinburgh: Edinburgh Univ. Press.

Allen, Danielle S. 2000. *The World of Prometheus: The Politics of Punishing in Democratic Athens.* Princeton: Princeton Univ. Press.

Amossy, Ruth. 2001. "*Ethos* at the Crossroads of Disciplines: Rhetoric, Pragmatics, Sociology." *Poetics Today* 22: 1–23.

Amouretti, Marie-Claire. 1979. "Les céréales dans l'Antiquité: Especes, mouture et conservation, liaison et interférences dans la Grèce classique." Pp. 57–69 in Marceau Gast and François Sigaut, eds., *Les Techniques de conservation des grains à long terme: Leur rôle dans la dynamique des systèmes de cultures et des sociétés.* Paris: Editions du Centre national de la recherche scientifique.

Amyx, D. A. 1958. "The Attic Stelai, Part III." *Hesperia* 27: 163–310.

Andrewes, A. 1974. "The Arginousai Trial." *Phoenix* 28: 112–22.

Andrews, James A. 1994. "Cleon's Ethopoetics." *Classical Quarterly* n.s. 44: 26–39.

Arnaoutoglou, Ilias. 1998. *Ancient Greek Laws.* New York: Routledge.

Arnott, W. Geoffrey. 2000. *Menander III.* Cambridge, Mass.: Harvard Univ. Press.

Azoulay, V. 2004. "Exchange as Entrapment: Mercenary Xenophon?" Pp. 298–304 in Robin Lane Fox, ed., *The Long March: Xenophon and the Ten Thousand.* New Haven: Yale Univ. Press.

Baldriga, Roberto. 1994. "Mopso tra Oriente e Grecia: Storia di un personaggio di frontiera." *Quaderni Urbinati di Cultura Classica* n.s. 46: 35–71.

Barbaro, Michael. 2006. "Clothes That Fit the Women, Not the Store." *New York Times* March 31, 2006, Section C p. 1.

Barzel, Yoram. 1982. "Measurement Cost and the Organization of Markets." *Journal of Law and Economics* 25: 27–48.

Bers, Victor. 1985. "Dikastic *Thorubos.*" *History of Political Thought* 6: 1–15.

Bettalli, Marco. 1985. "Case, botteghe, ergasteria. Note sui luoghi di produzione e di ven-
dita nell'Atene classica." *Opus* 4: 29–42.

Bickford, Susan. 1996. "Beyond Friendship: Aristotle on Conflict, Deliberation, and Attention." *Journal of Politics* 58: 398–421.

Billows, R. A. 1990. *Antigonos the One-Eyed and the Creation of the Hellenistic State.* Berkeley:
University of California Press.

Bissa, Errietta M. A. 2009. *Governmental Intervention in Foreign Trade in Archaic and Classical
Greece.* Leiden: Brill.

Blank, David L. 1985. "Socrates Versus Sophists on Payment for Teaching." *Classical Antiquity* 4: 1–49.

Bogaard, Paul A. 1979. "Heaps or Wholes: Aristotle's Explanation of Compound Bodies." *Isis* 70: 11–29.

Bourdieu, Pierre. 1977. *Outline of a Theory of Practice.* Trans. Richard Nice. Cambridge:
Cambridge Univ. Press.

———. 1990. *The Logic of Practice.* Trans. Richard Nice. Cambridge: Polity Press.

Bousquet, Jean. 1985. "Inscriptions de Delphes." *Bulletin de Correspondance Hellénique* 109:
221–53.

Braet, Antoine. 1987. "The Classical Doctrine of *Status* and the Rhetorical Theory of Ar-
gumentation." *Philosophy and Rhetoric* 20: 79–93.

Bresson, Alain. 2000. *La cité marchande.* Bordeaux: Ausonius.

———. 2008. *L'économie de la Grèce des cites, II: Les espaces de l'échange.* Paris: Armand
Colin.

Brock, Roger. 1994. "The Labour of Women in Classical Athens." *Classical Quarterly* n.s.
44: 336–46.

Brown, Vivienne. 1994. "Higgling: The Language of Markets in Economic Discourse."
Pp. 66–93 in Neil De Marchi and Mary S. Moran, eds., *Higgling: Transactors and Their
Markets in the History of Economics.* Durham: Duke Univ. Press.

Bureau of Labor Statistics. 1997. "Measurement Issues in the Consumer Price Index."
U.S. Department of Labor. (Cited from http://www.bls.gov/cpi/cpigm697.htm on
June 8, 2003.)

Burford, Alison. 1960. "Heavy Transport in Classical Antiquity." *Economic History Review*
12: 1–18.

———. 1993. *Land and Labor in the Greek World.* Baltimore: Johns Hopkins Univ. Press.

Buttrey, T. V. 1981. "More on the Athenian Coinage Law of 375/4 B.C." *Numismatica e
Antichita Classiche* 10: 71–94.

Cahill, Nicholas. 2002. *Household and City Organization at Olynthus.* New Haven: Yale
Univ. Press.

Carey, C. 1996. "*NOMOS* in Attic Rhetoric and Oratory." *Journal of Hellenic Studies* 16:
33–46.

Carruthers, Bruce G., and Wendy Nelson Espeland. 1991. "Accounting for Rationality:
Double-Entry Bookkeeping and the Rhetoric of Economic Rationality." *American
Journal of Sociology* 97: 31–69.

Cary, M. 1928. "A Constitutional Inscription from Cyrene." *Journal of Hellenic Studies* 48:
222–38.

Cason, Timothy N., Daniel Friedman, and Garrett H. Milam. 2003. "Bargaining Versus
Posted Price Competition in Customer Markets." *International Journal of Industrial Organization* 21: 223–251.

Casson, Lionel. 1956. "The Size of Ancient Merchant Ships." Pp. 231–8 in *Studi in Onore
di Aristide Calderini e Roberto Paribeni.* Milan: Casa Editrice Ceschina.

————. 1986. *Ships and Seamanship in the Ancient World*. Rev. ed. Princeton: Princeton Univ. Press.

Cavanaugh, Maureen B. 1996. *Eleusis and Athens. Documents in Finance, Religion and Politics in the Fifth Century B.C.* Atlanta: Scholars Press.

Chrimes, K. M. T. 1932. "On Solon's Property Classes." *Classical Review* 46: 2–4.

Christ, Matthew R. 1998. *The Litigious Athenian*. Baltimore: Johns Hopkins University Press.

————. 2002. Review of Rubinstein 2000. *Bryn Mawr Classical Review*. http://bmcr .brynmawr.edu/2002/2002–04–01.html.

————. 2007. "The Evolution of the *Eisphora* in Classical Athens." *Classical Quarterly* n.s. 57: 53–69.

Christophilopoulos, A. 1950. "ΑΘΑΝΑΤΟΣ en Droit Grec." *Revue International de Droits de l'Antiquité* 4: 297–301.

Cohen, David. 1991. *Law, Sexuality, and Society: The Enforcement of Morals in Classical Athens*. Cambridge: Cambridge Univ. Press.

Cohen, Edward E. 1992. *Athenian Economy and Society: A Banking Perspective*. Princeton: Princeton Univ. Press.

Cohen, Jean. 1999. "Trust, Voluntary Association and Workable Democracy: The Contemporary American Discourse of Civil Society." Pp. 208–48 in Mark E. Warren, ed., *Democracy and Trust*. Cambridge: Cambridge Univ. Press.

Cole, Susan G. 1981. "Could Greek Women Read and Write?" Pp. 219–45 in Helene Foley, ed., *Reflections of Women in Antiquity*. New York: Gordon and Breach Science Publishers.

Cole, Thomas. 1991a. "Who Was Corax?" *Illinois Classical Studies* 16: 65–84.

————. 1991b. *The Origins of Rhetoric in Ancient Greece*. Baltimore: Johns Hopkins Univ. Press.

Compton-Engle, Gwendolyn. 1999. "From Country to City: The Persona of Dicaeopolis in Aristophanes' *Acharnians*." *Classical Journal* 94: 359–73.

Connor, W. Robert. 1987. "Tribes, Festivals and Processions: Civic Ceremonial and Political Manipulation in Archaic Greece," *Journal of Hellenic Studies* 107: 40–50.

————. 1996. "Civil Society, Dionysiac Festival, and the Athenian Democracy." Pp. 217–26 in Josiah Ober and Charles Hedrick, eds., Demokratia: *A Conversation on Democracies, Ancient and Modern*. Princeton: Princeton Univ. Press.

Corey, David. 2002. "The Case against Teaching Virtue for Pay: Socrates and the Sophists." *History of Political Thought* 23: 189–210.

Couloubaritsis, Lambros. 1996. "La notion de 'jugement' dans la *Rhétorique* d'Aristote." Pp. 181–96 in André Motte and Joseph Denooz, eds., *Aristotelica secunda: Mélanges offerts à Christian Rutten*. Liège: Centre Informatique de Philosophie et Lettres.

Cox, Cheryl Anne. 1998. *Household Interests: Property, Marriage Strategies, and Family Dynamics in Ancient Athens*. Princeton: Princeton Univ. Press.

Crawford, M. H. 2001. Review of Figueira 1998. *Journal of Hellenic Studies* 121: 199–201.

Cronon, William. 1991. *Nature's Metropolis: Chicago and the Great West*. New York: W. W. Norton.

Cunningham, I. C. 1964. "Herodas 6 and 7." *Classical Quarterly* ns. 14: 32–35.

————. 1971. *Herodas Mimiambi*. Oxford: Oxford Univ. Press.

Dalby, Andrew. 1992. "Greeks Abroad: Social Organisation and Food among the Ten Thousand." *Journal of Hellenic Studies* 112: 16–30.

————. 2000. "Lynceus and the Anecdotists." Pp. 372–94 in David Braund and John Wilkins, eds., *Athenaeus and His World*. Exeter: Univ. of Exeter Press.

Davidson, James. 1997. *Courtesans and Fishcakes: The Consuming Passions of Classical Athens.* New York: St. Martin's Press.

Davies, John K. 1971. *Athenian Propertied Families.* Oxford: Clarendon Press.

De Brauw, Michael. 2001. "'Listen to the Laws Themselves:' Citations of Laws and Portrayal of Character in Attic Oratory." *Classical Journal* 97: 161–76.

De Ligt, L., and P. W. de Neeve. 1988. "Ancient Periodic Markets: Festivals and Fairs." *Athenaeum* 66: 391–416.

De Marchi, Neil, and Mary S. Moran, eds. 1994. *Higgling: Transactors and Their Markets in the History of Economics.* Durham: Duke Univ. Press.

de Moraes Farias, P. F. 1974. "Silent Trade: Myth and Historical Evidence." *History in Africa* 1: 9–24.

de Romilly, Jacqueline. 1975. *Magic and Rhetoric in Ancient Greece.* Cambridge, Mass.: Harvard University Press.

de Ste. Croix, G. E. M. 1953. "Demosthenes' TIMHMA and the Athenian Eisphora in the Fourth Century B.C." *Classica et Mediaevalia* 14: 30–70.

———. 1956. "Greek and Roman Accounting." Pp. 14–74 in A. C. Littleton and B. S. Yamey, eds., *Studies in the History of Accounting.* Homewood, IL: Richard D. Irwin.

———. 1966. "The Estate of Phaenippus (Ps.-Dem. xlii)." Pp. 109–14 in *Ancient Society and Institutions: Studies Presented to Victor Ehrenberg on his 75th Birthday.* New York: Barnes & Noble.

———. 2004. *Athenian Democratic Origins and Other Essays.* David Harvey and Robert Parker, eds. Oxford: Oxford Univ. Press.

Delhey, Jan, and Kenneth Newton. 2003. "Who Trusts? The Origins of Social Trust in Seven Societies." *European Societies* 5: 93–137.

Delebecque, Édouard. 1978. *Xénophon: De l'art équestre.* Paris: Société d'édition "Les belles lettres."

Descat, R. 2000. "L'État et les marchés dan le monde grec." Pp. 13–29 in *Mercati permanenti e mercati periodici nel mondo romano: Atti degli Incontri capresi di storia dell'economia antica, Capri, 13–15 ottobre 1997.* Bari: Edipuglia.

Develin, Robert. 1986. "Prytany Systems and Eponyms for Financial Boards in Athens." *Klio* 68: 67–83.

Donlan, Walter. 1989. "The Unequal Exchange between Glaucus and Diomedes in Light of the Homeric Gift-Economy." *Phoenix* 43: 1–15.

Dover, Kenneth J. 1960. "ΔΕΚΑΤΟΣ ΑΥΤΟΣ." *Journal of Hellenic Studies* 80: 61–77.

———. 1974. *Greek Popular Morality in the Time of Plato and Aristotle.* Berkeley: Univ. of California Press.

———, ed. and trans. 1993. *Aristophanes: Frogs.* Oxford: Clarendon Press.

Dow, Sterling. 1976. "Companionable Associates in the Athenian Government." Pp. 69–84 in Lirissa Bonfante and Helga von Heintze, eds., *In Memoriam Otto J. Brendel.* Mainz: Verlag Philipp von Zabern.

Drexhage, Hans-Joachim. 1991. *Preise, Mieten/Pachten, Kosten und Löhne im römishcen Ägypten bis zum Regierungsantritt Diokletians.* Sankt Katharinen: Scripta Mercaturae Verlag.

Duncan-Jones, Richard. 1990. *Structure and Scale in the Roman Economy.* Cambridge: Cambridge Univ. Press.

Engen, Darel Tai. 2005. "'Ancient Greenbacks': Athenian Owls, the Law of Nikophon, and the Greek Economy." *Historia* 54: 359–81.

Étienne, Roland, and Léopold Migeotte. 1998. "Colophon et les abus des fermiers de taxes." *Bulletin de Correspondance Hellénique* 122: 143–57.

Evans, Richard J. 2001. Review of Figueira 1998. *Mnemosyne* 54: 619–23.

Fanselow, Frank S. 1990. "The Bazaar Economy or How Bizarre is the Bazaar Really." *Man* 25: 250–265.

Feyel, Christophe. 2003. "À propos de la Loi de Nicophon: Remarques sur le sens de δόκιμος, δοκιμάζειν, δοκιμασία." *Revue de Philologie de Littérature et d'Histoire Anciennes* 77: 37–65.

Feyel, Michel. 1942. *Contribution à l'épigraphie béotienne*. Le Puy: Imprimerie de "La Haute-Loire."

Figueira, Thomas. 1981. *Aegina. Society and Politics*. New York: Arno Press.

———. 1986. "*Sitopolai* and *Sitophylakes* in Lysias' 'Against the Graindealers:' Governmental Intervention in the Athenian Economy." *Phoenix* 40: 149–71.

———. 1998. *The Power of Money*. Philadelphia: Univ. of Pennsylvania Press.

Fine, Gary Alan, and Brooke Harrington. 2004. "Tiny Publics: Small Groups and Civil Society." *Sociological Theory* 22: 341–56.

Finley, Moses I. 1951. *Studies in Land and Credit in Ancient Athens, 500–200 B.C. The Horos Inscriptions*. New Brunswick: Rutgers Univ. Press.

———. 1974. "Athenian Demagogues." Pp. 1–25 in M. I. Finley, ed., *Studies in Ancient Society*. London: Routledge and Kegan Paul.

Finnegan, R. J. 1992. "Women in Herodian Mime." *Hermathena* 152: 21–37.

Forbes, R. J. 1964. *Studies in Ancient Technology*. Vol. 4. 2nd ed. Leiden: E. J. Brill.

Ford, Andrew. 1999. "Reading Homer from the Rostrum: Poems and Laws in Aeschines' *Against Timarchus*." Pp. 231–56 in Simon Goldhill and Robin Osborne, eds., *Performance Culture and Athenian Democracy*. Cambridge: Cambridge Univ. Press.

Forman, Shepard, and Joyce F. Riegelhapt. 1970. "Market Place and Marketing System: Toward a Theory of Peasant Economic Integration." *Comparative Studies in Society and History* 12: 188–212.

Fowler, David. 1999. *The Mathematics of Plato's Academy: A New Reconstruction*. Second ed. Oxford: Clarendon Press.

Fox, R. J. Lane. 1996. "Theophrastus' *Characters* and the Historian." *Proceedings of the Cambridge Philological Society* 42: 127–70.

Fraser, P. M. 1956–58. "Inscriptions from Cyrene." *Berytus* 12: 101–128.

Fröhlich, Pierre. 2004. *Les cités grecques et le contrôle des magistrats (IVe-Ier siècle avant J.-C.)*. Geneve: Droz.

Gabrielsen, Vincent. 1987. "The Antidosis Procedure in Classical Athens." *Classica et Mediaevalia* 38: 7–38.

———. 1994. *Financing the Athenian Fleet: Public Taxation and Social Relations*. Baltimore: Johns Hopkins Univ. Press.

Gagarin, Michael. 1989. *The Murder of Herodes: A Study of Antiphon 5*. Frankfurt: Peter Lang.

———. 1992. "The Poetry of Justice: Hesiod and the Origins of Greek Law." *Ramus* 21: 61–78.

———. 2003. "Telling Stories in Athenian Law." *Transactions of the American Philological Association* 133: 197–207.

Gallant, Thomas W. 1991. *Risk and Survival in Ancient Greece: Reconstructing the Rural Domestic Economy*. Stanford: Stanford Univ. Press.

Gallo, Luigi. 2000. "Le imposte dirette nelle 'poleis' greche: Un istituto tirannico?" *Minima Epigraphica et Papyrologica* 3.4: 17–36

Gargola, Daniel J. 1992. "Grain Distributions and the Revenue of the Temple of Hera on Samos." *Phoenix* 46: 12–28.

Garlan, Yvon. 2000. *Amphores et timbres amphoriques grecs: Entre érudition et idéologie.* Paris: Boccard.

Garnsey, Peter. 1988. *Famine and Food Supply in the Gaeco-Roman World.* Cambridge: Cambridge Univ. Press.

Gärtner, Thomas. 2004. "Mitleid in rhetorischer Theorie und Praxis des klassischen Griechenlands." *Rhetorica* 22: 25–48.

Geertz, Clifford. 1978. "The Bazaar Economy: Information and Search and Peasant Marketing." *American Economic Review* 68: 28–32.

Gellrich, Michelle. 1994. "Socratic Magic: Enchantment, Irony, and Persuasion in Plato's Dialogues." *Classical World* 87: 275–307.

Gera, Deborah Levine. 1993. *Xenophon's* Cyropaedia: *Style, Genre, and Literary Technique.* Oxford: Clarendon Press.

Gibbins, David. 2001. "Shipwrecks and Hellenistic Trade." Pp. 273–312 in Zofia Archibald *et al.*, eds., *Hellentistic Economies.* London: Routledge.

Giddens, Anthony. 1990. *The Consequences of Modernity.* Stanford: Stanford Univ. Press.

———. 1992. *The Transformation of Intimacy: Sexuality, Love and Eroticism in Modern Societies.* Cambridge: Polity Press.

Gofas, Dimitri C. 1969. "Les Carpologues de Thasos." *Bulletin de Correspondance Hellénique* 93: 337–70.

———. 1993. *Études d'Histoire du Droit grec des Affaires: Antique, Byzantin et Post-Byzantin.* Athens: Bibliothèque de la Société archéologique a Athènes.

Goldhill, Simon. 1994. "Presenting Democracy: Women at the Great Dionysia." Pp. 347–69 in R. Osborne and S. Hornblower, eds., *Ritual, Finance, Politics (for D. Lewis).* Oxford: Oxford University Press.

———. 1998. "The Seductions of the Gaze: Socrates and His Girlfriends." Pp. 105–24 in Paul Cartledge, Paul Millett, and Sitta von Reden, eds., *Kosmos: Essays in Order, Conflict and Community in Classical Athens.* Cambridge: Cambridge Univ. Press.

Gomme, A. W., A. Andrews, and K. J. Dover. 1981. *A Historical Commentary on Thucydides,* vol. 5. Oxford: Clarendon Press.

Gorton, Gary. 1999. "Pricing Free Bank Notes." *Journal of Monetary Economics* 44: 33–64.

Gray, Vivienne. 2002. "Short Stories in Herodotus' *Histories.*" Pp. 291–317 in Egbert J. Bakker, Irene J. F. de Jong, and Hans van Wees, eds., *Brill's Companion to Herodotus.* Leiden: Brill.

Grayson, C. H. 1975. "Greek Weighing." Doctoral diss., Oxford University.

Greene, Elizabeth S., Mark L. Lawall, and Mark E. Polzer. 2008. "Inconspicuous Consumption: The Sixth-Century B.C.E. Shipwreck at Pabuç Burnu, Turkey." *American Journal of Archaeology* 112: 685–711.

Grenfell, Bernard P., and Arthur S. Hunt. 1906. *The Hibeh Papyri, Part I.* London: Egyptian Exploration Society.

Grimaudo, Sabrina. 1998. *Misure e pesare nella Grecia antica: Teoria, storia, ideologie.* Palermo: L'Epos.

Hamel, Debra. 1998. *Athenian Generals: Military Authority in the Classical Period.* Leiden: Brill. (*Mnemosyne* suppl. 182.)

Hammer, Dean. 2005. "Plebiscitary Politics in Archaic Greece." *Historia* 54: 107–31.

Hammond, N. G. L. 1983. "Army Transport in the Fifth and Fourth Centuries." *Greek, Roman, and Byzantine Studies* 21: 27–31.

Hansen, Mogens Herman. 1975. *Eisangelia: The Sovereignty of the People's Court in Athens in the Fourth Century B. C. and the Impeachment of Generals and Politicians.* Odense: Odense Univ. Press.

———. 1991. *The Athenian Democracy in the Age of Demosthenes*. Trans. J. A. Crook. Oxford: Blackwell.

———. 2009. "A Note on Agyrrhios' Grain Tax Law of 374/3 BC." Pp. 145–54 in Lynette Mitchell and Lene Rubinstein, eds., *Greek History and Epigraphy: Essays in Honour of P. J. Rhodes*. Swansea: Classical Press of Wales.

Harries, Byron. 1993. "'Strange Meeting': Diomedes and Glaucus in 'Iliad' 6." *Greece and Rome*, 2nd ser. 40: 133–146.

Harris, Edward M. 1989. "The Liability of Business Partners in Athenian Law: The Dispute Between Lycon and Megacleides ([Dem.] 52.20–1)." *Classical Quarterly* n.s. 39: 339–43.

———. 1999. "Notes on the New Grain-Tax Law." *Zeitschrift für Papyrologie und Epigraphik* 128:269–72.

———. 2002. "Workshop, Marketplace and Household: The Nature of Technical Specialization in Classical Athens and its Influence on Economy and Society." Pp. 67–99 in Paul Cartledge, Edward E. Cohen, and Lin Foxhall, eds., *Money, Labour and Land: Approaches to the Economies of Ancient Greece*. London: Routledge.

Harris, William. 1989. *Ancient Literacy*. Cambridge, Mass.: Harvard Univ. Press.

Harrison, A. R. W. 1971. *The Law of Athens*, vol. 2: *Procedure*. Oxford: Oxford University Press.

Harvey, F. D. 1965. "Two Kinds of Equality." *Classica et Mediaevalia* 26: 101–46.

———. 1985. "*Dona Ferentes*: Some Aspects of Bribery in Greek Politics." *History of Political Thought* 6: 76–113.

Heisserer, A. J. 1980. *Alexander the Great and the Greeks: The Epigraphic Evidence*. Norman: Univ. of Oklahoma Press.

Henderson, Jeffrey. 1991. "Women and the Athenian Dramatic Festivals." *Transactions of the American Philological Association* 121: 133–47.

———, ed. and trans. 1998a. *Aristophanes: Acharnians, Knights*. Cambridge, Mass.: Harvard Univ. Press.

———, ed. and trans. 1998b. *Aristophanes: Clouds, Wasps, Peace*. Cambridge, Mass.: Harvard Univ. Press.

———. 2003. "Demos, Demagogue, Tyrant in Attic Old Comedy." Pp. 155–79 in Kathryn A. Morgan, ed., *Popular Tyranny: Sovereignty and Its Discontents*. Austin: Univ. of Texas Press.

Hesk, Jon. 1999. Review of Yunis 1996. *Journal of Hellenic Studies* 119: 183.

———. 2000. *Deception and Democracy in Classical Athens*. Cambridge: Cambridge Univ. Press.

———. 2006. "Combative Capping in Aristophanic Comedy." *Cambridge Classical Journal* 53: 124–160.

———. 2007. "'Despisers of the Commonplace': Meta-topoi and Para-topoi in Attic Oratory." *Rhetorica* 25: 361–384.

Hill, Lowell D. 1990. *Grain Grades and Standards: Historical Issues Shaping the Future*. Chicago: Univ. of Illinois Press.

Hodkinson, Stephen. 1992. "Sharecropping and Sparta's Economic Exploitation of the Helots." Pp. 123–34 in Jan Motyka Sanders, ed., *ΦΙΛΟΛΑΚΩΝ: Lakonian Studies in Honour of Hector Catling*. London: The British School at Athens.

Hoffman, David C. 2008. "Concerning *Eikos*: Social Expectation and Verisimilitude in Early Attic Rhetoric." *Rhetorica* 24: 1–29.

Hopkins, Keith. 1980. "Taxes and Trade in the Roman Empire (200BC—AD 400)." *Journal of Roman Studies* 70:101–25.

Horden, Peregrine, and Nicholas Purcell. 2000. *The Corrupting Sea: A Study of Mediterranean History*. Oxford: Blackwell.

Hornblower, Simon. 2004. "This Was Decided (*edoxa tauta*): The Army as *Polis* in Xenophon's *Anabasis*—and Elsewhere." Pp. 243–63 in Robin Lane Fox, ed., *The Long March: Xenophon and the Ten Thousand*. New Haven: Yale Univ. Press.

Hunter, Virginia. 1988. "Thucydides and the Sociology of the Crowd." *Classical Journal* 84: 17–30.

Isager, Signe, and Mogens H. Hansen. 1975. *Aspects of Athenian Society in the Fourth Century B.C.* Odense: Odense University Press.

Isager, Signe, and Jens Erik Skydsgaard. 1992. *Ancient Greek Agriculture*. New York: Routledge.

Jameson, Michael H. 1955. "Seniority in the *Strategia*." *Transactions of the American Philological Association* 86: 63–87.

Jeacle, Ingrid. 2003. "Accounting and the Construction of the Standard Body." *Accounting, Organizaitons and Society* 28: 357–77.

Johnson, Nathanael. 2006. "Swine of the Times: The Making of the Modern Pig." *Harper's* vol. 312, no. 1872: 47–56.

Johnson, William A. 2000. "Toward a Sociology of Reading in Classical Antiquity." *American Journal of Philology* 121: 593–627

Johnstone, Christopher Lyle. 1980. "An Aristotelian Trilogy: Ethics, Rhetoric, Politics, and the Search for Moral Truth." *Philosophy and Rhetoric* 13: 1–24.

Johnstone, Steven. 1994. "Virtuous Toil, Vicious Work: Xenophon on Aristocratic Style." *Classical Philology* 89: 219–40.

———. 1998. "Cracking the Code of Silence: Athenian Legal Oratory and the History of Slaves and Women." Pp. 221–35 in Sheila Murnaghan and Sandra Joshel, eds., *Women and Slaves in Classical Culture: Differential Equations*. New York: Routledge.

———. 1999. *Disputes and Democracy: The Consequences of Litigation in Ancient Athens*. Austin: Univ. of Texas Press.

———. 2002. "Apology for the Manuscript Dem. 59.67." *American Journal of Philology* 123: 229–56.

———. 2003. "Women, Property, and Surveillance in Classical Athens." *Classical Antiquity* 22: 247–74.

Jones, Nicholas F. 1999. *The Associations of Classical Athens: The Response to Democracy*. New York: Oxford Univ. Press.

Jordan, Borimir. 1979. *Servants of the Gods: A Study in the Religion, History and Literature of Fifth-Century Athens*. Göttingen: Vandenhoeck & Ruprecht.

Jordan, David R. 2000. "A Personal Letter Found in the Athenian Agora." *Hesperia* 69: 91–103.

Jouanna, Jacques. 2008. "La nozione di misura e la sua problematica nella medicina ippocratica." *Annali dell'Istituto Universitario Orientale di Napoli. Sezione Filologico-Letteraria.* 30: 39–54.

Kahn, Charles H. 1979. *The Art and Thought of Heraclitus*. Cambridge: Cambridge Univ. Press.

Kahrstedt, Ulrich. 1969. *Untersuchungen zur Magistratur in Athen: Studien zum öffenlichen Recht Athens,* Teil II. Aalen: Scientia Verlag.

Kaplan, Steven Laurence. 1984. *Provisioning Paris: Merchants and Millers in the Grain and Flour Trade during the Eighteenth Century*. Ithaca: Cornell Univ. Press.

Kapparis, K. A. 1998. "Assessors of Magistrates (Paredroi) in Classical Athens." *Historia* 47: 383–93.

Karavites, Peter. 1990 "*Gnome*'s Nuances : From Its Beginning to the End of the Fifth Century." *Classical Bulletin* 66: 9–34.

Katz, Barry R. 1976. "The *Birds* of Aristophanes and Politics." *Athenaeum* 54: 353–81.

Knoepfler, Denis. 1988. "L'intitulé oublié d'un compte des naopes béotiens." Pp. 263–94 in Jacques Tréheux, ed., *Comptes et inventaires dans la cité grecque*. Genève: Librarie Droz.

Konstan, David. 1985. "The Politics of Aristophanes' *Wasps*." *Transactions of the American Philological Association* 115: 27–46.

———. 2000. "Pity and the Law in Greek Theory and Practice." *Dike: Rivista di Storia del Diritto Greco ed Ellenistico* 3: 125–45.

Kula, Witold. 1986. *Measures and Men*. R. Szreter trans. Princeton: Princeton Univ. Press.

Kurke, Leslie. 1999. *Coins, Bodies, Games, and Gold: The Politics of Meaning in Archaic Greece*. Princeton: Princeton Univ. Press.

Lambert, S. D. 1997. *Rationes Centesimarum: Sales of Public Land in Lykourgan Athens*. Amsterdam: J. C. Gieben.

Lang, Mabel, and Margaret Crosby. 1964. *The Athenian Agora*, vol. 10: *Weights, Measures and Tokens*. Princeton: American School of Classical Studies at Athens.

Lang, Mabel L. 1990. "Illegal Execution in Ancient Athens." *Proceedings of the American Philosophical Society* 134: 24–9.

Lanni, Adriaan M. 1997. "Spectator Sport or Serious Politics? οἱ περιεστηκότες and the Athenian Lawcourts." *Journal of Hellenic Studies* 117: 183–89.

———. 2006. *Law and Justice in the Courts of Classical Athens*. Cambridge: Cambridge Univ. Press.

Laronde, André. 1987. *Cyrène et la Libye hellénistique. Libykai Historiai de l'époque républicaine au principat d'Auguste*. Paris: Éditions du Centre National de la Recherche Scientifique.

Lattimore, Richmond. 1939. "The Wise Adviser in Herodotus." *Classical Philology* 34: 24–35.

Lave, Jean. 1986. "The Values of Quantification." Pp. 88–111 in John Law, ed. *Power, Action and Belief: A New Sociology of Knowledge*. London: Routledge and Kegan Paul.

Law, John. 1994. *Organizing Modernity*. Oxford: Blackwell.

Lawall, Gilbert. 1976. "Herodas 6 and 7 Reconsidered." *Classical Philology* 71: 165–169.

Lawall, Mark L. 2000. "Graffiti, Wine Selling, and the reuse of Amphoras in the Athenian Agora, ca. 430 to 400 B.C." *Hesperia* 69: 3–90.

Le Rider, G. 1989. "À propos d'un passage des *Poroi* de Xenophon." Pp. 159–72 in Georges Le Rider, ed., *Kraay-Mørkholm Essays: Numismatic Studies in Memory of C.M. Kraay and O. Mørkholm*. Louvain-la-Neuve : Institut supérieur d'archéologie et d'histoire de l'art, séminaire de numismatique Marcel Hoc.

Lee, John W. I. 2007. *A Greek Army on the March: Soldiers and Survival in Xenophon's Anabasis*. Cambridge: Cambridge University Press.

Levin, D. N. 1976. "A Herodean Diptych." *Ziva Antika* 26: 345–55.

Levinson, Daryl J. 2003. "Collective Sanctions." *Stanford Law Review* 56: 345–428.

Lewis, David M. 1955. "Notes on Attic Inscriptions (II): XXIII. Who Was Lysistrata?" *Annual of the British School at Athens* 50:1–36.

———. 1959. "Law on the Lesser Panathenaia." *Hesperia* 28: 239–47.

———. 1966. "After the Profanation of the Mysteries." Pp. 177–191 in E. Badian, ed., *Ancient Society and Institutions: Studies Presented to Victor Ehrenberg on his 75th Birthday*. New York: Barnes and Noble.

Loomis, William T. 1998. *Wages, Welfare Costs and Inflation in Classical Athens*. Ann Arbor: Univ. of Michigan Press.

Luhmann, Niklas. 1979. *Trust and Power*. New York: John Wiley & Sons.

———. 1986. *Love as Passion: The Codification of Intimacy*. Trans. Jeremy Gaines and Doris L. Jones. Cambridge: Polity Press.

MacDowell, Douglas M. 1978. *The Law in Classical Athens*. Ithaca: Cornell Univ. Press.

———. 1983. "Athenian laws about bribery." *Revue internationale des droits de l'antiquité* 30: 57–78.

Macve, Richard H. 1985. "Some Glosses on 'Greek and Roman Accounting.'" Pp. 233–64 in P. A. Cartledge and F. D. Harvey, eds., *Crux: Essays Presented to G. E. M. de Ste. Croix on his 75th Birthday*. London: Duckworth.

Mader, Gottfried. 2007. "Dramatizing *Didaxis*: Aspects of Demosthenes' 'Periclean' Project." *Classical Philology* 102: 155–79.

Mahir, Saul. 1987. "The Organization of a West-African Grain Market." *American Anthropologist* 89: 74–95.

Mansouri, Saber. 2002. "L'agora athénienne ou le lieu de travail, des discussions et des nouvelles politiques : chercher la politique là où elle n'est apparemment pas." *Dialogues d'Histoire Ancienne* 28: 41–63.

Mattingly, Harold B. 1999. Review of Figueira 1998. *American Journal of Archaeology* 103: 712–13.

Mayerson, Philip. 1998a. "The Sack (*sakkos*) Is the Artaba Writ Large." *Zeitschrift für Papyrologie und Epigraphik* 122: 189–94.

———. 1998b. "ΣΗΚΩΜΑΤΑ—'Standard' Measures for Decanting Wine." *Bulletin of the American Society of Papyrologists* 35: 153–58.

———. 2002. "P. Oxy. IV 708: *deigmata* Found to be *ou kathara* and Their Implications." *Bulletin of the American Society of Papyrologists* 39: 111–17.

Mayhew, Anne. 1994. "Transactors and Their Markets in Two Disciplines." Pp. 295–312 in Neil De Marchi and Mary S. Moran, eds., *Higgling: Transactors and Their Markets in the History of Economics*. Durham: Duke Univ. Press.

McAdon, Brad. 2004. "Reconsidering the Intention or Purpose of Aristotle's *Rhetoric*." *Rhetoric Review* 23: 216–234.

McDiarmid, John B. 1941. "Note on Heraclitus, Fragment 124." *American Journal of Philology* 62: 492–494.

Mehl, Andreas. 1982. "Für eine neue Bewertung eines Justizskandals. Der Arginusenprozess und seine Überlieferung vor dem Hintergrund von Recht und Weltanschauung im Athen des ausgehenden 5. Jhs. v. Chr." *Zeitschrift der Savigny-Stiftung für Rechtgeschichte (Romanistische Abteilung)* 99: 32–80.

Meiggs, Russell. 1972. *The Athenian Empire*. Oxford: Clarendon Press.

Merker, I. L. 1975. "A Greek Tariff Inscription in Jerusalem." *Israel Exploration Journal* 25: 238–44.

Mickwitz, G. 1937. "Economic Rationalism in Graeco-Roman Agriculture." *English Historical Review* 52: 577–89.

Migeotte, Léopold. 1993. "Un fonds d'achat de grain à Coronée." *Boeotia Antiqua: Papers on Recent Work in Boeotian Archaeology and History* 3: 11–23.

Miller, Jeff. 2002. "Warning the Demos: Political Communication with a Democratic Audience in Demosthenes." *History of Political Thought* 23: 401–17.

Miller, Peter. 1998. "The Margins of Accounting." Pp. 174–93 in Michel Callon, ed., *The Laws of the Markets*. Oxford: Blackwell.

Millett, Paul. 1984. "Hesiod and His World." *Proceedings of the Cambridge Philological Society* n.s. 30: 84–115.

———. 1990. "Sale, Credit and Exchange in Athenian Law and Society." Pp. 167–94 in

Paul Cartledge, Paul Millett, and Stephen Todd, eds., *NOMOS: Essays in Athenian Law, Politics, and Society*. Cambridge: Cambridge Univ. Press.

———. 1991. *Lending and Borrowing in Ancient Athens*. Cambridge: Cambridge Univ. Press.

Mirhady, David C. 2000. "Demosthenes as Advocate: The Private Speeches." Pp. 181–204 in Ian Worthington, ed., *Demosthenes: Statesman and Orator*. London: Routledge.

———. "Athens' Democratic Witnesses." *Phoenix* 56: 255–274.

Misztal, Barbara. 1996. *Trust in Modern Societies*. Cambridge: Polity Press.

Moline, Jon. 1969. "Aristotle, Eubulides and the Sorites." *Mind* 78: 393–407.

Moreno, Alfonso. 2003. "Athenian Bread-Baskets: The Grain-Tax Law of 374/3 B.C. Reinterpreted." *Zeitschrift für Papyrologie und Epigraphik* 145: 97–106.

———. 2007. *Feeding the Democracy: Athenian Grain Supply in the Fifth and Fourth Centuries BC*. Oxford: Oxford Univ. Press.

Morgan, T. J. 1999. "Literate Education in Classical Athens." *Classical Quarterly* n.s. 49: 46–61.

Mørkholm, Otto. 1982. "Some Reflections on the Production and Use of Silver Coinage in Ancient Greece." *Historia* 31: 295–305.

Mossé, Claude. 1979. "Citoyens actifs et citoyens 'passifs' dans les cités grecques: Une approche théorique du problème." *Revue des Études Anciennes* 81: 241–79.

Mueller-Goldingen, Christian. 1995. *Untersuchungen zu Xenophons Kyrupädie*. Leipzig: B.G. Teubner.

Mullineaux, Donald J. 1987. "Competitive Monies and the Suffolk Bank System: A Contractual Perspective." *Southern Economic Journal* 53: 884–898.

Murray, James S. 1990. "Plato's Psychology of Rhetoric: *Phaedrus* 270 D- 272 B." *Echos du Monde Classique* 34: 17–26.

Nadon, Christopher. 1996. "From Republic to Empire: Political Revolution and the Common Good in Xenophon's *Education of Cyrus*." *American Political Science Review* 90: 361–374.

Nannestad, Peter. 2008. "What Have We Learned about Generalized Trust, If Anything?" *Annual Review of Political Science* 11: 413–36.

Nelson, Stephanie. 1996. "The Drama of Hesiod's Farm." *Classical Philology* 91: 45–53.

Netz, Reviel. 2002. "Counter Culture: Towards a History of Greek Numeracy." *History of Science* 40: 321–52.

Nevett, Lisa C. 1999. *House and Society in the Ancient Greek World*. Cambridge: Cambridge Univ. Press.

Newman, W. L. 1902. *The Politics of Aristotle*. Oxford: Clarendon Press.

North, Douglass C. 1984. "Government and the Cost of Exchange in History." *Journal of Economic History* 44: 255–64.

———. 1987. "Institutions, Transactions Costs and Economic Growth." *Economic Inquiry* 25: 419–28.

———. 1991. "Institutions." *Journal of Economic Perspectives* 5: 97–112.

Nussbaum, G. B. 1967. *The Ten Thousand: A Study in Social Organization and Action in Xenophon's* Anabasis. Leiden: Brill.

Ober, Josiah. 1989. *Mass and Elite in Democratic Athens*. Princeton: Princeton Univ. Press.

———. 2008. *Democracy and Knowledge: Innovation and Learning in Classical Athens*. Princeton: Princeton Univ. Press.

Oliverio, G. 1928. "Inscrizioni di Cirene. 1. La Stele della Constituzione." *Rivista di Filologia e di Istruzione Classica*. 56: 182–222.

Olson, S. Douglas, and Alexander Sens. 2000. *Archestratus of Gela: Greek Culture and Cuisine in the Fourth Century BCE*. Oxford: Oxford Univ. Press.

Olson, S. Douglas. 1991. "Firewood and Charcoal in Classical Athens." *Hesperia* 60: 411–20.

Osborne, Robin. 1985. *Demos: The Discovery of Classical Athens*. Cambridge: Cambridge Univ. Press.

———. 1988. "Social and Economic Implications of the Leasing of Land and Property in Classical and Hellenistic Greece." *Chiron* 18: 279–323.

———. 1994. "Athenian Democracy: Something to Celebrate?" *Dialogos* 1: 48–58

O'Sullivan, Neil. 1993. "Plato and *e chaloumene retoriche*." *Mnemosyne* 4th ser. 46: 87–89.

Pagliaro, Antonio. 1956. "Osservazioni sull ΔΙΑΓΡΑΜΜΑ di Cirene." Pp. 101–9 in *Studi in Onore di Aristide Calderini e Roberto Paribeni*, vol. 1. Milan: Ceschina.

Parker, A. J. 1992a. "Cargoes, Containers and Stowage: The Ancient Mediterranean." *International Journal of Nautical Archaeology* 21: 89–100.

———. 1992b. *Ancient Shipwrecks of the Mediterranean and the Roman Provinces*. British Archaeological Reports International Series 580. Oxford: Tempus Reparatum.

Pébarthe, Christophe. 2006. *Cité, démocratie et écriture: Histoire de l'alphabétisation d'Athènes à l'époque classique*. Paris: De Boccard.

Peppler, Charles W. 1910. "The Termination -κός, as Used by Aristophanes for Comic Effect." *American Journal of Philology* 31: 428–44.

Piérart, Marcel. 1971. "Les ΕΥΘΥΝΟΙ Athéniens." *Antiquite Classique* 40: 526–73.

Plax, Martin J. 2005. "Profit and Envy: The *Hipparchus*." *Polis* 22: 85–108.

Poddighe, Elisabetta. 2001. "*L'atimia* nel *diagramma* di Cirene: La definizione della cittadinaza tra morale e diritto alla fine del IV secolo A.C." *Aevum* 75: 37–55.

Pomeroy, Sarah B. 1994. *Xenophon, Oeconomicus: A Social and Historical Commentary*. Oxford: Oxford Univ. Press.

Porter, James I. 1993. "The Seductions of Gorgias." *Classical Antiquity* 12: 267–99.

Pownall, Frances Skoczylas. 2000. "Shifting Viewpoints in Xenophon's *Hellenica*: the Arginusae Episode." *Athenaeum* 88: 499–513.

Préaux, Claire. 1939. *L'économie royale des Lagides*. Brussels: Fondation égyptologique reine Élizabeth.

Prier, Raymond Aldoph. 1976. "Some Thoughts on the Archaic Use of Metron." *Classical World* 70: 161–9.

Pritchett, W. Kendrick. 1956. "The Attic Stelai, Part II." *Hesperia* 25: 178–317.

———. 1991. *The Greek State at War*, vol. 5. Berkeley: Univ. of California Press.

Putnam, Robert D. 1993. *Making Democracy Work: Civic Traditions in Modern Italy*. Princeton: Princeton Univ. Press.

———. 2000. *Bowling Alone: The Collapse and Revival of American Community*. New York: Simon & Schuster.

Raepsaet, Georges. 2008. "Land Transport, Part 2: Riding, Harnesses, and Vehicles." Pp. 580–605 in John Peter Oleson, ed., *The Oxford Handbook of Engineering and Technology in the Classical World*. Oxford: Oxford Univ. Press.

Rathbone Dominic W. 1983. "The Weight and Measurement of Egyptian Grains." *Zeitschrift für Papyrologie und Epigraphik* 53: 265–275.

———. 1991. *Econcomic Rationalism and Rural Society in Third-Century Egypt: The Heroninos Archive and the Appianus Estate*. Cambridge: Cambridge Univ. Press.

———. 1997. "Prices and Price Formation in Roman Egypt." Pp. 183–244 in Jean Andreau, Pierre Briant, and Raymond Descat, eds., *Économie antique: Prix et formation des prix dans les économies antiques*. Saint-Bertrand-de-Comminges: Musée archéologique départemental.

Raven, E. J. P. 1950. "The Amphyctionic Coinage of Delphi, 336–334 BC." *Numismatic Chronicle* 6th series, 10: 1–22.

Redfield, James. 1985. "Herodotus the Tourist." *Classical Philology* 80: 97–118.

Reed, C. M. 1984. "Maritime Traders in the Archaic Greek World: A Typology of Those Engaged in the Long-Distance Transfer of Goods by Sea." *Ancient World* 10: 31–44.

Reger, Gary. 1993. "The Public Purchase of Grain on Independent Delos." *Classical Antiquity* 12: 300–334.

Remer, Gary. 2008. "Genres of Political Speech: Oratory and Conversation, Today and in Antiquity." *Language and Communication* 28: 182–196.

Revermann, Martin. 2006. "The Competence of Theatre Audiences in Fifth- and Fourth-Century Athens." *Journal of Hellenic Studies* 126: 99–124.

Rhodes, P. J. 1972. "The Five Thousand in the Athenian Revolutions of 411 B. C." *Journal of Hellenic Studies* 92: 115–127.

———. 1985. *The Athenian Boule*. Oxford: Clarendon Press.

———. 1993. *A Commentary on the Aristotelian* Athenaion Politeia. Oxford: Clarendon Press.

Rhodes, P. J., and Robin Osborne. 2003. *Greek Historical Inscriptions 404–323 BC*. Oxford: Oxford Univ. Press.

Rickman, Geoffrey. 1980. *The Corn Supply of Ancient Rome*. Oxford: Clarendon Press.

———. 1998. "Problems of Transport and Storage of Goods for Distribution: 'Les traces oubliées.'" Pp. 317–24 in Claude Moatti, ed., *La mémoire perdue: Recherches sur l'administration romaine*. Rome: École française de Rome.

Rist, Anna. 1993. "That Herodean Diptych Again." *Classical Quarterly* ns. 43: 440–444.

Roberts, Jennifer Tolbert. 1982. *Accountability in Athenian Government*. Madison: Univ. of Wisconsin Press.

Roller, Lynn E. 1983. "The Legend of Midas." *Classical Antiquity* 2: 299–313.

Rosivach, Vincent J. 2000. "Some Economic Aspects of the Fourth-Century Athenian Market in Grain." *Chiron* 30: 31–64.

———. 2002. "The Requirements for the Solonic Classes in Aristotle, *AP* 7.4." *Hermes* 130: 36–47.

———. 2005. "Notes on the Pentakosiomedimnos' Five Hundred Medimnoi." *Classical Quarterly* n.s. 55: 597–601.

Roy, James. 2004. "The Ambitions of a Mercenary." Pp. 264–88 in Robin Lane Fox, ed., *The Long March: Xenophon and the Ten Thousand*. New Haven: Yale Univ. Press.

Rubinstein, Lene. 1998. "The Athenian Political Perception of the *Idiotes*." Pp. 125–43 in Paul Cartledge, Paul Millett, and Sitta von Reden, eds., *Kosmos: Essays in Order, Conflict and Community in Classical Athens*. Cambridge: Cambridge Univ. Press.

———. 2000. *Litigation and Cooperation: Supporting Speakers in the Courts of Classical Athens*. Stuttgart: Steiner.

———. 2003. "Volunteer Prosecutors in the Greek World." *Dike* 6: 87–113.

Rusten, Jeffery, and I. C. Cunningham, eds. and trans. 2002. Theophrastus: *Characters*. Cambridge, Mass.: Harvard Univ. Press.

Saïd, Suzanne. 2002. "Herodotus and Tragedy." Pp. 117–47 in Egbert J. Bakker, Irene J. F. de Jong, and Hans van Wees, eds., *Brill's Companion to Herodotus*. Leiden: Brill.

Samuel, Alan E. 1966. "The Days of 'Hesiod's' Month." *Transactions of the American Philological Association* 97: 421–29.

Scafuro, Adele. 1997. *The Forensic Stage*. Cambridge: Cambridge Univ. Press.

Schaps, David M. 1977. "The Woman Least Mentioned. Etiquette and Women's Names." *Classical Quarterly* n.s. 27: 323–330.

————. 2004. *The Invention of Coinage and the Monetization of Ancient Greece*. Ann Arbor: Univ. of Michigan Press.

Schiappa, Edward. 1992. "*Rhetorike*: What's in a Name? Toward a Revised History of Early Greek Rhetorical Theory." *Quarterly Journal of Speech* 78: 1–15.

————. 1994. "Plato and *e chaloumene retoriche*: A Response to O'Sullivan." *Mnemosyne* 4th ser. 47: 512–14.

————. 1999. *The Beginnings of Rhetorical Theory in Classical Greece*. New Haven: Yale Univ. Press.

Schilbach, Jürgen. 1999. "Massbecher aus Olympia." *Bericht über die Ausgrabungen in Olympia* 11: 323–56.

Schmitt-Pantel, Pauline. 1990. "Collective Activities and the Political in the Greek City." Pp. 199–213 in O. Murray and S. Price, eds., *The Greek City from Homer to Alexander*. Oxford: Oxford Univ. Press.

Schmitz, Thomas A. 2000. "Plausibility in the Greek Orators." *American Journal of Philology* 121: 47–77.

Schofield, Malcolm. 1996. "Sharing in the constitution." *RMeta* 49 (4): 831–58.

————. 1998. "Political Friendship and the Ideology of Reciprocity." Pp. 37–51 in Paul Cartledge, Paul Millett, and Sitta von Reden, eds., *Kosmos: Essays in Order, Conflict and Community in Classical Athens*. Cambridge: Cambridge Univ. Press.

————. 1999. *Saving the City : Philosopher-Kings and Other Classical Paradigms*. London: Routledge.

Scodel, Ruth. 1992. "The Wits of Glaucus." *Transactions of the American Philological Association* 122: 73- 84.

Seaford, Richard. 2004. *Money and the Early Greek Mind: Homer, Philosophy, Tragedy*. Cambridge: Cambridge Univ. Press.

Seager, Robin. 1966. "Lysias Against the Corndealers." *Historia* 15:172–84.

Segal, Charles P. 1962. "Gorgias and the Psychology of the Logos." *Harvard Studies in Classical Philology* 66: 99–155.

Shear, Jr., T. Leslie. 1978. *Kallias of Sphettos and the Revolt of Athens in 286 B.C.* Princeton, N.J.: American School of Classical Studies at Athens.

Shultz, Thomas R., Elène Léveillé, and Mark R. Lepper. 1999. "Free Choice and Cognitive Dissonance Revisited: Choosing 'Lesser Evils' versus 'Greater Goods.'" *Personality and Social Psychology Bulletin* 25: 40–48.

Sigaut, François. 1988. "A Method for Identifying Grain Storage Techniques and Its Application for European Agricultural History." *Tools and Tillage* 6: 3–32, 46.

Skydsgaard, Jens Erik. 1988. "Solon's *Tele* and the Agrarian History. A Note." Pp. 50–4 in Damsgaard-Madsen, Aksel, Erik Christiansen, and Erk Hallager, eds., *Studies in Ancient History and Numismatics Presented to Rudi Thomsen*. Aarhus: Aarhus Univ. Press.

Small, Jocely Penny. 1997. *Wax Tablets of the Mind: Cognitive Studies of Memory and Literacy in Classical Antiquity*. New York: Routledge.

Stadter, Philip A. 1989. *A Commentary on Plutarch's* Pericles. Chapel Hill: Univ. of North Carolina Press.

Stern, Jacob. 1979. "Herodas' *Mimiamb 6*." *Greek, Roman and Byzantine Studies* 20: 247–54.

Strauss, Barry S. 1996. "The Athenian Trireme, School of Democracy." Pp. 313–25 in Josiah Ober and Charles Hedrick, eds., *Demokratia: A Conversation on Democracies, Ancient and Modern*. Princeton: Princeton Univ. Press.

Stroud, Ronald S. 1974. "An Athenian Law on Silver Coinage." *Hesperia* 43: 157–88.

————. 1998. *The Athenian Grain-Tax Law of 374/3 B.C.* Princeton: American School of Classical Studies at Athens.

Swiny, Helena Wylde, and Michael L. Katzev. 1973. "The Kyrenai Shipwreck: A Fourth-Century B.C. Greek Merchant Ship." Pp. 339–55 in D. J. Blackman, ed., *Marine Archaeology*. London: Archon Books.

Sylla, Richard. 1976. "Forgotten Men of Money: Private Bankers in Early U.S. History." *Journal of Economic History* 36: 173–88.

Tacon, Judith. 2001. "Ecclesiastic *Thorubos*: Interventions, Interruptions, and Popular Involvement in the Athenian Assembly." *Greece and Rome* 48: 173–92.

Taylor, Claire. 2007. "From the Whole Citizen Body? The Sociology of Election and Lot in the Athenian Democracy." *Hesperia* 76: 323–45.

Thalmann, William G. 2004. "'The Most Divinely Approved and Political Discord': Thinking about Conflict in the Developing Polis." *Classical Antiquity* 23: 359–99.

Thomas, Keith. 1987. "Numeracy in Early Modern England." *Transactions of the Royal Historical Society* 37: 103–132.

Thompson, Homer A., and R. E. Wycherley. 1972. *The Agora of Athens: The History, Shape and Uses of an Ancient City Center*. Princeton: American School of Classical Studies at Athens.

Thompson, Wesley E. 1970. "Notes on the Treasurers of Athena." *Hesperia* 39: 54–63.

———. 1982. "The Athenian Entrepreneur." *L'Antiquité Classique* 51: 53–85.

Thür, Gerhard, and Hans Taeuber. 1994. *Prozessrechtliche Inschriften der griechischen Poleis: Arkadien*. Vienna: Verlag der Österreichischen Akademie der Wissenschaften.

Timberlake, Jr., Richard H. 1981. "The Significance of Unaccounted Currencies." *Journal of Economic History* 41: 853–866.

Todd, Stephen C. 1993. *The Shape of Athenian Law*. Oxford: Clarendon Press.

Trevett, J. C. 1996. "Aristotle's Knowledge of Athenian Oratory." *Classical Review* 46: 371–9.

Trundle, Matthew. 2004. *Greek Mercenaries: From the Late Archaic Period to Alexander*. London: Routledge.

Tsetskhladze, Gocha R. 1998. "Trade on the Black Sea in the Archaic and Classical Periods: Some Observations." Pp. 52–74 in Helen Parkins and Christopher Smith, eds., *Trade, Traders, and the Ancient City*. London: Routledge.

Turfa, Jean MacIntosh, and Alwin G. Steinmayer, Jr. 1999. "The *Syracusia* as a Giant Cargo Vessel." *International Journal of Nautical Archaeology* 28: 105–25.

Uguzzoni, Arianna, and Franco Ghinatti. 1968. *Le tavole greche di Eraclea*. Rome: L'erma di Bretschneider.

Ussher, R. G. 1960. *The Characters of Theophrastus*. London: MacMillan.

van Alfen, Peter G. 2005. "Problems in Ancient Imitative and Counterfeit Coinage." Pp. 322–54 in Zofia H. Archibald, John Davies, and Vincent Gabrielsen, eds., *Making, Moving and Managing: The New World of Ancient Economies, 323–31 BC*. Oxford: Oxbow Books.

van Effenterre, Henri, and Françoise Ruzé. 1994. *NOMINA. Recueil d'Inscriptions Politiques et Juridiques de l'Archaïsme Grec*, vol 1. Rome: Ecole française de Rome.

Vanderpool, Eugene. 1968. "METRONOMOI." *Hesperia* 37: 73–6.

Vélissaropoulos, Julie. 1980. *Les nauclères grecs: Recherches sur les institutions maritimes en Grèce et dans l'Orient hellénisé*. Paris: Libairie Minard.

Vial, Claude. 1984. *Délos indépendante*. Athens: École Française d'Athènes.

Vlassopoulos, Kostas. 2007. "Free Spaces: Identity, Experience and Democracy in Classical Athens." *Classical Quarterly* n.s. 57: 33–52.

Walker, Jeffrey. 1996. "Before the Beginnings of 'Poetry' and 'Rhetoric': Hesiod on Eloquence." *Rhetorica* 14: 243–64.

Wallace, Robert W. 1989. "The Athenian *Proeispherontes*." *Hesperia* 58: 473–90.

———. 1992. Review of Develin, *Athenian Officials 684–321 B.C. American Journal of Philology* 113: 103–7.

———. 2005. "'Listening to' the Archai in Democratic Athens." Pp. 147–57 in Michael Gagarin and Robert W. Wallace, eds., *Symposion 2001: Vorträge zur griechischen und hellenistischen Rechtsgeschichte*. Vienna: Verlag der Österreichischen Akademie der Wissenschaften.

Warnick, Barbara. 1989. "Judgment, Probability, and Aristotle's *Rhetoric*." *Quarterly Journal of Speech* 9: 299–311.

Weber, Max. 1978. *Economy and Society*. Guenther Roth and Claus Wittich, eds. Berkeley: Univ. of California Press.

West, Martin L. 1978. *Works and Days. Hesiod*. Oxford: Clarendon Press.

Westbrook, Raymond. 1992. "The Trial Scene in the *Iliad*." *Harvard Studies in Classical Philology* 94: 53–76.

Whidden, Christopher. 2007. "The Account of Persia and Cyrus's Persian Education in Xenophon's *Cyropaedia*." *Review of Politics* 69: 539–67.

Whitby, Michael. 1998. "The Grain Trade of Athens in the Fourth Century BC." Pp. 102–28 in Helen Parkins and Christopher Smith, eds., *Trade, Traders, and the Ancient City*. London: Routledge.

Whitehead, David. 1986. *The Demes of Attica, 508/7– ca. 250 B.C. A Political and Social Study*. Princeton: Princeton Univ. Press.

Whitley, James. 1997. "Cretan Laws and Cretan Literacy." *American Journal of Archaeology* 101: 635–661.

Whitman, James Q. 1995. "At the Origins of Law and the State: Supervision of Violence, Mutilation of Bodies, or Setting of Prices?" *Chicago-Kent Law Review* 71: 41–84.

Whittaker, John C. 1999. "*Alonia*: The Ethnoarchaeology of Cypriot Threshing Floors." *Journal of Mediterranean Archaeology* 12: 7–25.

Willetts, Ronald F. 1967. *The Law Code of Gortyn*. Berlin: Walter de Gruyter.

Wilson, John-Paul. 1997/98. "The 'Illiterate Trader'?" *Bulletin of the Institute of Classical Studies* 42: 29–56.

Wohl, Victoria. 2002. *Love among the Ruins: The Erotics of Democracy in Classical Athens*. Princeton: Princeton Univ. Press.

Wycherley, R. E. 1956. "The Market of Athens: Topography and Monuments." *Greece and Rome* 3: 2–23.

Wyse, William. 1904. *The Speeches of Isaeus*. Cambridge: Cambridge Univ. Press (reprint: New York: Arno, 1979).

Yadin, Yigael. 1963. *The Finds from the Bar Kokhba Period in the Cave of Letters*. Jerusalem: Israel Exploration Society.

Yunis, Harvey. 1991. "How do the People Decide? Thucydides on Periclean Rhetoric and Civic Instruction." *American Journal of Philology* 112: 179–200.

———. 2005. "The Rhetoric of Law in Fourth-Century Athens." Pp. 191–208 in Michael Gagarin and David Cohen, eds., *The Cambridge Companion to Greek Law*. Cambridge: Cambridge Univ. Press.

Zelizer, Viviana A. 1989. "The Social Meaning of Money: 'Special Monies.'" *American Journal of Sociology* 95: 342–77.

———. 1994. *The Social Meaning of Money*. New York: Basic Books.

INDEX OF PASSAGES CITED

I have included passages discussed, but generally not those cited in catalogues of evidence. Page references point to the primary discussion, whether in the chapters or the notes.

LITERARY SOURCES

Aeschines
  1.110–12, 140
  1.111–12, 132
  2.1, 215n124
  2.21, 147
  2.22, 120
  2.43–47, 147
  2.55, 116
  2.107, 118
  2.178, 135
  3.18, 130
  3.166, 41
Aesop
  88, 22
Aineias
  2.2.3, 41
  18.10.2, 41
  29.3, 82–83
  32.2.2, 41
  32.8.8, 41
Alexis
  fr. 16, 21, 22
  fr. 125, 129
  fr. 126, 21
  fr. 128, 178n74
Amphis
  fr. 30, 21
Antiphanes
  fr. 68, 15
  fr. 125, 20
  fr. 166, 21
  fr. 206, 23

Antiphon
  6.10, 165
  6.12–15, 136
  fr. 218, 21
Archestratus
  fr. 36, 22
  fr. 45, 22
  fr. 53, 22
Aristophanes
  Achar. 34–36, 20
  Achar. 656–58, 212n52
  Achar. 837–38, 178n77
  Birds 1213, 183n29
  Birds 1565–1685, 120ff.
  Clouds 245–46, 151
  Clouds 643–45, 63
  Ekk. 25–30, 168
  Ekk. 149ff., 168
  Ekk. 244, 157
  Ekk. 507, 168
  Ekk. 817–20, 194n83
  Frogs 971–79, 195n96
  Knights 724–1128, 152
  Knights 1375–80, 157
  Lys. 404–19, 15
  Lys. 1199, 195n90
  Peace 1144, 63
  Peace 1246–49, 195n101
  Thes. 418–28, 78
  Wasps 496–99, 23
  Wasps 605–19, 194n83
  Wasps 725–26, 167

Aristotle
  Ath. Pol. 4.2, 100
  Ath. Pol. 7.3–4, 70
  Ath. Pol. 7.3, 86
  Ath. Pol. 7.4, 86, 87, 108
  Ath. Pol. 8.1, 86
  Ath. Pol. 13.2, 108
  Ath. Pol. 16.4, 191n21
  Ath. Pol. 29.5, 100
  Ath. Pol. 34.1, 134
  Ath. Pol. 36.2, 101
  Ath. Pol. 39.6, 85
  Ath. Pol. 43.1–62.3,
    202n3
  Ath. Pol. 47.1, 86
  Ath. Pol. 49.2, 88
  Ath. Pol. 49.4, 96
  Ath. Pol. 51.1, 54
  Ath. Pol. 51.1–4, 28
  Ath. Pol. 51.3, 29
  Ath. Pol. 55.2–4, 92
  fr. 63, 184n39
  fr. 558R, 21
  fr. 598, 177n61
  HA 596b26, 74
  HA 629a13, 44
  NE 1164a22–28, 19
  Oik. 1344b31–34, 15
  Oik. 1344b33–34, 76
  Oik. 1345a19–24, 75–76
  Oik. 1346b24–26,
    181n145

INSCRIPTIONS

PAPYRI

INDEX